P9-DVV-115

SMOKE SCREEN

Smokescreen: What the Marijuana Industry Doesn't Want You to Know

Published by Forefront Books.

Cover Design by Bruce Gore, Gore Studio Inc.
Interior Design by Bill Kersey, Kersey Graphics

ISBN: 978-1-948677-87-5
e-Book ISBN: 978-1-948677-88-2

SMOKE SCREEN

WHAT THE MARIJUANA INDUSTRY DOESN'T WANT YOU TO KNOW

KEVIN A. SABET, Ph.D.

Foreword by REP. PATRICK J. KENNEDY

To all those I've met who are affected by addiction

Those who do not learn history are doomed to repeat it.

—George Santayana

Table of Contents

PART TWO: BECOMING A FULL-FLEDGED MOVEMENT

PART THREE:
ADDRESSING THE CONSEQUENCES

Acknowledgments

This book would not exist without the unending support of my wife, Shahrzad. Since almost the moment we met, my work has been elevated by her brilliance, intuition, clear thinking, skillful writing, and commitment to justice. I am especially grateful for her continual reminder that in any work worth doing, means and ends must be consistent. She and our daughter are the bright lights of my life.

Much of *Smokescreen* was written during the coronavirus pandemic, and thus in the home of my wife's parents, Afsaneh and Saeed Sabet, who not only provided perpetual encouragement, a roof over my head, loving childcare, and some of the best food I've ever tasted, but also a valuable sounding board for many of these ideas. To have received so much of their help during this book project, during a global health crisis to boot, is a gift I do not deserve and one I can't pay back.

I would not be where I am today without the unflinching support of my parents, Sohie and Zabih Sabet, who always pushed me to do better while supporting my "drug work." They, along with my sisters, Homa, Mina, and Shayda; their husbands, Alex, Christopher, and Saba; and my nieces and nephew, provided substantive help for this book, moving me to delve deeper into my own past and to add more color to some of these chapters than would have otherwise been there. Shahrzad, Sohie, Zabih, Homa, Mina, Afsaneh, Saeed, and Shayda read the manuscript—either specific chapters or in its entirety—and provided invaluable feedback. I am also indebted to Shayda for providing my wife and me countless hours of support by helping to care for our new baby during the first few months of the pandemic.

I feel exceedingly (almost embarrassingly) fortunate to do this work with so many extraordinary, talented colleagues. They are far too many to list here. But a few stand out so much that this book would feel incomplete if I didn't name them. Luke, my soul-brother, without whom I would be far less happy and far more cynical. My deepest thanks to your family, especially Eliza, Shiloh, and Eden, for encouraging you to take these leaps with me and for enduring the sacrifices they entail. The whole rest of the team at SAM—Will, Beth, Colton, Brendan, Dana, Katie, and Jordan—who in very profound ways inspired every page in this book. The moms and dads I've met along the way, many of whom have opened their courageous hearts to me, and most of whom I interviewed for this book. The former marijuana regulators and insiders who, with incredible humility, recognized the folly of this industry and with enormous strength, told me about it.

I'll also be forever grateful for my mentors, all of whom I consider family: wise sages Bob DuPont and Mitch Rosenthal; former bosses turned confidants, Gil Kerlikowske and Barry McCaffrey; my three favorite "Sues"—Foster, Rusche, and Thau—who have known me since I was a teenager; the ever kind and generous David Frum and his wife, Danielle Crittenden; and the world's brightest (and with me, most patient) drug policy analyst, Jon Caulkins; and so many others. The late David Musto and Bruce Johnson gave me a chance early in my career; I wouldn't be here without them. And the three dear colleagues I lost during the conception and writing of this book who were a constant source of knowledge and inspiration: Herb Kleber, ever my encourager; Christopher Kennedy Lawford, who would always find a way to make me laugh; and Mark Kleiman, the drug policy researcher-practitioner I loved to hate (not really), who made it his goal to always teach me something new, even if it made me uncomfortable. Invaluable research assistance from Jacqueline Grace, the SAM staff and board, David, Jon, Steven, Mike, Ian, and Ben Cort (who also happens to be one of the finest people I know), and many others made this book a possibility. I am indebted to my editor, Hope Innelli, who jumped into this with fervor and drove me to make something good into something much better, all the while taking my Sunday afternoon calls with enthusiasm and excitement. Jennifer, Jana, and the Epic powerhouse have been a pleasure to work with. And I will be forever grateful to my publisher, Jonathan Merkh and everyone at Forefront Books for taking a chance on me and this book with little to go on. For carefully reading the manuscript, in part or in whole, I am also grateful to Luke Niforatos, William Jones, Colton Grace, Garth Van Meter, Brendan Fairfield, Katie Gallop, Theodore Caputi, and Jordan Davidson.

Few are so blessed as me to have found a true comrade in arms in the work they do every day, especially work that is so emotionally and mentally draining. For that I will forever be grateful to Patrick Kennedy. He is always willing to jump in headfirst with me, even when it would be much safer to stand and watch from the sidelines. Equal gratitude goes to his wife, Amy, and his five children, for giving him the space to do that. I am honored he agreed to write the foreword to this book.

Foreword by Patrick J. Kennedy

The U.S. elections in November 2020 were among the most closely watched in history. I was paying attention for many reasons beyond the obvious. Yes, I wanted to see who would be president and how the House and Senate would shape our future; and how my wife, Amy Kennedy, who was running for the 2nd district house seat in New Jersey, would fare. But I was also watching to see the outcome of ballot measures in four states—Arizona, Montana, South Dakota, and New Jersey (where I now live). When the results were tallied, all of these jurisdictions legalized marijuana by popular vote, bringing the total count to fifteen states. Currently one in every three Americans lives in a state where the recreational use of marijuana is legal.

When a substance is that ubiquitous, its use naturally rises. In the case of marijuana, use has more than doubled since the first state legalized it. Unlike alcohol and tobacco use, which have been waning among kids, marijuana is going in the wrong direction. And the actual amount of marijuana consumed is off the charts.

The entities who stand to gain tens of billions of dollars from the legal sale of marijuana are masters at using sophisticated techniques to produce, package, brand, market, and upsell consumer goods. The one hurdle most other industries have to surmount—building a repeat clientele—is no obstacle for them. The products they have traditionally marketed to the public are naturally habit forming. And today's marijuana, with its increased THC concentration, shares this trait. In other words, no matter how "homegrown" or even "citizen-initiated" the marijuana movement looks to you from where you view it, it is anything but that.

The seasoned drivers behind this industry are pros at normalizing the use of harmful substances. As they seek to expand their market, they know they must target ever-younger users. Hence the addition of highly potent, albeit innocuous-looking, candies and soft drinks with catchy names.

The vulnerable stand the most to lose in a world of addiction for profit. This should be evident to anyone who has watched similarly exploitative industries, such as the alcohol industry, expand. In some cities, there are eight times the number of liquor stores in poor communities of color versus white communities. Similarly you will see more pot shops in vulnerable communities where political power is often less potent, and harms mount at higher rates.

This is one of many reasons why I co-founded SAM (Smart Approaches to Marijuana) with David Frum, and with the remarkable author of this revelatory book, Kevin Sabet. Kevin's record in fighting the disinformation campaign regarding this drug is unparalleled, not only in his role at SAM, but also in his drug advisory capacity to several White House administrations across party lines. While the new Big Tobacco industry begins rolling in the profits, and while local governments fall victim to legal marijuana's promise of a quick revenue fix, Kevin and the whistleblowers he has assembled in this book are fighting for your health and your right to be protected from such harm.

By calling out the marijuana industry's duplicitous and misleading marketing tactics, their irresponsible development of a more potent and palatable range of pot products, and their lax safety practices,

Kevin and his front-line team of contributors have put together one of the most comprehensive guides to combating predatory industry.

Smokescreen: What the Marijuana Industry Doesn't Want You to Know offers an unvarnished 360-degree perspective of the industry from those who hail from all aspects of the business. Among them are people who have used, sold, grown, tested, or regulated legal marijuana, and have either been adversely affected or appalled by its rampant contamination, toxicity, harm, and misrepresentation. Their first-hand accounts are not just compelling, they are necessary. They deepen our understanding of the many problems that emerge as legal marijuana gains an even stronger foothold in our nation. Equally valuable in this era of alternative facts is the science supporting their claims, which is provided in the book's robust appendix.

The time to halt and reassess the alarming trend of legalized marijuana is now. Standing on the precipice of a déjà vu experience, we can learn from the mistakes of the opioid crisis and avoid repeating such a grave error. The fact that we are, as I write these words, in the midst of a large settlement with Purdue Pharma—a company whose executives lied about the addictiveness of OxyContin and effectively held the medical system hostage—should teach us something about how damaging corporations that put profits ahead of public health can be. Public health didn't stand a chance against the onslaught of big money then. What makes us think that this time it will be any different?

As the adage goes, "Fool me once, shame on you; fool me twice, shame on me." The earlier we push back against these companies' greed, the better. The decision to see marijuana for the increasing danger it is, and to cast an informed vote on the subject in subsequent elections, is in your hands. So, too, is the book that can help inform these decisions.

Patrick J. Kennedy
Former Congressman D-RI
Author of the Mental Health Parity and Addiction Equity Act
Cofounder, SAM (Smart Approaches to Marijuana)

PROLOGUE

Exposed

It's a Saturday afternoon like every other for these workers. They stand in a windowless basement. There isn't much to occupy the confined space except the task itself, which lasts for hours at a stretch.

How many hours? The workers aren't really sure, as one hour blends uneventfully into the next.

There is a meticulousness to their task, which involves the use of scissors. One of the workers calls it "trimming." What he does, over and over again, is cut the big leaves of countless mature marijuana plants, dropping the refuse into a bucket so as not to make a mess.

His coworker trims the lucrative product as well. It can be, they say, a hard, tiring, and monotonous chore.

Rarely do they set foot upstairs on the main level—the public face of the shop—where there's a waiting room furnished with couches, a coffee table and a set of chairs, and where occasional customers mill about, perusing products. When they do venture into this space, these workers never utter a word to the customers.

Sometimes, though, they help deliver product to people's homes. The two of them also water the pot plants on Sundays when the store is closed. They used to help make gummy bears—not the kind you buy at the concession counter in movie theaters, mind you, but the variety that makes you high. Now their employer buys the gummies wholesale from a supplier. These days, the workers prepare a different concoction to sell to customers. It's something one worker calls "chocolate medicine." She stirs the cocoa in a pot, infusing it with THC, the active ingredient in marijuana.

The two workers don't look forward to the manual labor. They confess they'd rather be doing something else, such as watching TV. They each make a dollar a day, which works out to 25 cents an hour—slave wages by any measure. But they don't complain because they don't have a choice.

One worker is five years old.

The other, his sister, is seven.

Shocking.

How could this be?

Children their age should be outdoors involved in sports, enjoying play dates with friends, or going to birthday parties, not supplying a trove of laced candies for pot parties. But on the weekends, when their dad has custody, he puts them to work at his shop in Montana where he sells "medical" marijuana. This substance is legal there, as it has also become in several other parts of the United States.

Marijuana isn't the first thing you think of when your eyes take in the sweeping vistas of Montana—an expanse of snow-capped mountains where clouds hover under rugged peaks, creeks run alongside meandering valley trails, and cows graze in the open fields. But even here, where hardworking people labor on ranches carved out of the wilderness, marijuana has arrived.

Following California's lead in the mid-1990s, Montana voters approved so-called "medical" marijuana in 2004. Although the legislators set limits on the number of patients whom providers could serve at that time, a dozen years later another ballot initiative loosened the rules, allowing for the wider sale of medical marijuana in Big Sky country. And in 2020, Montana dropped the "medical" pretense and legalized the drug for any purpose, as is what often happens after a state flirts with so-called therapeutic weed.

For the stay-at-home mother of the two small children who work in their father's pot shop, the legalization of marijuana in Montana is personal.

At least it became so when she discovered her ex-boyfriend was putting their children to work there without her consent.

When she questioned him about it, he told her, "It's medical" and tried to assure her that the work wouldn't hurt the kids. He was convinced marijuana was a good thing.

A yelling match ensued.

In the months and years that followed, the mother sought to stop her ex-boyfriend from involving their children in his business for many obvious reasons—most notably, her fear of what the exposure to pot could do to their still developing brains. Her efforts were in vain. When she contacted the police, they told her that they couldn't help because medical marijuana is now legal. When she reached out to child protective services, they told her the same thing. When she went to the courts to seek a judge's order requiring her ex to keep their children away from the marijuana he sells, again she had no luck.

"Why isn't anyone helping me?" the distraught mom wanted to know. "I'm being treated like this is a normal thing. This is *not* normal."

But the truth is that America's mad dash to commercialize marijuana in recent years has indeed led to it becoming normalized.

"I just don't know how to help my children," she lamented.

The children's mom has since remarried, and her husband is equally stunned by the acceptance of marijuana despite its dangers. The motivation for this acceptance, as he sees it, is obvious: "There's money in it. And so, people are turning a blind eye."

One might wonder how this could really happen, especially since weed remains prohibited under federal law, and, more importantly, since studies demonstrate that marijuana is especially dangerous to children and their development. In fact, research shows marijuana use among youth can lead to a permanent 8-point drop in IQ,[1] as well as a significant increase in the risk of schizophrenia and suicidal thoughts.[2] Since pot was legalized in Colorado, the state has continued to see increases in youth suicide coinciding with an increase in marijuana, which far outweighs alcohol, showing up in their toxicology reports.[3]

The stepfather of the five- and seven-year-old kids employed by their dad in the pot shop has said, "They're little kids with little brains and little bodies. They're not of age to do anything. I don't understand how this isn't [an] open and shut [case]. It just blows my mind."

And it may very well be destroying theirs. Both of these young children recently tested positive for levels of Tetrahydrocannabinol—THC—the principal psychoactive constituent in pot.

The mom and her husband aren't sure how their children have been exposed, whether through secondhand inhalation, skin contact, or some other means. All they know is, it's a nightmare.

Although the five-year-old son has been working at the pot shop since he was three, he doesn't have any idea what marijuana is. He simply knows he'd rather be doing something else. As this young boy with the thick tuft of blond hair says, "I just like playing with Hot Wheels."

The seven-year-old daughter doesn't understand the nature of their work either. "I don't know really about the medicine," she said, "but I want to save enough money to buy a horse. Or a phone."

So they keep doing what their father asks them to do.

The mom tries to explain to her children that even though the product looks like candy and is called medicine, it's neither; it's a drug that affects one's mental abilities. "The kids keep calling it medicine, and I keep correcting them," she said. "It's weed. But in their minds, it's no different than taking Tylenol."

The concerned mom smells the skunklike stench of pot on the kids when they come home from a weekend with their dad. She worries because her ex-boyfriend and his girlfriend smoke it in front of the children. And though big mounds of weed sit in bowls on their father's kitchen table, as readily accessible as salt and pepper, she must continually point out to her children that it's not good for them.

But in today's era of sweeping legalization in state after state, this is not an easy message to transmit. While the word "legal" means "safe" to a lot of kids, today's marijuana is anything but that.

Of course, this is contrary to what many people believe—but it is, in fact, the informed opinion of the National Academies of Sciences, the World Health Organization, and every other major medical association.

The hazards of today's high-potency marijuana have been demonstrated in study after study. The pot available to Americans right now is a mind-altering drug so strong that it can lead to a fatal car crash. It can also lead to addiction, debilitating mental illness, and a host of other devastating outcomes.

Bloggers in search of clicks, pot merchants in pursuit of cash, and politicians in the hunt for votes cast these as controversial statements. But for scientists who know and care about facts, this is an incontrovertible truth.

A mysterious lung illness in America, which broke out in the late summer of 2019, made the risks of marijuana all too clear. Scores of people became ill and several died. Authorities at the U.S. Centers for Disease Control and Prevention said the illness was closely associated, in most cases, with THC infused e-cigarette products and vape pens. (It later became known as EVALI, an acronym for e-cigarette or vape product use-associated lung injury.) What made the crisis all the more alarming was that a heavy portion of the products causing illness and death was sold via the "legal" industry.

And yet, America continues its headlong dive into the green rush.

For the mother of these young children and her husband, the fear of the unknown is relentless. Just recently, their seven-year-old daughter started coming home from her father's pot shop complaining of being sick to her stomach, feeling lethargic, and experiencing muscle cramps and headaches.

Whether her ailments are due to her exposure to marijuana isn't fully known, but the questions loom large. The children's parents want to know, how can this go on? When will people begin to heed the dangers of marijuana—and worse, the dangers of a hyped-up industry hell-bent on profiting off addiction?

I have often asked the same question.

It's a question for all of us.

What's happening in America is a silent and sanctioned epidemic of sorts—an emerging public health crisis over a drug that has been clothed, stunningly, in acceptability. What is being overlooked is the simple fact that today's high potency marijuana is a different drug than it was in the past—too dangerous a drug for many who consume it—and for those, like these two children, who have been exposed to it.

Marijuana's acceptance, and its increasing legalization, is hid under a veneer of social justice—and a thin one at that. It's what Ron Rice, the chairperson of the New Jersey Legislative Black Caucus calls "the big cover":

> *"The only way they can sell [legalization] is with social justice. But if there is more pot on the streets, it'll set us back. Beyond being a bad idea, it's trickery."*[4]

Make no mistake: The scourge of systemic racism thoroughly permeates our justice system. Like so many of our institutions, it requires a fundamental overhaul. But marijuana legalization will perpetuate racial injustice, not lessen it. The depth and ubiquity of systemic racism in this country is such that loosening pot laws will make little difference. If pot is legal, a dozen other laws will be used to ensnare young Black men in the criminal justice system, even as they are heavily targeted by a now legal and emboldened addictive industry. Addiction-for-profit industries rely on the vulnerable and disenfranchised to make money. You're their best customer if you are less likely to get help and stop using. This is the well-documented playbook of Big Tobacco. And it will be the playbook of Big Marijuana.

As Rice continues, "When I hear my colleagues pushing for legalization 'in the name of social justice,' I can't apologize for my instinct to suspect that it's really about helping political friends profit from an industry that should not be allowed a foothold in our state."[5] He also wrote, "I hate to be suspicious of marijuana industry investors lurking as shills in the background, but I really believe this whole exercise had nothing to do with social justice . . . ."[6]

The senator along with the various chapters of the National Association for the Advancement of Colored People (NAACP), who have pushed back on this industry, are right. In the eight years since pot has been legalized in some states, it is clear disadvantaged communities have not come out ahead. Their voices are being drowned out by a chorus of (almost exclusively white) marijuana-industry zealots who want to make a buck. As Teresa Haley, head of the Illinois chapter of the NAACP put it recently: "I'm tired of rich people getting richer off the backs of poor people. We see that every day. Addictions are real . . . We believe people of color still are going to be disproportionately targeted and lose their jobs or places to live."[7]

To be clear, opposing legalization does not mean supporting criminalization—which, indeed, is borne disproportionately and unjustly by people of color. The decriminalization of marijuana use, which I strongly support, would remove criminal penalties *but avoid* creating a for-profit marijuana industry that exploits the most vulnerable. Decriminalization, however, will not enrich for-profit weed companies and other business moguls looking to cash in. So they continue touting the supposed benefits of full marijuana legalization, confusing the American people in the process.

America's attitude toward ramped up marijuana legalization and commercialization can be summed up by the children's stepfather: "Nobody," he says, "seems to be listening."

I've written this book to make sure this message is heard. It's about how we're *all* affected by the commercialization of marijuana in this nation, whether we are innocent children, such as these two young people, or seemingly aware adults. Through my past work as a White House Office of National Drug Control Policy advisor (under Democratic and Republican administrations alike), and my present work as cofounder of the advocacy group SAM (Smart Approaches to Marijuana), I've met countless people with moving and eye-opening stories to share, many of whom willingly do so in these pages.

The personal accounts contained in this book come from real people—some who have sold marijuana "legally"; some who have sold it illegally; some who have used it and barely survived ordeals associated with it; some who love and have cared for people whose health has been compromised or whose lives have been lost to a marijuana incident or addiction; some who have witnessed gross negligence and malpractice on the regulatory side of the business in states where the drug is legalized; some who have been victims of the social injustice that results from it all; and finally, some who see how major corporations and their investors are sowing widespread misinformation and chaos for the sake of enormous profit.

You will hear from brave whistleblowers, people of conscience, people with sincere regrets, and people with only Americans' well-being in mind. Of course, I add my own unique perspective, and by way of an expansive appendix, I include the perspective of many others whose exhaustive research corroborates the dangers our contributors' accounts reveal.

Collectively, we believe it's high time the spin ends and the truth be told.

PART ONE
The Green Rush

CHAPTER ONE

Taking on Goliath

In the early days of 2019, I was asked to speak at a drug policy conference in the middle of the Phoenix desert. During my remarks I asked the crowd of 500 if they remembered John Boehner. There were some puzzled looks: why would I mention the former Republican speaker of the U.S. House of Representatives? Then I reminded my audience of what Mr. Boehner had said in a marijuana infomercial aimed at investors.

"I used to sit on the board of a major tobacco company, Reynolds," he said. "You think Big Tobacco is staying on the sidelines? I've talked to these guys. They're not gonna sit this one out. And they have the dollars to acquire whoever they want. We're just beginning to see some action in the space." What Boehner neglected to mention at the time was how he stood to have a $20 million payday as a board member and shareholder of a marijuana-investment firm, Acreage Holdings, if marijuana became legal nationally.[8]

I had given versions of this talk hundreds—maybe thousands—of times across the country in my capacity as the cofounder and president of Smart Approaches to Marijuana (otherwise known as SAM), a nonprofit, nonpartisan organization I started with my friend, former Rhode Island Congressman Patrick Kennedy. SAM's mission is to educate the public about marijuana, and this is exactly what I was doing in the scorching desert heat that afternoon.

The pot promoters of today, I continued to explain, were creating a dangerous atmosphere, exactly like what Big Tobacco created generations ago when it hooked countless people on cigarettes, an addictive product that has killed hundreds of thousands of people each year (and still does). Tobacco only became a tool of mass murder once big corporations got a hold of it and turned it from a leaf to a cigarette—from a single plant into thousands of chemicals.

As the late Mark Kleiman, a scholar distraught both by prohibition and legalization, said:

> *"The people now being hired by the guys in suits doing cannabis-business stock promotions play by different rules. I expect them to have about the same ethical standards as lobbyists for the alcohol, tobacco, pharmaceutical, food, and fossil-fuels industries: that is, I expect them to be utterly willing to sacrifice human health and welfare on the altar of the operating statement, just like those folks at VW who decided it would be a cute idea to poison the air just a little bit to goose the performance of their diesel-driven cars."*[9]

"Did you know," I asked the audience, "that today's marijuana can be up to 99.9 percent potent?" I urged them to compare that with the 3 percent potency of the weed that was smoked at Woodstock. "Throw away what you think you know about marijuana. We are talking about an entirely different drug now."

Forging ahead, I referenced the voluminous studies documenting the rise of teenage pot smoking. Today there are more than *ten times as many daily users* of marijuana than there were when Bill Clinton was president.[10] There has also been a major jump in marijuana-related hospitalizations and drugged-driving fatalities,[11] as well as demonstrated links between THC and psychosis, schizophrenia, suicide, and depression.[12] In fact, the world-renowned British medical journal *The*

Lancet recently published research indicating regular users of today's highly potent weed are *five times more likely* than nonusers to develop psychosis.[13]

Whenever I deliver these talks, I am always prepared for some resistance. We live in a time when Americans are largely unaware of the growing health hazards associated with marijuana. I'm accustomed to feedback from people who've never heard what I'm saying. They wonder if I'm making it up. Exaggerating. Stretching the truth.

I've seen people shrug off critics of pot like me. "What's the big deal?" they ask. "It's just pot. It helps with pain, doesn't it? You're not all about reefer madness, are you?" (The short answer is no; the longer one can be found in my first book, *Reefer Sanity*.)

Other times, I field *this* common refrain: It's harmless, right?

Wrong.

But as I addressed the Phoenix audience that day, something completely unanticipated was gnawing at the back of my mind.

The problem was more sartorial than oratorical. It began when I received an urgent call in my hotel room earlier in the day from the conference organizers. They wanted me to hurry over and give my talk an hour earlier than planned because the previous speaker had finished sooner than expected. They didn't want conference attendees sitting around cooling their heels with nothing to do, or worse yet, leaving the event before it was over.

In the name of full disclosure, I should mention that when I got that call, I was still dressed in a T-shirt and wrinkled slacks. What's more, I was unshaven, having just arrived after a delayed flight from New York.

But not for long.

I jumped in the shower, threw on a checkered button-down shirt, a dark suit, and a tie, and ran over to the tent. That's when it hit me. Standing onstage, against a backdrop of glowing red and green lights, I realized there was nothing under my pair of tan cordovan lace-ups.

I forgot to put on socks.

I paused, smiled, and moved on.

After all, my time was ticking. My speech was just about up.

I'm happy to say the audience left the event a lot wiser about marijuana and none the wiser about my bare feet, but the feeling that time is almost up is not a new one to me. The clock is running out for taking on well-funded interests who want to make money off addiction. We've become inured to many of these special interest groups—the alcohol, gambling, tobacco, pharmaceutical, and now, marijuana, lobbies. From Wall Street to Davos, some of the most well-funded and wide-ranging interests have a stake in this new business. Among these many groups are Big Tobacco, Big Pharma, and Big Alcohol.

It's big business.

These guys—and I say "guys" because they're almost exclusively white men—are repackaging and spinning weed into countless other forms. Gummy bears and lollipops—the province of children—are now being sold with unprecedented levels of THC, pot's active ingredient, all the while luring new and younger users. Yes, they're enticing them with cookies, sodas, wax, budder, dabs, and shatter.

Did I lose you at budder, dabs, or shatter?

If so, you're not alone.

Most of the crowd in Phoenix didn't get it either. They didn't realize that THC can be extracted and heated to produce a high 50 to 99 times more powerful than that of an old '60s-style joint. One form resembles peanut butter on a stick, but it's basically hot marijuana oil on a nail. Pretty far from the days of using roach clips. Another is a tab no bigger than a throat lozenge that's intended to give you a faster, more intense high. Yet another is heated until it forms a sheet so thin and pure it delivers a powerful hit. The latter is so brittle, it can easily shatter, hence its name.

In a sense, this is just history repeating itself. A century ago, dangerous substances were marketed to look and sound completely benign. Doctors were featured in advertisements, including my favorite in which one peddled "asthma cigarettes" without blinking an eye. The ad cautioned, "Not recommended for children under 6."

Another ad, unfathomable in retrospect, boasted, "More doctors smoke Camels than any other cigarette!"

Another equally bewildering endorsement went like this: "As your dentist, I would recommend Viceroys."

These weren't jokes, though they're laughable now.

Americans were duped by the tobacco industry for decades.

And it's happening again.

I asked the audience at that Phoenix summit if they were aware that cigarette makers, like those who produced Marlboro, are moving into the marijuana market?

Many were not.

"So, too, is Big Pharma," I told them. The former CEO of Purdue Pharma, one of the purveyors of Oxycontin, which was behind the opioid crisis in America, was later the president and head of a newly established "pharma" division at Emblem, a marijuana company.[14]

Constellation Brands, one of the country's largest alcohol conglomerates, has also invested billions into pot, so it's safe to say that Big Alcohol has already jumped onto the marijuana bandwagon.

Would it surprise you to learn that no one in the states where pot is now legal has a clear idea of what precisely people are smoking, ingesting, vaping, and otherwise consuming? That today's "regulated" marijuana often contains mold, pesticides, bacteria, and other additives? That some of the state agencies charged with oversight are woefully understaffed and that so-called state inspectors often miss key safety issues? In some areas, known drug dealers have been granted licenses and are now operating in the legal market—while continuing their illegal work. There's a naive public assumption that with legalization and the introduction of government licensing and oversight, illegal activity has curtailed.

Perhaps worst of all, is the fact that regulators and politicians regularly lie about what they know or *think* they know. Some take cuts from the businesses and even hand out licenses to friends and associates.

Take Illinois for example. The *Chicago Tribune* and *Chicago Sun-Times* have published stories detailing how the newly legal state pot trade is an insider's game. To start, Candice Gingrich—Newt's half-sister *and* the wife of the legalization bill's lead sponsor—is in the business. "It's not a conflict," legislator Kelly Cassidy, Candice's wife, reportedly said, noting that legalization bill had passed before her wife took the pot job. Still, Cassidy is basically one of the reasons why marijuana is legal in Illinois. And it's now making her and her wife a lot of money.

There's also the example of Green Renaissance Illinois, a marijuana company whose leaders include a former Chicago police commander (who has since resigned), a Republican Party operative, a former Transit Authority official, a pot industry insider related to a former state lawmaker, and a former director of the state agency that oversees the marijuana dispensaries. Although licenses are granted via lottery in Illinois, there's some concern that such an influential group will reap more success than the odds would dictate. The company has submitted 25 license applications that could net it a maximum of 10 licenses worth more than $130 million.

The company's listed address raised eyebrows even more: they're located in the same building as numerous influential lobbyists in the state. It's hard to imagine how this company, with all of its power players, warrants being included in a pool of social equity applicants, or applicants from traditionally underrepresented communities.

The social equity licensing process has been mocked by many in the state, including State Representative La Shawn Ford (D-Chicago) who said, ". . . the well-connected [are] having their way in this cesspool of state government. Anybody that thought that they had a chance to get into cannabis with a fair shot, it seems as though they were wrong."

Unfortunately, these concerns aren't just confined to the Land of Lincoln. In Missouri, the medical marijuana licensing process seemed rigged from the start. In fact, lawmakers are investigating Governor Mike Parson's questionable appointments to positions regulating the industry. Those include his appointment of former Republican state representative Lyndall Fraker to be the state's medical marijuana czar. Of note: Fraker, a former Walmart manager, has no previous medical experience. The administration also hired Amy Moore to serve as Fraker's deputy after serving at the Missouri Public Service Commission. Moore's husband is a lawyer who has numerous marijuana industry clients.

In Maryland, elected officials are going to jail—the ones we know about, at least. State legislator Cheryl Glenn, who created Maryland's medical marijuana program, was sentenced to two years in prison for taking bribes totaling $33,750 for legislative favors.

In Massachusetts, the mayor of Fall River, Jasiel Correia, was arrested and charged with extorting marijuana vendors for hundreds of thousands of dollars in bribes. Correia allegedly offered non-opposition letters (required documents for operation in Massachusetts) in return for payments of $100,000 to $200,000 and campaign contributions as well as mortgage discharges. Correia, who denies any wrongdoing, had reportedly issued 14 non-opposition letters at the time of the indictment, including two that were issued to his girlfriend's brother. Furthermore, Correia vetoed an order made by the Fall River City Council that would limit marijuana licenses.

In Nevada, the state's marijuana efforts have drawn the attention of the FBI because of "how regulators deleted disciplinary records of dispensary sales to minors, bent the rules to favor certain establishments, and stored undocumented, unsecured and unknown quantities of seized marijuana in a state office."[15] In addition, the deputy director of licensing is on a leave of absence after being accused of favoritism and bribes. Jon Ralston, the dean of Nevada political media, noted that the state's industry regulatory scheme is "at best inept and at worst corrupt."

Corruption extends to the D.C. crowd, too, of course. Remember the name Jack Abramoff? He's your run-of-the-mill convicted felon, sentenced to federal prison for mail fraud, conspiracy to bribe public officials, and tax evasion. Abramoff pleaded guilty in 2019 to criminal conspiracy related to marijuana lobbying. And how about Lev Parnas? Parnas is known for his ties to Rudy Giuliani. He and his partner, Igor Fruman, were charged with creating a scheme to pay out political contributions totaling up to $2 million to politicians they hoped would help them win licenses for a marijuana retail business in California, Nevada, and Florida.

The pot industry has problems. And they extend beyond the dangerous product they are selling.

Why, then, would we be willing to make ourselves and our children the guinea pigs of a mind-altering substance known to be harmful to our health and largely distributed by folks with no regard for the public good? Perhaps *The Economist* answered that question for us when it suggested, "While lab animals are an expensive way of understanding the risks of cannabis use, North Americans come free."

Imagine stopping by your neighborhood grocery store and blithely buying, say, a soda, assuming it must be safe, but it isn't because no one has actually checked its contents—no one has the foggiest notion of what's in it, except that it might get you kind of high. Or realllllly high.

That would be crazy, right? But that's what's happening today when people buy marijuana in loosely regulated pot shops. They're assuming the products sold there are safe when they have little reason to make that assumption.

Let me be clear about one thing.

I don't care if an adult smokes a joint and falls asleep on their couch. Nor is this about sick people seeking some relief from their pain. But we don't need to create Philip Morris 2.0. Shouldn't we slow down before we make pot shops as ubiquitous on Main Street as CVS and Walgreens stores? Doesn't it make sense to figure out what's actually in the marijuana being sold today?

This isn't a call for a renewed war on drugs, or greater police presence, or the New Jim Crow. We can remove criminal penalties (including arrests and mandatory minimum sentences) for pot without recreating Big Tobacco. We can choose treatment instead of criminal sanctions. In short, we can choose *decriminalization* without *legalization*.

But why as a nation should we rush headlong into legalizing highly potent THC products without understanding the consequences?

As I detail in this book, it is not just the direct health dangers we need to be worried about.

It's the calamity of mismanagement in pot shops where customers are given the wrong dosages.

It's the way regulators who are tasked to protect the public have turned a blind eye to the shady players who are taking over the pot business.

It's the state-sanctioned labs that fail to catch and stop shipments of marijuana tainted with mold, hazardous pesticides, and heavy metals.

It's the shocking message from hard-core marijuana insiders who are now frightened by what the industry has wrought.

It's the tragic story of a teenager who almost lost her life to pot.

It's the stunning account of an underground-market dealer who admits legalization has actually expanded her business, not thwarted it, as the advocates for legalization promised.

This discussion is being had all over the globe, most acutely in our nation's capital, of course, where there's a pitched battle over whether the federal ban on pot should be scrapped altogether.

I knew something had to be done after a meeting I had on Capitol Hill when a young congressional staffer told me she would be perfectly fine if a commercial airline pilot lit up a joint before taking the controls in the cockpit.

"It's not like the pilot's actually impaired," she said. "Besides, alcohol is worse."

I tried to muster a polite smile.

Houston, we have a problem, I couldn't help thinking. A *big* problem.

But to the rich investors everywhere—and the bureaucracies and systems supporting them—this misinformed and ignorant attitude represents a golden opportunity.

CHAPTER TWO

An Unexpected Ally

"If you had the chance to stop the tobacco industry before they got everyone unknowingly addicted to their products, you would, wouldn't you? If you could have raised the alarm on the over-prescription of opioids before they destroyed the lives of other brothers and sisters, you would have, right?"

These are the words of "Gentleman Toker" Joe Tierney as expressed during an interview with him for this book.

No, really, that's his self-anointed title.

The "Gentleman" was once a hardcore marijuana user, but he began to sing a different tune.

In 2015, when Washington, D.C., legalized marijuana use, Joe, a thirty-something-year-old man who had been smoking pot since his teen years, absolutely rejoiced. Actually, he did more than that. Within a year he seized on the excitement and launched Gentleman Toker, a website that functioned as a forum for D.C. denizens who wanted to know where to get the best weed in the nation's capital. Even the august *Washingtonian* magazine referred to Tiernan as the district's "go-to source" for pot.

At the time, Joe was an executive of a small print shop. But his beloved avocation was marijuana—not just telling people where to get it, but, writing reviews of the partaken products.

Joe was not only having fun, he reckoned he was offering the pot-imbibing crowd a public service. His website also happened to morph into a profitable business, which ultimately became a full-time gig for him. Gentleman Toker got so big, it reached a critical mass, garnering thousands of dollars a month in paid advertisements. Joe wasn't merely a blogger anymore. He was at the vanguard of a movement. Or so he thought—until he began to feel an increasing sense of unease.

At a marijuana pop-up event, Joe was standing next to an open "dab bar" that offered free gifts of marijuana concentrates and waxes when suddenly a partygoer fell into a fit of seizures. It happened "right on top of me," he recalled.

"Wow," he thought. "This is going to get out of hand very quickly."

He didn't know how prescient he was.

Not much later, Joe's mother got sick. She was suffering from a rare inflammatory disease. One of his first actions was to stop by a pot dispensary where he sought to buy her CBD oil to help ease her pain. As an extract from the marijuana plant, cannabidiol products are available in tinctures, skin patches, massage oils, and other forms, which contain *no* THC, the psychoactive ingredient that makes you high. Though some people believe CBD reduces pain, anxiety, and inflammation, these claims have not been approved by the FDA and are certainly open to doubt.

At the store counter, Joe was greeted by an in-house nurse. He asked her what dosage he should get for his ailing mother. The nurse gave him a vague, ballpark answer—nothing to suggest she knew what she was talking about or what she was dispensing.

"It was," he said, "shocking."

Even more surprising was what Joe came to learn about the burgeoning industry to which he had latched his star. During his sojourns, as he sampled marijuana products for his online users, he said he noticed "plants were not being flushed and cured properly."

This was precisely what other whistleblowers you will hear from later in this book confided in me.

Marijuana, even under state-sanctioned regulation, was not being monitored for safe consumption.

"A lot of the products I would find on my travels were really bad," Joe told me.

He defined "bad" as legally sold marijuana that included the use of "unlicensed pesticides."

Further corroborating reports from other whistleblowers, Joe said it wasn't simply benign neglect that resulted in pot being pitched to the public with contaminants. "It's an open secret in the industry that lab results are for sale," he said. Consumers may "think their items are getting the CSI treatment," referring to the idea that regulators give all products a thorough forensic analysis, but "that's not the case at all."

According to Joe and other insiders I've spoken with, marijuana operators are shopping their weed to different labs, often selecting the ones that yield the most favorable results, regardless of the facts. And this means falsely labeling the strength of the product as well as overlooking the contaminants. A pot product can be marked by these labs as having a high—or low—percentage of THC, whichever the operator desires, even though this assessment doesn't reflect the true quality of the product or, in some cases, have any semblance of accuracy whatsoever.

As Joe explains, "There are a number of different ways to cheat."

The problem, from the standpoint of consumers, is that they have no idea what they are consuming. "The risks they're taking are poorly understood," he said. "The labs are not testing for every single possible contaminant." So what concerns Joe and other whistleblowers is not only that the level of THC in many products is being misreported; it's that the product is being undertested for known toxins and impurities too.

Adding to the confusion is the lack of uniformity in the way testing is carried out from state to state. "The real damning thing to me," Joe said, is that "the state regulations are different everywhere." Each state where pot is legal oversees the drug in different ways, leading to a patchwork of oversight that is decidedly less than effective.

Remember, these are the unvarnished words of someone who was at the heart of the green rush. Joe wasn't just pro pot. He was a long-time user who *wanted* to believe in the legalization process. But the facts convinced him otherwise.

In some cases, he said, it wasn't clear to him whether the problem was premeditated.

"The industry is moving too far, too fast without consideration of the consequences," he observed. "Either they don't know what they're doing, or they don't care what they're doing."

Joe wasn't the first top name in the D.C. pot world to forcefully critique the industry. Dan Riffle, the federal affairs and lobbying head for the biggest pro-marijuana legalization group in the country, the Marijuana Policy Project (MPP), shocked the pot world in 2015 when he announced his abrupt departure. (I'd like to say he left the scene because I beat him in a long C-SPAN debate we did a year earlier, but alas, that was not the case! He now works for Alexandria Ocasio-Cortez.)

It was bombshell news. In a November email to his colleagues, he explained his reasoning, writing "industry is taking over the legalization movement and I'm not interested in the industry." In a subsequent interview with the *International Business Times*, he went further. "I felt for the last few months the industry was kind of dominating the legalization movement's work in general, and MPP's specifically." After his employer launched a "Pledge 4 Growth campaign," asking the industry to dedicate .420 percent of their revenue to MPP, Riffle commented, "I think it is a pretty stark example of the kinds of things I was concerned about and [those] were the reasons why I left . . . ." He continued, saying he had "concern about the industry's interest being in conflict with public health interests . . . I've even had people within the industry reach out to say they have similar concerns based on what they're seeing . . . As the industry grows and they see the type of people it's attracting, they're turned off by it."

Gentleman Toker was feeling uneasy about the industry as well. As he pointed out, "Everybody's being taken advantage [of] for their ignorance." He was quick to add, though, that it's "not all malicious." Perhaps, as he says, some people "don't know any better."

But by the summer of 2019, it didn't matter to Joe whether it was malicious or not. That's when he started feeling chest pains. First he had trouble breathing, then he found himself coughing up wads of phlegm.

"It started to concern me," he admitted. "No warning, I'd suddenly cough up a big friggin' thing across the room." However, his concern quickly turned to alarm when he coughed up blood for the first time.

It didn't take long for the man who was promoting the benefits of toking on his highly trafficked website to stop toking.

"I quit immediately," he said.

Almost as quickly, Joe stopped hacking up blood. The wetness in his lungs went away too. His chest didn't feel tight anymore. There was no question in Joe's mind that the cure was giving up inhaling concentrates of marijuana. "I'm absolutely 100 percent convinced that it was the dabs," he said.

His belief that potent concoctions of pot caused him harm was confirmed by the similar experiences of a friend working in a legal pot dispensary in Maryland. "She was getting sick from vape cartridges way before any of this stuff hit," he said.

The "stuff "Joe was referring to was the EVALI vaping crisis afflicting people across the country, leaving many dead. It was such a serious public emergency that it warrants its own chapter later in this book. But even before the crisis had a name and became a full-blown national scandal, Joe had heard troubling things about vaping: how there was lead contamination in the products and how the lead leaked into the vape juice. The way Joe described it, after the metal coils within the vape device heated to a certain point, contaminants leach into the oils inhaled by users. And yet, until a critical mass of people became ill and died, the problem went undetected by users *and* authorities.

It wasn't his own illness that prompted Joe to take matters into his own hands; nor was it learning his friend, who worked in a dispensary, got sick from vaping. Sadly, what set him into action was learning that vaping was actually *killing* some Americans.

"A lot of people aren't raising their hand because they just don't know any better," he said.

Finally, Joe raised his hand.

By the fall of 2019, at the height of the vaping crisis, he decided to shut down his popular Gentleman Toker website. It was an act that garnered another *Washingtonian* article about Joe's work. This time the headline read, "A Major Cannabis-Review Site Is Shutting Down Because Its Founder Doesn't Think There's Any Safe Way to Consume Weed."

On October 1, Joe launched a final salvo with a post on his website titled, "Going Down Swinging."

"I'm not arrogant enough to think that I can stop the wave of commercial cannabis simply by walking away, but I had to do something, and this is the last card in my deck."

To underscore his conversion, Joe wrote in capital letters, "I'M ABSOLUTELY DISGUSTED WITH THE INDUSTRY."

Perhaps not completely though. When this book went to press, his website was back up. He didn't respond to any calls or inquiries about what had happened.

Was the lure of the pot industry too strong?

And just *who* is this industry?

CHAPTER THREE

Forces behind the Revolution

The man with the mic swayed restlessly in a white swivel chair. He cut a dashing figure—youthful in a buzz cut, a dark V-neck shirt, burgundy slacks, and white Nike sneakers.

No socks for him either.

I don't think he forgot them as I had. This was actually part of the image he cultivated as a controversial cofounder and chief executive of MedMen, one of the leading purveyors of pot in the nation.

It was in February 2019, on a snowy day in Boston, that Adam Bierman—the fashionably sockless pot poster child—delivered the opening keynote address, holding court before a standing-room-only crowd in a huge auditorium at a convention called "Seed to Sale Show: Navigating the Next Wave in the Cannabis Revolution."

To Adam and this industry desperate to break away from Cheech and Chong stereotypes, it's not called marijuana, pot, or weed anymore. Rather, the more refined term "cannabis" is preferred, as if it were some kind of special reserve Chablis from the Burgundy region of France. Which, to hear Adam tell it, it was.

"Cannabis makes the world a safer, happier place," he crowed on stage, much like Steve Jobs did about the iPhone.

With an almost giddy glibness, Adam claimed, "Cannabis saved my marriage," though details were less than forthcoming—*hazy* even. He also credited marijuana with helping him "fall asleep at night." Then he went on to say that he was convinced pot would "change the world." In the not-so-distant future, he envisioned weed being sold in upscale retail locations—places that look more like Whole Foods. There would be gleaming aisles of neatly packaged products. After all, Adam boasted, most people who partake of pot in the United States do so for what he called the purposes of "wellness."

But what of all the recent news articles, including one from marijuana skeptic Malcolm Gladwell in *The New Yorker*, raising concerns about whether pot is safe?

"Four people read that stuff," Adam said dismissively. "It's just noise, man."

Drowning out that noise, as he indicated, is the promise of profit. "Fundamentals will prevail," he said, sounding more like a Wall Street analyst than a man selling a federally illegal product that induces a mind-bending high.

Adam began to brag about how "suits" from ten top banks paid their respects, visiting his office in the hopes of winning his business. He touted the benefits of normalizing marijuana, stating that it would generate jobs and tax revenue, albeit without disclosing any of the fine print. (Don't worry, I will in a moment.) Everyone wants a piece of the pot pie, including Big Tobacco, Big Pharma, and Big Alcohol, all of which were making moves to get into the marijuana business.

According to Adam, this thing is so big that it earned a nickname inspired by the Gold Rush of 1849.

The Green Rush.

"This is my purpose on this planet," Adam declared, before concluding his remarks to an enraptured audience.

Let me give Adam his due. He was right about at least one thing: There was a mad dash among corporate interests—especially the trinity of tobacco, pharmaceutical, and alcohol companies—to make a quick buck on pot. But they rushed in ignoring the potential effects on consumer health as if they had learned nothing from past mistakes, except perhaps how to sidestep them. To wit:

- After Big Tobacco was exposed for the health dangers cigarettes pose, Philip Morris, the maker of Marlboro, rebranded itself as the more innocuous, if unrecognizable, Altria. Seeking new financial frontiers as cigarette smoking waned, Altria made a flurry of marijuana deals, spending $1.8 billion to purchase a 45 percent stake in Cronos Group, the biggest pot company in Canada. Altria also spent $12.8 billion for a 35 percent stake in Juul, the e-cigarette maker. Juul is widely considered a stalking horse for the marijuana business through its former parent company PAX, which shares the same technology, allowing users to vaporize weed with its products. Also worth noting is that Juul has come under fire for the surge in use of its products among high school students, hooking them on nicotine. In fact, the FDA launched an investigation into Juul's alleged predatory marketing to underage children via social media. While Juul took its ads down, PAX's similar branding and youth-appealing ads remain up.
- A 2014 report[16] by researchers at the University of California, San Francisco and the University of Helsinki demonstrate the interactions between Big Tobacco and marijuana in the fledgling e-cigarette market:

"E-cigarettes are another nexus between tobacco and marijuana. E-cigarettes can be used as marijuana-delivery devices using hash oil and are difficult to distinguish from conventional e-cigarettes. In 2014, Altria (formerly Philip Morris) purchased Florida-based Green Smoke, an e-cigarette company whose logo and website suggests crossover marijuana use, and as of 2014, NORML [National Organization for the Reform of Marijuana Laws] was assisting the tobacco and e-cigarette companies in opposing efforts to include e-cigarettes in clean indoor air laws."

- Tobacco giant Imperial Brands, the fifth-largest tobacco company on earth and the manufacturer of Winston cigarettes, recently made an equity investment in a British firm that researches, develops, and licenses marijuana products.
- Leaked internal documents show that Big Tobacco considers marijuana as just "a natural expansion of current smoking habits which, if a more tolerant attitude were ever taken . . . would be a change in habit comparable to moving over to cigars."[17]
- The Marijuana Policy Project (MPP), one of the largest organizations seeking to legalize marijuana, openly collaborates with tobacco companies, soliciting their donations to continue expanding the market for marijuana nationally.[18] (Its board chair is a cousin of billionaire Illinois Governor J.B. Pritzker.)
- The former head of the company that produced OxyContin—a drug largely responsible for the opioid epidemic—recently moved into the medical marijuana market. The state of Massachusetts alleged John Stewart, as Purdue Pharma's CEO, directed his company's sales reps to visit prescribers more than 70,000 times. Meanwhile, Sandoz, a generic drug unit of Novartis, the Swiss pharmaceutical maker, recently struck a global distribution deal with Tilray, a major Canadian marijuana maker, for co-branded marijuana oils and other products to allegedly treat ailments, such as epilepsy, sleep disorders, and post-traumatic stress, all claims open to significant doubt.
- Constellation Brands, the producer of Corona Beers, recently made a multibillion-dollar investment in Canopy, another big Canadian pot company. Tilray, its Canadian brethren in pot, recently formed a $100 million partnership with Anheuser-Busch InBev, the behemoth behind Budweiser, aimed at creating a pot-infused substitute for beer. Not to be outdone, Molson Coors, as well as smaller beermakers, such as the creator of Blue Moon, are developing lines of custom marijuana-infused so-called craft beers. Weed-infused wine is already on the market via CannaVines. Meanwhile, our intelligence reports indicate that the Beer Institute, the Wine & Spirit Wholesalers of America, and the Distilled Spirits Council

have begun to work with the pot industry as their reps meet quietly to collaborate.

Despite their products' legal status, society has had numerous disastrous experiences in the past with all three industries—pharmaceuticals, alcohol, and tobacco. Legal tobacco and alcohol combined kill more than 500,000 Americans a year. That's ten times the number of deaths from all illegal drugs—methamphetamine, heroin, crack, and more—put *together*. And these legal killers incur at least $15 in social costs for every $1 in taxes we rake in. If we're being honest, we've never regulated those drugs in a responsible way. (Alcohol and tobacco are most certainly drugs, in case you're wondering.) Lobbyists and special interests essentially own the rule-marking when it comes to such drugs. Why in the world would we think we could get it right *this time*?

The substance of choice now just happens to be marijuana. But it could be any substance. Already, there are moves to legalize other drugs. Denver, for instance, became the first city to decriminalize hallucinogenic mushrooms, followed by Washington, D.C. And Oregon has decriminalized heroin in an effort funded by a group whose goal is to legalize all drugs, including crack and methamphetamine.

Again, I ask, do we really want to repeat history?

Actually, some do.

The Green Rush—or the Marijuana Revolution—attracts more than those who are already in the business of peddling mind-altering products. Even ScottsMiracle-Gro, the giant gardening supply firm, has joined the fray. Miracle-Gro doesn't just produce big tomatoes anymore. It produces big lobbying efforts in Washington, D.C., too. Today this company is one of the strongest proponents of the legalization of marijuana. What's the connection?

The almighty dollar.

Sensing a financial windfall, Miracle-Gro is spending hundreds of millions of dollars purchasing ancillary companies in the pot business, such as manufacturers of grow lights and hydroponic equipment. And in November 2020 they helped finance the successful effort to firmly ensconce marijuana legalization in New Jersey's state constitution.

The numbers are hard to ignore. Legal pot sales have rocketed, rising 259 percent in just four years, from $3.4 billion to $12.2 billion worldwide in 2018. According to Roy Bingham, the chief executive of BDS Analytics, this is the largest growth of any product in the consumer industry.

By 2022, Bingham predicts legally licensed marijuana will be a $31.7 billion global industry—dwarfing Hollywood's annual box office gross.

But what's happening with marijuana isn't just about greed, for lack of a better word.

It's also about hubris.

We return to Greek tragedy.

But the key figures in today's drama are the major financiers of the pot resurgence—über-wealthy capitalists whose names remain largely shrouded in mystery. They operate in the shadows of anonymity, pulling the trigger on multimillion-dollar deals from laptops in the perch of high-rises, unbothered by a lack of notoriety, consumed by an acquisitiveness bordering on obsession. They don't want you to know who they are. They just want to gather expensive toys: personal jets, palatial villas, Ferraris.

That's how one such financier keeps score. He resides in Canada, one of the epicenters of the legal pot boom, which has spun off a series of initial public stock offerings à la the dot-com boom of an earlier generation. To borrow a touchstone phrase, the "irrational exuberance" of investors in the early aughts created a stampede of newly minted millionaires not unlike today's marijuana moguls.

If the analogy holds, however, investors in the marijuana boom should remember what happened during the internet boom. It busted.

In the meantime, they count their earnings and try to score bigger and better objects of desire. This is happening at the same time the Auditor-General of Canada's most populated province, Ontario, is saying the marijuana industry does not have proper oversight (a damning December 2020 report from the office criticized "inventory controls over recreational cannabis sold in retail stores" and found that 80 percent of the marijuana sold was on the illegal market, among other major concerns).[19]

On a recent pot stock deal, this Canadian financier netted tens of millions of dollars—on paper. While sitting in a quiet lunch joint one afternoon shortly after his windfall, he looked unhappy. Apparently, he couldn't find a suitable second home to buy. You can't get what you used to for north of $10 million.

His buddy, a venture capitalist, also from Canada, looked to match his unhappy compadre. This other multimillionaire recently recruited a small team, including a farmer from New England, to work out the logistics of boarding a private jet and flying off on a secret mission to the Caribbean. Their goal: to persuade the prime minister of a small island nation to allow them to purchase a hundred acres to grow marijuana. Their investment: a couple million dollars. Their anticipated profit: upward of $100 million.

That's not a typo.

They expected to make an unheard-of fiftyfold return on their money in a single year.

There is a notable difference, though, between the internet bubble and what we're experiencing today with the mad rush to normalize marijuana. Executives of various pot enterprises worry about being arrested while crossing the U.S. border from Canada. And for good reason.

Despite being clothed in fine linen, these chieftains are, at a basic level, operating as drug dealers according to federal law.

Not that you can tell by their behavior. They acted as if there wasn't a whiff of impropriety about their business during the aforementioned pot convention in Boston. The frenzied floor had the look and feel of almost any other buzzing industry trade show in love with itself.

Off in one corner of the bustling Expo sat salesmen from a Chinese maker of industrial LED lighting. Pivoting to pot as a new opportunity, they were now marketing grow lights for the burgeoning marijuana cultivation business. (Miracle-Gro wasn't the only one trying to corner this market early!) The same principle applied to the startups hawking their services at other nearby tables. Such services included specialty packaging, social media, sales software management, downloadable apps—and, of course, there were those offering all manner of "advisory solutions to cannabis businesses." As one company's handout put it: "We understand the unique cultural, political, and legal environment in which our clients operate and can assist with navigating through complex industry solutions." From another vendor came the promise of "Turnkey cultivation solutions," whatever that means. *Emerald*, a slick lifestyle magazine, promoted a "boutique cannabis culture." In another corner stood Karson Humiston, looking mildly unimpressed with all the attention she was drawing as a millennial prodigy of the industry.

At the age of twenty-two, she founded Vangt. Heralded as the über for weed workers, the firm connected rapidly expanding companies, desperate for employees, with people to fill their ranks. Karson started the business in 2015 with two employees. About four years later, she oversaw more than seventy-five. Not unlike the siren call of the dot-com boom, venture capitalists (aka, VCs) are now rushing to the marijuana market, throwing money at it with wild abandon in the hope of reaping outrageous returns. In her first round of funding, Karson netted a cool $10 million.

"Total blast," she said about the experience of building a pot business.

Down another row of the Expo, a couple of youthful sales reps were overjoyed with their company's prospects for success. They worked for MJ Freeway, a pot consultancy helping entrepreneurs break into the business. The underlying cause of their optimism? They stand to reap millions when their firm is listed on Nasdaq, one of the leading stock market exchanges. This, too, harkens back to the days of the internet bubble when high-flying stocks, often based on little more than an idea, produced a phalanx of admins who promptly quit their jobs and retired as millionaires after cashing in their stock options. The weed reps for MJ Freeway were confident about their future given the robust growth of the marijuana market. "Women between the ages of thirty and fifty-five are the biggest spenders [on] cannabis," said one of the reps.

The calculus was simple. Their demographic sweet spot was what one rep called "soccer moms." These are women whom the reps said possess two qualities perfectly aligned with the industry's best customers: Soccer moms are stressed out and they have lots of disposable income to spend.

The free flow of money was palpable at an invitation-only pot party held after convention hours that evening.

Weed wasn't being passed around. Oysters were. An old Boston hand was hired to shuck the expensive ocean delectables as partygoers ate, drank, and generally enjoyed the exclusive soirée hosted in a funky gallery where original art in bold, bright hues was handsomely displayed. There was a sense of comradery as the guests mingled in the dark, intimate space—a feeling that they were in this together. They all seemed to know and root for one another, presumably having seen one another before at similar conventions. The guy who marketed wine-storage solutions was familiar with the pair who launched a pot magazine for moms. And everybody seemed to know the person circulating in the middle of the room. She was Ashley Picillo, the head of a women-owned and -operated marijuana consulting firm. She also coauthored the book *Breaking the Grass Ceiling: Women, Weed & Business*.

What's more, Ashley—as with so many others in the room—believed in what she was doing. She sincerely looked after her employees and was known to be kind to the many acquaintances and newcomers who introduced themselves and paid their respects to her. Many in this business are well-meaning people, even if they don't recognize the dangers inherent in the product.

But everyone in the industry, to be sure, is taking advantage of the gray policy area in which we are living—the world where something is illegal federally yet allowed on the state level. The challenge with living in this gray zone is that sometimes even the regulators don't know or haven't yet established the parameters. A former executive partner of Adam Bierman's, the MedMen exec whose popular chain of marijuana shops was modeled after the Apple Store aesthetic, had this observation about the industry: "I hate to say it . . . you're dealing with regulators who are just kind of making it up."[20]

This kind of latitude can make it easy for the misuse of corporate money, as was alleged in a 2019 lawsuit brought against MedMen.

If the suit's allegations are accurate (the company maintains they are not), the company's spending didn't just rival the renowned excesses of previous dotcom and housing booms and busts; it crossed legal lines. The MedMen lawsuit alleged that Adam Bierman and Andrew Modlin, the company's other cofounder, instructed the company's CFO to wire hundreds of thousands of dollars to a so-called consultant in Canada to "buy up" the company's flagging stock as it was under attack. A "sham office" was allegedly created in Vancouver to fool regulators.

What's more, their ousted CFO also claimed that he was forced to contribute to Democrat Steve Sisolak's successful campaign for governor of Nevada in 2018. When *Politico* revealed that the donations may have circumvented campaign finance rules, the state began an investigation into whether they were illegal or not. (The investigation is still ongoing.) An Associated Press story discovered that in October, the same month as the donations were made, "Sisolak, serving then as chairman of the Clark County Commission, attended the opening of a MedMen store in Las Vegas, presented a placard to Bierman and Modlin and declared it 'MedMen Day,' praising the company for creating jobs."[21]

By late 2019, the company was starting to show even more cracks. The flagship MedMen store lost its bid for a permanent license from the city of West Hollywood, putting its main retail location on shaky legal ground. In January 2020, with MedMen under financial pressure, Bierman resigned as CEO. In May 2020, in another signal of distress, MedMen closed five of its eight Florida stores.

And it's becoming increasingly hard to ignore other troubling news emanating from the pot industry. For instance, an attorney for FusionPharm, a Colorado marijuana supply company, was recently found guilty in connection with $12.2 million in securities fraud, conspiracy, money laundering, and wire and mail fraud.

Even more troubling are the blatant conflicts of interest that have begun to emerge, with officials trading their government badges for more profitable gigs in marijuana. For instance, in Colorado a marijuana enforcement official quit her job and immediately began working for Harmony & Green, a weed cultivation company, as a compliance consultant, disregarding the state's required six-month post-termination restrictive covenant period.

Another whopper: a Washington State marijuana licensing specialist leased 25 acres he owned to a pot entrepreneur.[22]

And another: an official of the Massachusetts public health agency that issues medical marijuana licenses applied for a medical marijuana license while employed by the department.

Illinois, America's original beacon of organized crime, isn't immune either. Almost all of the state reps (and even their loved ones) pushing for legalization there received contributions from the marijuana industry.[23]

The bad behavior extends into more subtle realms, including marijuana marketing, which continues to move ahead full throttle. The pot industry can't nationally advertise its illicit product, but it skirts federal media restrictions anyway, employing social media by contracting with those quick-to-fame stars of our age: Instagram influencers.

They are, for the most part, hyperlocal celebs—big names and wealthy people who post alluring Instagram content promoting pot. Images of product in the hands of bikini-clad models beckon attention. Packaging is professional, commoditized, appealing.

Their target: young users.

One marijuana marketer who was quoted in a 2019 issue of *Wired* magazine explained that she pays influencers to place product in their Instagram post or story to make the messaging more organic.

Who needs traditional promos?

"People don't like to be advertised to, so when they're seeing something that an influencer is using, they're going to want to have that," she said.

That strategy is borrowed from another playbook—that of Big Tobacco, which famously used product placement to make smoking look cool. By paying to place their cigarettes in the hands of actors in movies, Big Tobacco was doing much the same thing in print and television ads that the marijuana industry is doing today with Instagram influencers—using subtle but powerful persuasion.

Weed chocolate bars and fruit-flavored Kush pops that look identical to the unadulterated versions of these snacks are also being used to lure young consumers. And there's yet another tactic that Big Tobacco taught to the marijuana trade by example. When Ohio was trying to legalize pot (an effort that subsequently failed), one major marijuana company introduced "Bud Man," a cartoon mascot that was basically an anthropomorphic marijuana bud. It's an image that harkens back to Big Tobacco's Joe Camel mascot. We all know the power of cartoon characters on the psyches of our children.

The appeal to teens is also evident in the billboards that adorn California's freeways. Their message reads, "Delivering more joy than dogs and babies combined. Marijuana delivered." Sure, people of all ages love the convenience of home delivery, but this service also makes pot readily available to teens who don't drive yet!

Meanwhile, Eaze, a pot delivery service in California, doesn't even hide that it is collecting customer data, paying close attention to demographics including what it calls the "Gen Z" market—sixteen to twenty-two year-olds—because their spending is up.

Of course, broader celebrity branding is taking off too. Now Jonah Hill, Whoopi Goldberg, Snoop Dog, Kevin Durant, and Willie Nelson, among other stars, are unabashedly hawking pot products.

A big part of the problem, experts say, is that the media is also complicit; reporters are sending the wrong message, increasingly romanticizing marijuana while giving short shrift to its health risks.

This isn't entirely by accident.

The Influence Foundation Inc. is a nonprofit organization whose expressed mission is to advocate "through journalism for rational and compassionate approaches to drug use, drug policy, and human rights." It's funded by the usual suspects—such powerful vested marijuana interests as Altria, the American Vaping Association, Philip Morris International, and Reynolds American Inc. The Influence Foundation is all over Twitter using the hip name "Filter Mag," among others.

What's more, numerous journalists who've covered the marijuana phenomenon have jumped ship to actually join the industry. Several have started pot companies or firms supporting them. They include the savvy Ricardo Baca, who was the first full-time marijuana editor for a major American metro newspaper, *The Denver Post*. For three years, until December 2016, Baca produced the paper's *Cannabist* publication, which covers national marijuana news and culture.

Now Baca is something of an *éminence grise* for the pot industry—a powerbroker who knows just about everyone in the business. In his new capacity, he is founder and chief executive of Grasslands, a PR company that positions itself as a "journalism-minded" agency and whose clients include quite a number of players in the field. Baca also happens to be known for putting on a great party at pot conventions, including the oyster-shucking soirée in Boston mentioned earlier. He is known for his rather transparent tweets, such as, "Every time I consume psilocybin, regardless of my intentions for the trip, the mental health benefits are real." (It is possible there are benefits to some of these substances in specific, controlled conditions, but to be changing policy *en masse* via badly worded ballot initiatives and lobbying campaigns funded by greedy profit hunters is outright dangerous.)

Many other organizations, including the Marijuana Policy Project, Drug Policy Alliance, and Students for Sensible Drug Policy, dot the drug "reform" landscape and are funded and pushed, directly or indirectly, by an army of PR and corporate consultants such as Baca. It's a familiar pattern: medicalize or decriminalize to desensitize first, then legalize to make money.

So that's where we are. Neutral policy words have been coopted by these groups who define themselves as an "alliance" a "coalition" or simply as "sensible." Eaze, the pot delivery service, talks in its annual state-of-the-industry reports about the evils of marijuana "prohibition," a loaded term referring to the failed U.S. ban on alcohol that prevailed from 1920 to 1933. (By the way, the alcohol prohibition-drug law analogy is a bad one. Humans have been consuming alcohol for more than 5,000 years. Most people who drink today are part of that cultural continuum, making efforts to prohibit alcohol futile. By contrast, we don't have the same centuries-long, ingrained history with marijuana. Most people do not use and have never used illegal drugs and the laws reflect that. If properly applied, laws can deter and stop mass normalization of pot before it ever goes the way of alcohol. Did you know that during the brief period of alcohol prohibition in the U.S.—from 1920 to 1933—diseases such as cirrhosis of the liver dramatically declined in prevalence and that tens of thousands of lives have been saved since 1984 when Congress upped the national minimum drinking age to 21? These are not reasons to prohibit alcohol—again, because it is so ubiquitous—but these examples prove that access and availability are key factors of use with any substance prone to misuse.)

Eaze also casually throws around other well-scrubbed terms, calling pot—ahem, *cannabis*—a "wellness tool" and comparing its impact on health to the felicitous effects of wine, even though wine is not consumed for the sole reason of intoxication, unlike marijuana. And with today's 99.9 percent THC waxes readily available, intoxicate it does.

CHAPTER FOUR

Facts Matter, Money Talks

Where's Patrick? I wondered.

There we were—a group that included scientists from top universities, Democratic and Republican lawmakers, National Institutes of Health staffers, and the nation's first Black magistrate judge—but former Congressman Patrick Kennedy hadn't arrived yet. He was running late. He is such an integral part of our organization that it was important that he be present before we got started. It was April 20—the unofficial "stoner's holiday"—and C-SPAN was about to start filming our press conference live to millions of people. About thirty seconds before showtime, the dapper Kennedy made a stealth entrance through the doors in the back of the room, where he remained for the duration of the presentation, letting the others shine on camera, as is his style.

Great, he's here! I thought to myself with relief before going through the usual pre-presentation rundown in my head. Cameras. Check. Audience. Check. Nerves under control. Sort of.

Although I was feeling pretty good by then, and I was extremely grateful for the important purpose C-SPAN serves, a concern still lingered in the back of my mind: "Will enough people see this? Or will all of our hard work go unnoticed?"

It would be a shame if the message didn't get out to enough people because the data we were about to present was news. Actual news. News most Americans don't know:

- Today's marijuana isn't anything like it used to be. It can be up to 99 percent potent, and no one knows the effect this can have on the brain.[24]
- Marijuana use among youth—twelve- to seventeen-year-olds—continues to rise in states that have legalized pot.[25]
- Addiction rates have more than doubled. One in three marijuana users, according to one prominent study, meet the criteria for a "marijuana use disorder."[26]
- Emergency poison control calls for children, from newborns to age eight, more than tripled in Colorado after legalization.[27]
- The number of car crashes involving marijuana is skyrocketing. For instance, the percentage of traffic deaths related to pot more than doubled in Washington State the year retail sales were allowed there.[28]
- Despite pronouncements to the contrary, studies show the opioid crisis in America is worsening where marijuana has been legalized.[29]
- Smoking weed by pregnant women is linked to lower birth weights in newborns.[30]
- The more you use pot, the higher the likelihood it will create other (non-marijuana) substance abuse and dependency, according to no less an authority than the National Academy of Sciences, an independent nonprofit organization comprised of the country's leading researchers.[31]
- People in states where it's been legalized are testing positive for marijuana at much higher rates, and a recent survey showed that 25 percent of Americans living in pot-legal states admit to having gone to work stoned.[32, 33]

Heads nodded in understanding as each point was made. The top leaders who were gathered around the podium clearly got it. People in the room got it too.

But who else would get it? Say someone watching at home wasn't persuaded to believe the alarming statistics—say they still denied the harmful effects of marijuana— what would it take to convince them?

The answer, based on the past forty years of experience, is, in a word, *money*. After all, that's what it took to convince the powers that be in fifteen states and Washington, D.C., to sanction it.

Three men primarily laid the foundation for legalization in this country. According to *Forbes*, the elusive and powerful billionaire George Soros is one of them.[34] The philanthropist bankrolled many of the successful statewide initiatives to legalize marijuana over the past several years. It is estimated that Soros has contributed north of $200 million to relaxing drug laws, with several million dollars going to the Drug Policy Alliance, which promotes legalization. John Sperling, the

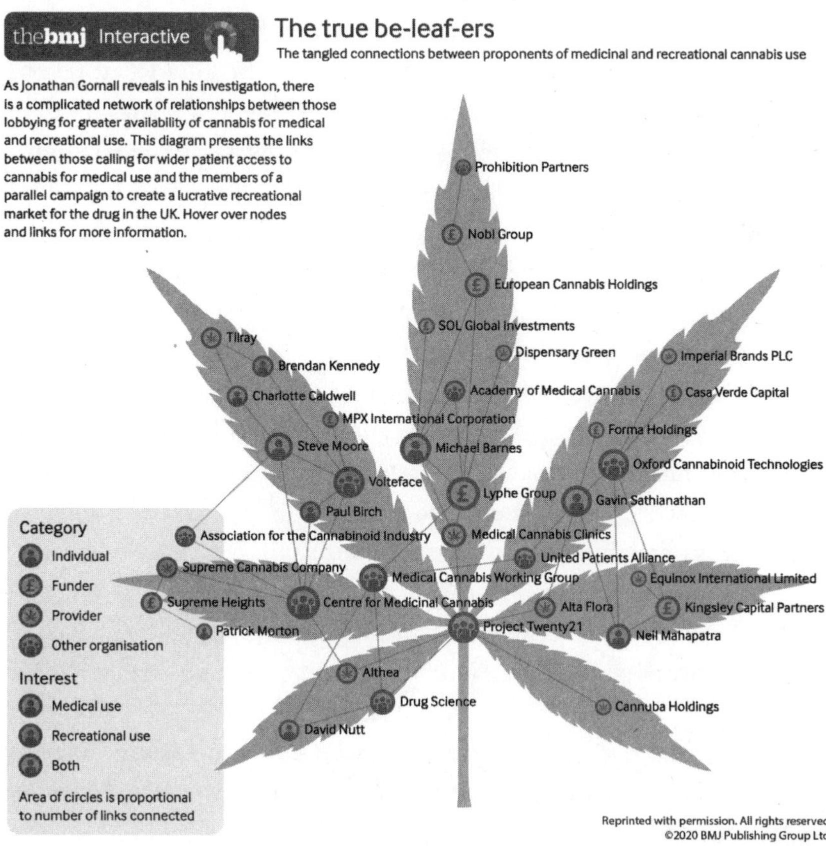

billionaire founder of the University of Phoenix, also helped bankroll the early move to legalize, as did Peter Lewis, the founder of Progressive Insurance, who discovered pot late in life and fell in love with it.

According to *Ballotpedia*, proponents have raised $145 million specifically for state ballot initiatives to legalize marijuana since 1996 (the vast majority coming in between 2010 to 2016). That's more than triple the amount of $35 million that opponents have raised.

Big money influences so alarmed academics in the UK that the *British Medical Journal* published a special article about it, in what was for them a highly unusual move. The piece highlighted the intertwined government, media, academic, and business interests—particularly those of Big Tobacco's—in pushing for legalization. In an investigative report, journalist Jonathan Gornall linked several commercial organizations that stood to gain from the creation of a recreational marijuana market with individuals and activists who were pushing for more access to medical marijuana. What's more, he found that several tobacco companies were funding studies on medical marijuana, an activity that calls for some questioning of the validity of that research.[35]

The big dollar figures behind pro-pot forces don't even take into account indirect "education" campaigns, think-tank manipulation, university recruiting, journalist training, federal lobbying efforts, and international initiatives. Those numbers are harder to track but are likely in the $1 billion or more range.

One egregious example of this was found by *The Washington Post*. In a piece by Tom Hamburger and Alexander Becker, titled, "At fast-growing Brookings, donors may have an impact on research agenda," the work of Peter Lewis, the billionaire founder of Progressive Insurance, was highlighted. The article begins:

> *Of all the topics the venerable Brookings Institution has examined in recent years, legalizing marijuana was rarely high on anyone's scholarly agenda.*
>
> *That changed after a November 2012 visit from a lawyer working with Peter B. Lewis, the billionaire insurance magnate who during the*

last years of his life made the legalization of marijuana his personal mission.

The article goes on to detail how "Brookings emerged as a hub of research that supported the views of the legalization movement." Op-eds, speaker series, dinners, and prominent papers were published to support the idea in Washington. The cost? At least $500,000. Money indeed talks. (In full disclosure, I was invited to one of these posh dinners—perhaps because they needed a token anti-pot spokesperson. As you might expect, my views clashed that night with those in attendance, including with a person who would later be nominated to a U.S. cabinet position.)

Wealthy individuals of all political stripes—think of Silicon Valley magnate Peter Thiel, natural soap producer David Bronner, and tech whiz Sean Parker—have donated tens of millions of dollars to legalize pot. That's not even to mention the known industry players who have contributed money.

Back to our April 20 event. To my surprise, more people were watching C-SPAN than I estimated because we received a record amount of donations after the press conference.

But beyond all the financial contributions that poured in (SAM relies on individual donations and foundation grants—we don't take a penny from industries such as Big Pharma, Big Tobacco, or Big Alcohol), were the manifold cries for help we fielded from parents grieving over their children's dangerous use of pot.

That's where Sally comes in.

CHAPTER FIVE

A Mother's Job

It was 8:33 on a quiet Sunday morning, but for Sally Schindel, it might as well have been a Wednesday afternoon or a Monday evening. Those who have been forever touched by devastating loss will tell you that the day never ends—it simply blends into all the others that follow.

Not long after my talk in Phoenix, Sally could be found just a few miles away, at the National Memorial Cemetery of Arizona. In many ways it had become her home away from home.

It was partly sunny along this wide flat expanse of barren land where symmetrical rows of graves stretched on as far as the eye could see. Saguaro cacti and palo verde trees dotted the landscape against the backdrop of the majestic Phoenix Mountains. The cemetery was nothing if not immaculate, with its neatly cropped asphalt roads, well-manicured bushes, and carefully appointed rocks. The only sound piercing the peace and solitude was the occasional chirp of a bird or a plane mimicking it beyond.

"Andy would love it," Sally said, taking in the beautiful vista under a pair of dark sunglasses.

After a few more moments of silence, she opened the trunk of her SUV and removed a clutch of long-stemmed white lilies.

"I carry these around with me," she said, then referred to her son in the present tense as if he were still here. "Andy has a fondness for houseplants. I always make sure he has a good-looking one."

These were faux flowers, but they would last—they were something that couldn't die. Sally placed her left hand on the marble façade of Section F, 39 A, caressing it with a motherly touch.

Behind it lay the remains of her beloved son, Andrew Steven Zorn, an Army veteran who served his country honorably after a deployment in Iraq.

Free at last
Truly loved
True friend
At peace.

Sally had those indelible words carved into the granite columbarium. Inside, along with the urn, is a snapshot of Andy's dog, Trit, a German Shepherd mix. Trit's tongue was wagging when the photo was taken, and he was standing tall before his master as if he were protecting him.

Andy would have wanted it that way.

Flanking his resting place are the remains of World War II and Korean War vets, not far from an Eternal Flame pyramid and a World War II Submarine Torpedo monument.

"I think about the people around him," Sally said. "They're old enough to be his grandpas. He'd like that."

The sound of birds tweeting caught Sally's attention. Holes in nearby cacti had become home to birds feeding their babies. "This is so full of life," Sally said of her surroundings.

So, too, was Andy once.

As a child, Andy used to build forts out in the open where coyotes roamed. Those were in the days before fresh air was replaced by AC. Those were also the days before a Walmart was plunked down and his hometown, like so many other places, became the land of strip malls. He was a tyke who loved hammers and the noises they made. He adored cowboy boots too. "That was his identity as a child," Sally recalled.

Andy was a happy boy—the kind who smiled a lot and whose face was animated even more by dark brown eyes and an unruly tuft of hair. He was funny and liked to be the center of attention, the class clown.

At the age of eight, Andy was named camper of the week. On the form saved by his mother, he said the thing he most liked about summer in Phoenix was swimming because, "It's fun." He also wrote that if he could go somewhere, it would be Italy because, "I don't know."

Andy was a planner as well. When he earned his first paycheck, he asked his mom, who was an accountant, how much he would have to save to become a millionaire by the time he was forty.

"Five percent every year," Sally replied.

He saved ten percent.

Everything began to change when he was fourteen, an eighth grader. That's when Sally discovered a big bag of weed in Andy's bedroom, which she promptly flushed down the toilet.

His reaction was utterly shocking for such a gentle kid. Raging, he locked himself in his bedroom, smashed his rented electric guitar, and broke the speaker. Sally figured it must've been an isolated incident. She had no idea that he continued smoking pot throughout high school since he masked it so well.

He was something of a poet then:

I feel as though,
There is two of me,
One wants peace and happiness,
All the other one does is destroy,
One smiles all day,
The other wants it the other way,
One has a future,
The other should not,
But without one, the other dies,

So like a shadow,
He is here to stay,
So what I need to do,
Is balance all day.

At 16, Andy worked at a call center for Choice Hotels. After high school, he enlisted in the army, becoming a paratrooper in the 82nd Airborne infantry division. It's true, he saw terrible things in Baghdad. Blown up body parts—the handiwork of insurgents' IEDs (improvised explosive devices). As a mechanic, Andy would clean up the remains. When he returned to civilian life, he was adamant that he did not have PTSD. A diagnosis was never completed to corroborate his assertions.

But it was clear, nevertheless, that something was not right.

Andy started calling suicide help lines. He'd text his older sister, Sarah, bizarre messages that made no sense. He claimed that she never talked to him anymore and that she didn't even know where he lived, though she did.

In 2011, Sarah got a more disturbing call than usual from Andy saying that he was going to hurt himself. When she frantically tried to call him back, he wouldn't answer. It was broad daylight when Andy's father came to his front door to check on him. Andy didn't recognize his own father. He came out of nowhere and attacked his dad with his fists. The police ultimately arrived and placed Andy in a straightjacket. The scene was chaotic as Andy cursed and yelled, threatening to come after whoever approached him.

"He was totally out of his mind," Sally said. "That was not him."

"I kept my phone on me for the rest of his life," his sister Sarah said. "I never knew when he'd call. But he never did."

After a period of hospitalization and another rocky patch, Andy seemed to fare better. He was hiking. He got a job as an electrician's apprentice. He had a girlfriend.

But when he broke up with his girlfriend in January 2014, he called another suicide hotline and was hospitalized once again. After his release later that February, he talked about wanting to quit, about wanting to die. He was smoking marijuana again. Lots of it.

In the darkness, at about 9 p.m. on March 1, 2014, Andy's father entered the house they shared. Mirrors were shattered. Houseplants were wrecked. Pool balls had been flung all over the place. After making his way to the backyard, Andy's father found his son hanging from a tree.

He cut him down, but it was too late. Andy was just 31 years old when he died.

"I will only get worse," he wrote in a handwritten note he left behind. "My soul is already dead. Marijuana killed my soul & ruined my brain. I am doing everyone a favor."

Police found another note in Andy's bedroom the night he passed away. "I ruined my brain with drugs," he wrote along with a litany of other self-recriminations.

In the aftermath, Sally called the coroner who conducted the autopsy on Andy's body. He told her, as a practice, he didn't test for marijuana.

Why not? she wanted to know.

Because, he told her, "Marijuana doesn't cause an overdose death."

Many of us have heard this phrase before.

But some people know it to be a patent lie.

Take, for example, the plight of Kevin Bright.

He was fifteen and suffering from depression when he started smoking pot in his small town just outside of San Francisco. When he couldn't stop, he admitted to his parents that he was afraid.

But his fear gave way to dependency, obstinacy, fits of rage, and worrisome threats, followed by rehab and hospitalizations, until, over the years, it all became too much. He was spending about $400 a week on marijuana, ingesting capsules filled with a tarlike oil containing high doses of THC.

People told his parents, a retired elementary school teacher and an insurance broker, that marijuana wasn't addictive. But Kevin's use proved otherwise. He simply couldn't shake the habit. Although he admitted at one point that marijuana had "ruined his life," he kept demanding that his parents buy him what he called "his medicine." Out of love and worry, they refused.

Subsequently, he overdosed on pills, but survived. Then he tried to hang himself, but a 911 call saved him. Later he drove his Honda Accord off a boat ramp, but didn't drown as he hoped he would. Finally, on August 14, 2018, at just 29 years of age, Kevin placed a plastic bag over his head in a hotel room in Davis, California, and inhaled nitrous oxide through a tube until he asphyxiated.

He finally succeeded in ending his life.

As Hazel Bright, Kevin's mother, said, "If we can convince one parent—to educate them so they can hopefully save their son or daughter—it will all be worth it, because it doesn't make sense to lose our children to marijuana."

Jacki Cosner knows this too.

A few years back, her daughter, Kayla Nicole, and her husband, Daniel Brian Amos, were celebrating their six-month anniversary. She was twenty; he was twenty-one. It was Valentine's Day. They had just left church and were headed for lunch. She was wearing a beautiful red lace skirt, which he had just bought for her. On their way home, a vehicle jumped the centerline and hit their car head-on.

The driver had been impaired by marijuana. Kayla and Daniel paid with their lives.

There are countless other tragic examples. Among them are Corrine LaMarca, Karen Bailey, Joe Tilton, and too many others to list here, though I mourn, almost daily in this work, for their suffering and loss of life too.

Yet the pot industry marches forward, unabashedly advertising more and more powerful strains of marijuana.

Some might suggest, in the case of veteran Andy Zorn, that he was the victim of the horrors he witnessed in the army in Iraq. Surely, these are nightmares no one would wish for their child to endure. It's very possible these experiences and the regular use of highly potent marijuana were mutually reinforcing. It should be noted that several studies, such as one conducted by researchers at Yale, find marijuana exacerbates PTSD symptoms.[36] Could marijuana have played a central role in Andy's demise?

"There is no doubt in my mind," Sally said.

What's more, Sally is certain Andy knew what she would do with his final note. "Save other lives," she said.

Sally is the cofounder of Moms Strong, a support group intended to educate and raise awareness about the mental health risks of marijuana. If you ever meet her, she is apt to have at the ready a glossy photo of Andy, looking chiseled in his Army beret and uniform. Under his steady gaze are the printed words, "Andy served our country. But marijuana took his freedom."

"This is what I do, and it's extremely important to me," Sally affirms. "It's my relationship with Andy. I feel like Andy's with me in everything I do. Andy's so much more alive to me now doing this than the five or six years when he was lost."

Sarah, Andy's sister, has witnessed the compassionate, meaningful, and tireless work her mother has done in Andy's honor. She has such admiration for her mom's spirit and resilience, and certainly for the impact she's making on others' lives. It's a job no mother should ever have to do, yet Sally perseveres.

CHAPTER SIX

Superman and Me

....

My mom was fixing dinner one day when she heard a big thump and ran up the stairs to find me holding my limp left arm. I was 2 years old. This, evidently, is what happens when you've just watched the movie *Superman* and you think *you're* the action hero.

My sister says that I didn't complain; I just stood there, with a smirk on my face as my horrified family rushed me to the ER. An X-ray delivered the news: My arm was broken. I couldn't have been more pleased my family would later tell me. I got to return to the neighborhood, holding out my cast like a badge of honor, delighted by the messages and graffiti my friends scribbled on it. I only cried when the doctor later removed the cast.

From the beginning of my life, I had a habit of leaping—some might say recklessly—into the impossible. I suppose there's an analogy between that early incident and my diving headlong into what some view as an interminable fight.

From an early age, I was exposed to socially conscious music by my socially conscious siblings. I listened to songs such as "Talkin' 'Bout a Revolution," Tracy Chapman's ode to people rising up against inequality, and "Don't Talk," Natalie Merchant's track about a person pleading with an alcoholic. Often one of my sisters would peer at me through the rearview mirror of our blue Toyota Corolla, and throw in a 10,000 Maniacs tape while the other would tell me about South Africa's revolutionary political leader, Nelson Mandela.

On one particular occasion, my sister asked me, "Do you know what the word 'apartheid' means?" She was 13 years my senior and an undergraduate student at UCLA at that time.

Not understanding, I responded by saying something to the effect of, "What 'apartment?'"

While we drove around our new neighborhood in Southern California, trying new foods such as frozen yogurt, my sister navigated the stick shift and explained that the white supremacist government of South Africa imposed a policy of strict segregation on its Black citizens. I didn't know what "segregation" meant then either, but I got it soon enough. A little sticker that hung in my childhood room read: "No room in my heart for prejudice."

"It's not really strange for me to bring up apartheid, considering our worldview," my sister now recalls. "That's who we are."

Nor was it odd that dinner-table conversations often revolved around the topic of injustice.

Credit my parents. Though they never experienced apartheid, they did know something about the harsh ways of the world. Systematic oppression. Knowing you had to forever leave your homeland. My father, the youngest of six children, grew up in deep poverty in Isfahan, an ancient capital of Iran. His father—my grandfather—was a young Muslim preacher until he was exposed to the teachings of the Bahá'í Faith, a nascent religion originating in Iran during the 1800s. It teaches the essential worth of all major religions and the oneness of humankind. As you might imagine, these teachings were threatening to the status quo—government and religion alike. When my grandfather became a Bahá'í in the early years of the 20th century, his home was ransacked and burned down, all his property was confiscated, and he was forced to flee his native town of Yazd with his wife and children, lest they all be killed.

My mother also was forced to leave her homeland, though under vastly different circumstances. Growing up in Yemen, she was the daughter of Jewish ancestors who had become Bahá'ís long before she was born.

My mother's father was the first pharmacist in the region, and the first to bring modern medicines to Yemen when the family moved there in the early 1950s. He introduced the Yemenis to a little product called aspirin.

I guess you could say drugs are the family business.

When a member of the royal family eyed my mom for marriage—she being more than 20 years his junior—my grandfather sent her to live in Europe with the little money he had.

After my parents met at a large Bahá'í conference in London, my father looked toward a future in America. It was a "dreamland" to him. He loved cowboy movies and was captivated by swaggering silver screen stars such as John Wayne, Burt Lancaster, and Kirk Douglas. His life in Iran, and the few opportunities it afforded him, was different than what these movies promised. And being a Bahá'í meant you were vulnerable to various forms of persecution, or worse. A first cousin of mine was hanged for his religious beliefs shortly after the 1979 Revolution. Even before this though, my father was restless and eager to leave Iran.

"The U.S. was considered the place to go," he said.

That's how my parents ended up in Cleveland in 1967, where my dad pursued graduate studies. Later they would move to Indiana, where I was born—my dad teaching at a local college and my mom earning a bachelor's degree in accounting. We stayed for a number of years before relocating to Southern California. My parents were the first in their family to come to America. Several dozen relatives would arrive later, many with the help of my parents.

Ours was a classic story of immigrant upbringing in America's suburbia, which is to say, we lived comfortably in a four-bedroom home with a two-car garage in a cul-de-sac. In archetypal fashion, I played soccer (I wasn't very good), water polo (I was much better), and tennis (I wanted to be the next Andre Agassi). I edited the high school newspaper. I didn't touch pot or booze. In fact, addiction had never been an issue in my family at all. I have never even *seen* alcohol in my house.

Yet I can give you a million reasons why I got into drug policy. Certainly my Bahá'í faith, which calls us to service, led me to this vocation. A local sheriff, who enlisted me in my youth to speak out about the dangers of drugs, was also a big influence. My parents and sisters, who instilled in me a mission to do good, had also been a driving force. My friends, some of whom got into trouble with drugs, and others who were victimized by impaired drivers, motivated me as well.

I can also say with certainty that talking with real people afflicted by addiction when I served as editor-in-chief of two teen newspapers—the high school paper, aptly called *Smoke Signals*, and a county-wide paper specifically focused on drug issues, auspiciously named *The Quest*—taught me more than I ever could have imagined about the drug and the aftermath of its use. Indelible lessons came from the crack-addicted mother I got to know while organizing a holiday party for drug-exposed children. They also came from the friend who hid his addiction while maintaining a 4.0 GPA until his world came crashing down, and from the girl I knew whose parents abused her because of their own addictions.

The deeper I dug, the more gunk I found. Orange County in the 1990s was not the kind of place where one could readily admit they had a problem. Not here, neighbors would say. Drug abuse happens *over there*, pointing hard north to Los Angeles. But while proudly wearing two student press passes (which really didn't entitle me to anything, of course) and developing my newly found interest in hearing people's stories, a fire was lit within me.

That's when I began raising my voice about drugs in public forums. One time, at an Orange County school board meeting, I challenged the libertarian majority who wanted to do away with afterschool counseling programs. "We don't need the federal government telling us what programs to implement here," said one irate attendee. Another time, when I was seventeen, the county sheriff threw me on stage at the last minute to engage in an impromptu debate with a federal judge and future candidate for U.S. vice president. "I'm here to debate the sheriff, not this kid," Judge Jim Gray exclaimed, with a look of disdain on his face I will never forget. Then there was that time at age eighteen, when a congressman from Cleveland allowed me to submit testimony about my experiences to Congress.

In the late 1990s, when I left home to become an undergraduate student at the University of California, Berkeley, my first order of business—taking cues from the feelingful music of Ms. Chapman—was to start a revolution. But this was Berkeley. Hundreds of revolutions were already underway when I got there! If I wanted to raise awareness about something new, I had to go big or go home.

I had no plans to go back to the O.C.

So I created a new civic group: Citizens for a Drug-Free Berkeley.

I'll be the first to admit it. Starting a group like this at a school known for its embrace of counterculture and its penchant for substances was likely to be as popular as starting the Coalition for a Wine-Free France. There were maybe ten recruits, all of whom I enlisted by offering free burgers and soft drinks. The term "organizational plan" wasn't even in our vocabulary. As was my wont, I wasn't intimidated by the challenges ahead of me. I met with some city councilmembers (duly taking note of their stunned reaction when they realized they were meeting a freshman who was *against* drugs), and the mayor, who, courageously, albeit quietly, supported me. I would slip into pro-legalization conferences in San Francisco to take notes and gather intelligence. It was there that I got to speak with the young future governor of California, Gavin Newsom, and with Willie Brown (nicknamed the "Ayatollah" of the California State Assembly), who by then was San Francisco's popular, larger-than-life mayor. (I made little to no impression on them, clearly, given their subsequent positions on marijuana.) The conference speakers discussed how kids should hear from "*successful* drug users."

"Why do they always have to bring in the failed drug addicts?" one presenter asked when speaking about how to conduct school assemblies on drugs. "Bring in people who use drugs sensibly!" *Did these folks really believe this?* I asked myself. Probably the most interesting part of that day for me, though, was when George Zimmer (the famous "I guarantee it!" guy who sold cheap suits on TV) charged right at me and angrily said, "I've heard of you!" to which I happily replied, "And I, you, sir!" Everyone knew Mr. Zimmer from his cheesy commercials, but how in the world did this somewhat famous guy know me, a Persian kid with black curly hair from Anaheim?

With my small band of cohorts, I resorted to unconventional tactics, showing up at nightclubs in San Francisco's Mission district, handing out fact-laden postcards, or propping up a linen sheet and flipping the switch on an old school projector to show images of what your brain *actually* looks like on drugs. (It doesn't look like a fried egg, in case you're wondering.) I think the club owners were so taken aback by my request to talk about the dangers of drugs that a combination of surprise and good heartedness convinced them to acquiesce to my rather odd request. I found that many of them were genuinely decent people with a conscience. I'm not sure if I made a huge difference. (When a friend showed me a *San Francisco Chronicle* article that had been written about me, titled "Tilting at Windmills at Berkeley," I felt both insulted and pleased.) But my peers often thanked me privately for these stunts, saying it sometimes gave them an excuse to forego using drugs that night, or at least have a conversation about it with a friend.

Then during my junior year, I got a call. "This is Pancho, head of White House drug strategy, Kevin. We've seen your work," the deep, almost militaristic voice on the other line said, as my heart started pounding. "Come work for us this summer. We'll pay you." Must be a prank call, I thought. But, alas, the call was real. I soon joined the Clinton ranks as a research assistant in the Office of National Drug Control Policy, working under the brilliant cabinet member and drug czar, Barry McCaffrey.

Two years later, the White House came calling again while I was a Marshall Scholar at Oxford. The Bush administration needed a speech writer on drug policy; so when they asked, I said yes, again. But the shine of D.C. wore off fast—my work seemed small compared to what many of my friends were doing as they shipped off to fight a new war. I decided to return to Oxford to get my PhD.

That's when I met the girl of my dreams.

Bear with me, this is relevant.

I met Shahrzad (yes, she is named after the mythical storyteller) at a Bahá'í meeting hosted in my Oxford flat. She was a Canadian who had come to Oxford on a prestigious scholarship for a master's degree in political philosophy. I was instantly taken.

She was ravishingly beautiful. Elegant and eloquent. Deep and stunningly brilliant. Just the kind of girl I had always dreamed of but thought I would never actually meet.

Then I found out we had the same last name, even though our families aren't related. I decided in that moment that we had to get married. Now I all I had to do was get her on board.

This was harder than I had hoped. It turns out I wasn't the only guy at Oxford with this plan. And as Shahrzad has teasingly recounted at many dinner parties since, she wasn't exactly taken by me at our first meeting. "The first time I met Kevin, I thought he was the furthest thing from my type. I thought he was *so* American."

Almost every week for the next five months, I asked her out on a date. And every week, she found a way to say no.

"Are you a Nancy Reagan minion?" she joked at one point.

"Just say yes!" I quipped back.

Nancy's anti-drug slogan (slightly edited) seemed to work. Shahrzad had dinner with me the next night.

Shahrzad challenged my thinking—on all things, but especially drugs—in ways nobody had before. For my birthday that year, she gave me a t-shirt that read "Pothead" on the front. I knew then that she really was the *one*. We would eventually get married, and today we are parents to our first child.

Giving up on her was never an option for me, just as giving up isn't an option when it comes to my work. This spirit came in handy again a year after we wed, when I received a call from Gil Kerlikowske, President Obama's newly nominated U.S. drug czar.

Gil had seen an op-ed I wrote—with Shahrzad's skillful help, I confess—in *The Seattle Times,* his hometown paper. He told me he was coming to the East Coast and asked if he could "pick my brain" for a "few minutes" about drug policy.

A few minutes turned into a few hours, and a few weeks later my phone rang again. It was Gil. "I just got confirmed!" he said jubilantly from the car, on the way home from Capitol Hill. "I want you to come work for me."

I was hesitant.

We had just moved to Cambridge, Massachusetts. Shahrzad was beginning a PhD. at Harvard, and I had already landed some drug policy consulting work that would allow me to lead a fulfilling yet flexible life. But the desire to do something more tugged at my heart. Barely 30, to be a senior advisor at the White House, under the leadership of the first Black president, was an opportunity I couldn't pass up. I could serve my country once more in a senior leadership role.

So I said yes, and plunged right in, shuttling from Boston to D.C. every week.

But not even Superman could save me from what was to come next.

PART TWO
Becoming A Full-Fledged Movement

CHAPTER SEVEN

What's Been Unleashed

The year was 2009. It was a beautiful fall morning in Virginia. Some of my fellow senior members of the White House drug office and I were assembled at an idyllic retreat in Williamsburg.

Suddenly my BlackBerry started buzzing.

Nonstop.

Something was wrong.

One angry email read, "Why is Obama legalizing marijuana, Kevin?" Another: "This is great news for the pot industry. Bad news for kids. WTH!?!?"

This wasn't good. I gathered my colleagues and headed to the business center so we could get to work using one of their computers (BlackBerrys weren't good for this kind of thing).

"It will not be a priority to use federal resources to prosecute patients with serious illnesses or their caregivers who are complying with state laws on medical marijuana," U.S. Attorney General Eric Holder's news statement read. It also went on to say, "Marijuana distribution in the United States remains the single largest source of revenue for the Mexican cartels, and authorities would continue to track down such nefarious characters as a 'core priority.'"

Hmm. I didn't get what the fuss was about at first. No administration—Republican or Democrat—had ever gone after sick people simply for smoking a joint. In fact, if Holder's words sounded familiar to me when I read them, it was probably because I had signed off on them months earlier—as did my boss—with little more than some minor edits and a shrug.

But the media inquiries began flooding in, and I hurried to respond. The adrenalin was pumping.

Even with a computer, a landline, and a BlackBerry, there wasn't much we could do. The media and pro-pot lobby were having a field day. They were reading into this what they wanted: that Obama would take a hands-off approach to pot. It's all they needed to march forward and gather investment.

The Justice Department's new directive was met in many quarters with immediate consternation by Republicans eager to seize on the news. Rep. Lamar Smith, then the senior Republican on the House Judiciary Committee, was quoted in *The New York Times* as saying, "By directing federal law enforcement officers to ignore federal drug laws, the administration is tacitly condoning the use of marijuana in the United States."

Was Holder speaking only as the chief law enforcement officer of the United States? Or was he possibly conveying the *laissez-faire* position on marijuana of his boss (and good friend), President Barack Obama? It was no secret that in his high school days, like many presidents before him, Obama was acquainted with the drug.

None of us knew, really.

"Obama had a softer stance [than previous presidents] in the way he wanted to deal with marijuana," Gil Kerlikowske, the former drug czar and my one-time boss, said when he was interviewed for this book.

The seminal declaration from the attorney general became known as the "Ogden Memo," which had the effect of insulating Holder and Obama from negative political fallout. The label is an obscure reference to a missive from David W. Ogden, then deputy attorney general, to his lieutenants—ninety-three U.S. attorneys, several of whom were grappling with the odd contradiction between state and federal law regarding marijuana at the time. This memo advised the U.S. attorneys *not* to focus federal resources in their states on "individuals whose actions are in clear and unambiguous compliance with existing state laws providing for the medical use of marijuana"—essentially the same policy as held by the previous administration of George W. Bush.

My reaction, from the quietude of my retreat in Virginia, was to wonder, *What just happened?*

Bob Troyer was asking himself the same question in Colorado.

Troyer had worked in the criminal division of Colorado's U.S. Attorney's Office prosecuting drug and violent crime cases before leaving to join the private sector for a number of years. But around the time all this went down, Bob was poised to return to Colorado's U.S. Attorney's Office, this time via an appointment in 2010 by President Obama to the position of first assistant U.S. attorney. He was steeped in trying to figure out exactly what had transpired in terms of law enforcement after voters approved medical marijuana in 2000. When he was interviewed for this book, he shared his findings. He summed up the situation during that first decade as a case of "benign neglect." He told me that he was absolutely mystified that no one noticed how much the industry quietly expanded in those intervening years.

When Bob got wind of the Ogden Memo, he knew the issue couldn't be ignored any longer.

As he put it, the memo was saying to him and others, "The feds will look the other way."

But Bob *wasn't* the kind of guy who looked the other way. He had always been—and still is—a straight shooter. He said, "You noticed atmospherically in Colorado a lot of talk about ease of access, the visible presence of marijuana." Even before law enforcement authorities really knew what commercialization was all about, "There was dope everywhere," he explained.

Guidance from the federal government—including messages to ease off—only created more confusion among local police chiefs and sheriffs. Debates ensued about whether to enforce marijuana laws or not. It was unclear to them who could have pot and who couldn't.

The confusion only grew worse a few years later, when in 2012 Colorado became the first state in the nation, along with Washington, to permit the sale of what is euphemistically termed "recreational" pot.

"Nobody in law enforcement was mobilized," Bob said.

But pro-pot forces were. They trotted out testimonials from soccer moms and touted all the economic benefits the community would enjoy, not the least of which was the additional tax revenue from pot sales—an illusion to be dispelled later. Military vets also vouched for marijuana, saying it helped stave off PTSD, despite evidence to the contrary. A former metro police chief even hit the airwaves, saying legalization would free up cops to go after real criminals—another specious claim to be refuted later.

"Did anyone say this is capitalism applied to addiction?" Bob asked rhetorically.

If people had known then what we know now about how much profit pot purveyors have made from sales to young people—who are among the heaviest users—Bob is convinced it "would have blown the minds of even the most thoughtful, long-term professional law enforcement representatives."

"Unfortunately," as he noted, "the only people who knew what was going on was the [marijuana] industry. People had their lunch money taken."

As pot shops began to open in Colorado, local law enforcement clamored for clarity from the U.S. Attorney's Office about what to do; marijuana, after all, was still federally illegal.

Bob recalled being inundated with questions such as, "What are you guys going to do about this?"

At some point he and his peers knew they had to halt the incursion of marijuana in their state without openly defying their bosses in Washington, D.C.

That's when an idea began to percolate in the U.S. Attorney's Office in Colorado: what if they filed a civil lawsuit seeking to strike down state Amendment 64, which permitted the commercial sale of pot in violation of federal law? Bob liked this idea, which is termed "preemption."

If you've never heard of this effort before, it's partly because it's being revealed in this book for the first time, and it's partly because preemption was in some ways *preempted.*

The sheer number and magnitude of other problems the U.S. attorneys were already addressing, including domestic terrorism, international terrorism, white-collar crime, not to mention the rise in use of other illicit drugs, including fentanyl, heroin, and stimulant drugs such as methamphetamine, got in the way.

Higher ups in the Justice Department in Washington, D.C., also told them, "We have much higher enforcement priorities."

He and some of his peers in the U.S. Attorney's Office in Colorado pushed back, but to no avail.

I, on the other hand, wasn't done with the Ogden Memo. I began working feverishly with a few allies at the Department of Justice and within the White House to lobby the Attorney General's Office. Armed with facts and statistics, we evidenced how this missive gave a "green light" to the marijuana industry to expand their operations–whether they were medical or not, or whether they were being carried out by caregivers or drug kingpins.

When I say 'feverishly" working, I meant it quite literally.

It was a sweltering day in June 2011. I was in New York for a United Nations meeting when I started to suffer from extreme stomach pains. Colleagues told me I looked gaunt and ghostly white. Doctors thought it was probably an aggravated gallbladder. They told me to monitor it.

But I couldn't even look at food (and if you know me, you know I love to eat—especially in New York).

By the time I went to the ER my fever was 105.1 degrees. "Wow, I haven't seen that high a level in an adult before!" the doctor who examined me exclaimed. I responded, "Okay, what should I do? I have to be back to work in a few hours." She laughed. Loudly. And before I could really figure out what was going on, I was promptly admitted. As it turned out, I was septic from a burst appendix. Fluids from the ruptured organ were leaking into the rest of my body. I'd be there for a bit more than a full week, but surgery had to wait because my body needed time to recover from the sepsis.

When two more stints in the hospital followed, I started thinking about what really mattered in life. I missed my wife. I wanted kids. I didn't want to be gone all the time. What's more, I saw what I could *and* couldn't do about it while working in a government position. I saw how marijuana legalization was gaining acceptance.

The proverbial writing was on the wall. I needed to be out in the real world doing this work. The jubilation and shine that came with working for the first Black president started to wane. Bureaucracy started to grate. It was time for me to go.

But I could not just fade gently into civilian life. I wanted one last hurrah.

From my hospital room, I reignited the Ogden Memo dispute via email (much to some of my superior's good-natured annoyance). I wanted us to correct the record about marijuana and acknowledge the abuses stemming from that memorandum. And after a lot of hemming and hawing, we did just that.

The June 29, 2011, memo from then Deputy Attorney General James M. Cole "sent a chill through the industry," according to one industry source. It acknowledged, in part, that there had "been an increase in the scope of commercial cultivation, sale, distribution and use of marijuana for purported medical purposes . . . ." and that, "The Ogden Memorandum was never intended to shield such activities from federal enforcement action and prosecution, even where those activities purport to comply with state law."

What I experienced with the release of that memo was the sweet feeling of redemption.

If only temporarily.

Shortly afterward, a multimillion-dollar effort put marijuana legalization initiatives on the ballots in Washington, Colorado, and Oregon. This development solidified my belief that I couldn't do my best work from D.C. I wanted and had to do more.

On November 4, 2012, my phone rang. It was former Congressman Patrick Kennedy. We had worked together on the Affordable Care

Act to ensure addiction was included in the law that is also known as Obamacare. We strongly believed that mental health had to be on par with physical health. "Kevin," Patrick said. "What happened last night was horrible for people like me." *But Obama won*, I thought to myself. *What's he talking about?* "How are people in recovery going to get the help they need if they are bombarded by pot advertisements and storefronts?" I quickly realized he wasn't referring to Obama winning a second term, of course. He was talking about the fact that Colorado and Washington had just voted to legalize marijuana. We knew we had to do something. Speak out. Lead. No one else really was. But neither "Reefer Madness" nor "Reefer Freedom" was the answer. The way to proceed, from our perspective, had to be sane, smart, and science-based. The next month, after I participated in a nationally televised, hour-long panel discussion on the recent vote, people such as former Bush speechwriter David Frum came calling. And then dozens—and *dozens*—of scientists also contacted us. Former state officials. Governors. Executives. They all said the same thing: *We need to stop, or at least slow down, the rush to commercialize marijuana.*

That desire to do more in this space was realized in January 2013, about a year or so after leaving my post in D.C., when Patrick and I, and top scientists and doctors, unveiled Smart Approaches to Marijuana (SAM) in the new capital of pot: Denver, Colorado.

At about the same time, President Obama requested a briefing on the legalization of marijuana with ONDCP Director Kerlikowske.

In describing that high-level meeting for the first time in this book, Kerlikowske said it was important enough to be held in the Situation Room of the West Wing—a wood-paneled, twenty-four-hour communications operation from which President Johnson orchestrated the Vietnam War and President Obama watched on monitors as Navy SEALS killed terrorist mastermind Osama Bin Laden.

In attendance at this marijuana meeting, along with the president, were Attorney General Eric Holder, Vice President Joe Biden, and Secretary of State John Kerry. The gathering was supposed to last forty-five minutes but extended for double that time. "The central questions," Kerlikowske recalled, were: "What should be the federal government's response to the states' initiatives [permitting marijuana]? And whether the federal government should step in because the initiatives were a violation of federal law and international law." Legalization had passed in Colorado and Washington, and there had to be a response.

Though largely overlooked, the United States is a signatory to three international treaties that are decidedly anti-pot. Among other things, the United States helped push through the 1961 United Nations Single Convention on Narcotic Drugs, which requires "special measures on control . . . having regard to the dangerous properties" of marijuana. It's worth noting that at the time no country in the world had violated the UN drug treaties. (There are two others in addition to the 1961 version: one from 1971 and one from 1988.) Marijuana is still technically outlawed in The Netherlands, a place often the butt of pothead jokes, even if the country does not enforce those laws. (You should hear what my Dutch colleagues say to me now when I see them at international meetings—they can't tease me enough for how puritanical their laws look compared to American-style pot legalization, or how quickly the U.S. went from staunch "drug free" sloganeering to a seemingly "free drugs" attitude.) But there are stricter limits there, for instance, on THC potency, than in any of the U.S. states, and they have scaled back their plans for expansion since the policy was instituted forty years ago. It's also worth noting that no other European country has followed The Netherlands' "non-enforcement" policy; strange for a country often touted as a "marijuana policy success" by the industry (despite popular myth, marijuana is not legal in Portugal). As of now, though, two more countries have legalized—Canada and Uruguay—with mixed results that I won't extrapolate on here. (In November 2020, Canada's UN Ambassador, Bob Rae, who had previously strongly advocated for legalization and industry expansion, disclosed that he had investments in the marijuana industry.[37]) Other countries have had national referenda on the policy and have rejected legalization, as New Zealand did in 2020.

Though the majority of its citizens opposed legalization, Mexico is also on the verge of commercializing and corporatizing marijuana because of a court case brought on by activists, some of whom are financed by the same billionaires funding legalization in the United States.[38]

But back to the gathering of minds in D.C. Suffice it to say, international concerns didn't carry the day at that Situation Room meeting. The government wanted to please both sides on the issue and thus a new memorandum was born.

On August 29, 2013, in what became known as the Second Cole Memo, the deputy attorney general sent a directive under his letterhead, along with his scribbled signature, to all U.S. attorneys, instructing prosecutors to do even less than what was proscribed by the Ogden Memo, which was limited to medical marijuana. Now under the Obama administration, the federal government was to take a looser position on all forms of marijuana, including so-called recreational pot.

Sometimes I wondered what it would have been like if I had stayed on long enough to attend this meeting. No matter. It had been decided. New state pot legalization laws would be able to move forward, though marijuana would remain federally illegal, and the Obama administration would not (nor ever) come out in favor of legalization, or even push for it behind the scenes.

It was clear what Jim Cole had in mind. He said the U.S. Justice Department would not enforce federal law prohibiting marijuana in states that had enacted "laws legalizing marijuana in some form" and followed that bombshell by saying it was up to states to tamp down on illegal markets, youth use, drugged driving, and the like. The Government Accountability Office (GAO) would later chide the administration, finding in a report that no meaningful action was ever taken by the Justice Department, even as states routinely violated the safeguards installed in the "Cole Memo." (Mr. Cole would later deliver a [paid] keynote address to a marijuana industry conference and rebuke his successors for rescinding his memo in 2018.)

Looking back, Bob Troyer described the response from the U.S. Attorney's Office in Colorado after the Cole Memo was issued as "a period of great unhappiness."

But some of his prosecutors remained restive. Is there something else we can do via prosecution to stem the tide of this industry? they asked, presumably thinking they could work within the parameters of the new directive to selectively go after parts of the business that violated points made in the Cole Memo.

This approach became known in the Colorado office as the "honey badger strategy."

But then, a dose of reality hit the federal prosecutors. They realized they were getting lured into the politics of pot.

"We are federal prosecutors," Bob said. Whether they liked it or not, "Our lane is the enforcement of federal law, not the use of federal law to change policy."

Soon after the second Cole Memo, the industry exploded. In no time at all, the business of staging "marijuana conventions" was almost as big as the industry selling THC. Pot lawyers defending users' rights and applying for product trademarks on their clients' behalf popped up everywhere. Consultants emerged to help businesspeople navigate regulations. And the lobbying class—oh, the huge lobbying class that sprang up in every single state capitol and D.C. was thirsty to please those who had hired them and even hungrier to make money. Lots of it. These people thrived on ensuring public health took a back seat to industry profits.

It wasn't only special interests that benefited from this new wave of acceptance. The increasing normalization of pot has led to more demand, and more demand has meant plenty of business for illegal drug dealers.

That's where Anna comes in.

CHAPTER EIGHT

The Marijuana Underground

The highway was pockmarked with telltale signs of poverty: junk yards, corrugated scrap metal, and busted trailers galore. In this remote part of Michigan, there was no one in sight. A low-slung, nondescript building housed an illegal pot den, a place where users could buy marijuana and get high.

Let me back up a second. Michigan had just gone legal weeks earlier, allowing so-called recreational marijuana to be sold in licensed venues. But legalization hadn't dampened the illicit market for pot. Quite the contrary. By all indications, black market dealers were doing gangbusters sales. Legalization was doing the opposite of what it promised—it was hastening the expansion of the illicit market. Such was also the case in other parts of the country that had legalized marijuana. And I certainly wasn't the only one to take note. A *Newsweek* headline shortly thereafter declared, "Black Market Marijuana Still Popular in States Where Pot Is Legal, Exported to Other States." A recent analysis by the United Cannabis Business Association also showed that illegal sellers outnumbered regulated pot businesses in California by nearly three-to-one. Oregon authorities had much the same findings: that legalization had only encouraged the expansion of the illicit market. Many illegal pot shops were operating in broad daylight, brashly marketing their products as if they expected no repercussions. How could this be?

Anna, age 36, cut an unlikely figure as a drug kingpin. "I'm the most mentally stable person you're going to find," she declared.

Anna was proud, and she was definitely among the unintended beneficiaries of Michigan's new marijuana legalization law. According to her own estimate, she has been raking in a whopping $13,000 a *day* in cash at her unlicensed pot lounge since marijuana legalization came to Michigan.

That was until state police raided her place.

The pot proprietor said authorities confiscated $176,000 worth of pot products, ranging from flowers and edibles to concentrates. Law enforcement sources told me the stash was remarkable in quantity: 35 pounds of marijuana, 231 THC vape cartridges; 128 THC edibles; 15 hash oils; and $3,200 in cash. This was not your ordinary mom-and-pop operation.

Authorities also said they retrieved *untested* marijuana products at Anna's illegal lounge.

"You don't know if it's laced with anything illegal," Lt. David Kaiser of the Michigan State Police was quoted as saying in the news. "They just found it on the black market."

Perhaps even more stunning was that little more than a week after police raided and shut down Anna's sprawling operation, she was already plotting her pot comeback. She was going to reopen at the same place—just bigger and better. She promised it would be a private social club with small membership dues, maybe $20. Anna already began brashly promoting her comeback on Facebook with alerts to her friends.

"Stay tuned!" she declared.

A new bar was being constructed at the backend of the long, wide-open space. Dry wall had already been thrown up—the precursor to what she said would be a VIP room. The cavernous place was already filled with games for patrons to play while they partook of pot. There was ping pong, air hockey, board games, pool tables, you name it. There was also a stage for open-mic nights and the occasional burlesque performer. "Tasteful," Anna was quick to point out. Her other plan: not to sell pot. At least not directly. Rather, she was considering selling other merchandise, including a $200 T-shirt. In return, customers would receive $200 worth of pot. This was what she called "gifting."

It was another term for skirting the law.

Her phone was ringing off the hook; customers wanted to know how they could buy weed.

I had the feeling, if Anna hadn't become a clever black market dealer, she would've been a brilliant operator in legal realms, whether it was on Wall Street or Main Street. But as she put it, she was born in poverty, grew up in a trailer, and started smoking pot when she was 17 years old.

"I loved weed my whole life," she said.

Anna believed pot kept her calm as a teenager—that it leveled her out. She thought it made her happy. And she was convinced that it even helps with decision- making.

Decision-making, in her case, included sneaking out at night, writing bad checks, and running away from home. It also included getting into the business.

Anna started selling pot in her early 20s.

Blame it on the Michigan law. Or give it credit, as Anna did. When Michigan permitted so-called medicinal marijuana in 2008, it created an army of pot growers—licensed caregivers—who could legally grow up to 72 plants that yielded a total of 15 ounces—nearly a pound—for a maximum of five patients. There was only one problem with those numbers.

It doesn't take 72 plants to produce 15 ounces of useable pot. A single plant can easily do the trick. What that meant was, caregivers often found themselves with a huge surplus of pot.

The way Anna put it, these weren't hardened criminals; these licensed caregivers were mainly men in their fifties who were "hillbilly-esque" and often people she knew from the area.

What were they to do with all this excess pot product?

In Anna's case, they sold it to her at what was effectively a wholesale rate, making a handsome profit nonetheless. "Guys started dumping weed on me," she said, and then she turned around and peddled it at retail from the door of her home.

Throwing herself into the trade, Anna created a pink business card with her name and phone number, which she attached to bags she sold to her burgeoning clientele.

"When I was making a thousand a week," she said, "I thought I was killing it."

This was back in 2010, and the Mexican drug cartel, which controlled much of the illicit market in Michigan, wasn't amused. Just to show Anna how unamused they were, cartel thugs threw bricks through the glass doors of her home, brandished semiautomatic weapons, and took all of her stash.

"I was so naïve," she recalled.

Leaving aside the threat to her life, there was another problem: without the product to sell, she owed tens of thousands of dollars to local growers who had lent her the product on consignment, so to speak. Her solution was that she moved to another place, a gated community, which allowed her to be more anonymous, and she hooked up with a different supplier—an Asian drug cartel.

"They dropped a hundred thousand on me," she said.

That is, a hundred thousand dollars' worth of pot.

This put Anna on a different level; the marijuana came from California, and she marveled at the packaged look and quality of the weed. "I'd seen nothing like this," she said.

The Asian cartel kept it coming, regularly sending her huge batches of pot through a middleman. "It was crazy," she confided. Selling it was no problem. "Effortless" is the way she described it. "Word spreads fast when you have good weed."

Harder, though, was figuring out where to store all of this incoming marijuana. She said a former local prosecutor, whom she knew well, let her use an old empty dentist's office he owned. Taking precautions, she installed bulletproof glass in the reception area, along with a "guy at the door with a gun."

A 9mm.

Anna found herself juggling zip-lock bags brimming with wads of cash—$20,000, $30,000, $50,000.

When it got to the point where she sold $100,000 worth of pot product, she used the money to fund her first unlicensed pot dispensary. "The Wild West," was how she saw the marketplace. Anna called the money she used to set up shop an "unapproved loan" from the Asian cartel. Naturally, when the drug lords got wind of her plan, they were none too pleased. She promised to pay them back quickly, which she did.

"I don't know how I'm alive," she mused.

Cut off from the cartel supply, Anna quickly came up with a new source of pot. She purchased the homes of local families struggling to make payments on their mortgages. Then she bought them new homes where they could live rent free. What's more, she paid them $1,000 a week. In return, they had to cultivate marijuana in their garage.

"I'd teach everybody how to grow," she explained.

Before long, Anna had more than twenty illegal "grow ops"—families operating out of their garages, churning out marijuana in their rent-free homes. As a result, Anna had a ready supply of cheap weed, which she could sell at $10 a gram, half the normal rate on the street in 2011.

Tens of thousands of dollars' worth of weed were being sold in a given day. It was the new norm for Anna. So, too, was the constant state of havoc that prevailed in the ensuing years. A Ford Crown Vic of indeterminant ownership plowed into her dispensary building, wrecking the place. Employees embezzled money. Another time, someone ignited a Molotov cocktail, burning her shop to the ground.

Known for operating a business—with lots of drugs and cash on hand—she was robbed at gunpoint multiple times, including just a couple of months prior to our interview.

And that's not all. Police have raided her establishment on several occasions. She got hit with a marijuana misdemeanor. No felony, though. Indeed, law enforcement sources pulled records showing that Anna continued to operate an illegal dispensary for two years before her case came to court and she pleaded guilty to possession—a misdemeanor. In the end, she was slapped with little more than a $500 fine.

Meanwhile, Anna kept at it, starting a marijuana delivery service and operating illegal dispensaries in different parts of Michigan. When one place was shut down, she'd simply open another. That is, until she opened her latest location.

This space was still scarred from a recent raid by the police. Parts of the ceiling were still caved in, spewing out insulation like the bloated innards of a carcass. Glass jars that had contained different varieties of pot sat empty. A massive safe door remained open, the shelves bare. Days before it had been lined with stacks of cash.

When she opened the place in December 2018, she hadn't planned to sell pot there. It was just going to be a gathering place where people could smoke weed or ingest it. But nobody wanted to come if they couldn't buy marijuana. "Everybody demanded weed, dude. It snowballed."

So Anna made a decision to sell. "I'm a street dealer," she conceded with a shrug.

It didn't take much effort. She already had the supply—a wide network of licensed caregivers acting as illicit growers—some of whom would sell her their voluminous leftover pot product and others who were indebted to her for their home and livelihood.

There are "hundreds of pounds waiting for me," she said. "No end to it."

The police raid put a damper on things, though. She said she's broke, but she knows she'll be able to recoup her losses when she reopens after the holidays. The period from January to March is "the busiest time for weed," Anna said, because that's when users get their tax refunds. Even in this economically depressed area, people will be flush with money to buy what she has to sell. What's more, she said her product is "better quality. It's fresh."

"Most humans actually need it," she said. "The human condition is tough."

Anna is opposed to pot for kids, but for the rest of us, she argues that pot is better than, say, aspirin. She also purports that marijuana is effective as a substitute for other illicit drugs.

"I watched a lot of people get off the opiates." Even more remarkable, she swears marijuana helped cure one of her employees of acute leukemia, though, of course, there is no scientific support for such a claim.

"Seen it first-hand," she vouched.

Anna also has seen first-hand the deleterious effects of alcohol. It's caused people to suffer, including a member of her own family. When she was a teenager, her father was killed by a drunk driver.

She's convinced that pot offers a safer alternative. "It's so harmless," she insisted. "It's good for people."

Anna also pointed to the benefit of employment in the pot trade. "I pay my employees good." And she was quick to note, "I have a good product and I don't rip people off."

Don Bailey has long been familiar with this particular illicit dealer. For years, he worked as a state trooper, putting away bad guys in the drug trade. He's retired now, but he still keeps track of Anna and her pot compatriots. In fact, Don is the one who told me about Anna. It wasn't difficult to keep tabs on her. Don has a fake Facebook account. Illegal dealers brashly market their wares online. Among those wares, by the way, is a baby blue baseball cap sold by pot purveyors throughout the state for $25. Embroidered just above the bill of the cap, in large white letters, are the words: "F- -K DON BAILEY."

Don remains one of the most hated people in the Michigan marijuana market.

The baseball cap was first advertised for sale in June of 2017. But Don alienated himself from the pro-pot forces long before then. It was not by design; it was a matter of circumstance. Without even trying, Don became their enemy number one.

"I was in dope for fifteen years," he said.

What he meant was, he served as a sergeant lieutenant on state police drug teams, making busts mostly for cocaine and crack. "Less than 5 percent were marijuana cases," he noted.

Later he worked on a state police team that roved Michigan, pursuing bad guys. He didn't write tickets for a "Joey bag of donuts." Forget about broken taillights. What he went after were "guns, drugs, fugitives." Sometimes he was called in when uniformed state troopers were needed at the scene of a drug bust, especially after so-called medical marijuana was legalized.

"All these dispensaries started popping up," he explained.

Many were illegal shops, meaning they were unlicensed and/or they were selling to recreational users, not just those with a medical need. After Michigan opened the door to medical marijuana, some prosecutors refrained from pursuing cases involving illicit pot dispensary. Some of Michigan's prosecutors "turned a blind eye to it," Don recalled.

He didn't though. He would show up in his dark blue wool uniform and cap to provide security or transportation when state police shut down illegal shops or executed search warrants.

"We were extra bodies" is the way he put it.

Don stands out. Now just about 60 years of age, he is still a powerhouse. He competes in the sport of discus throwing and not long ago, was ranked fifth in the world in his age category. What's more, he used to hold a world record in power lifting—squatting 950 pounds in his weight class of 275 pounds. Don also had a distinctive habit, which was to gab with whom he called the "stoners" he encountered on drug busts and protests. "I would talk to them," he said.

Argue might be more like it.

In one exchange, at a raid of an illegal pot dispensary in the summer of 2016, a high school dropout who was caught insisted that marijuana "personally cured two instances of brain cancer."

"Is this verified by the oncologist who treated these patients?" Don, who was on duty as a state trooper, asked her. "Can you tell me why this doctor isn't coming forward publicly? Because everyone wants a cure for cancer."

She replied, "He can't."

"Why can't he?" Don persisted.

"Big Pharma," she said. "He's paid off by Big Pharma to be silent."

Don resisted the temptation to become apoplectic. Instead he asked her, "Have you ever heard of George Washington, Abraham Lincoln, or Thomas Edison?"

"Yeah."

"Because," Don continued, "the guy who comes up with the cure for cancer will be known as a hero to mankind."

In another exchange at a pot demonstration in 2016, a protester proudly mentioned that he had been involved in shaping the law that brought medical marijuana to Michigan. In the midst of his bragging, this individual admitted that medical pot was never the point. "We wanted recreational" marijuana, he told Don. "But polling said that would fail."

This individual acknowledged that pro-pot forces knew "problems were going to occur" with the spread of illegal dispensaries. They also knew there would be raids, arrests and convictions. "We need to desensitize the public to the idea of marijuana."

Don was stunned. "I'm sure my jaw was a little agape."

The state trooper then turned to one of the pot dealers who had gotten into trouble. He tapped him on the shoulder and gestured at the pot protester who had just revealed his grand strategy.

"Did you hear that?" Don asked the pot dealer. "You're cannon fodder . . . he knew guys like you were going to fall victim, and they went ahead anyway."

Don enjoyed the give and take, even if he didn't have an active role in the raids of illegal pot dispensaries occurring periodically across the state in 2016 and 2017. "I was there just because I had a bright shiny car," he said.

His presence had an effect. Unbeknownst to him, as Don continued to show up at busts and raids and court appearances involving people facing marijuana charges, he became recognizable to the coterie of pro-pot forces across Michigan. They began to direct "all their angst and energy at me," he said with a hint of amusement. They concluded Don was "personally responsible for every marijuana investigation in the state of Michigan," he chortled.

In the age of social media, the specter of Don spread like wildfire. "It goes viral. They're talking all this trash about me—how I've done all this stuff across the state."

He even made the cover of a pro-pot magazine, the *MMM Report*. "Former MSP, Don Bailey and Friends, Want to Take Over Weed in Michigan," declared the headline set above a photo of the man in uniform.

Don didn't seem to mind the notoriety that came with the vitriol of pro-pot forces. In fact, he embraced it. After he retired from the state police on April Fools' Day of 2017, he accepted the governor's invitation to sit on a newly created state board to review license applications for medical marijuana dispensaries.

It was the worst nightmare for those sympathetic to the marijuana movement. Don vowed to vote against applicants who had already flouted the law by operating illegal pot shops.

"I'm not voting for you to get a license if you've already demonstrated to me what you're going to do on a law you don't like," he warned applicants.

"I became the most hated man in marijuana in the state almost overnight," he said gleefully.

That's about the time when the baseball cap bearing the words "F- -K DON BAILEY" surfaced.

"I wanted to get one," Don admitted.

The regulatory agency was disbanded in April 2019, but Don hasn't let go. "I have found through thirty-seven years in law enforcement, marijuana is addicting. What I also found out is the investigation and regulation of marijuana is also addicting."

That's why, even while he renovates a bathroom during his retirement, Don continues to keep tabs on pot dealers such as Anna. They keep emerging; every time one illicit shop is shut down, another appears. He equates it to an arcade game of "Whac-a-Mole." While the proverbial mallet gets rid of one illegal dealer, another pops up seconds later. He remains worried about how marijuana legalization is "allowing the black market to grow." And he fears, "Michigan is going to lead the country in the black market."

Strangely enough, some of Don's concerns about the black market are shared by Anna, the black market dealer herself. Both the retired state trooper and the drug dealer on hiatus are concerned about the effects the legalization of marijuana has had in their state.

"I was all for legalization but now I'm uncertain," she said. "I don't know if legalization is that great."

It's an entirely unexpected response from a true believer, who only a few years ago had a marijuana leaf tattooed on her ring finger, clinching her marriage to the product. "I'm committed" is how she described her relationship to the plant then.

When Michigan legalized marijuana—first medicinal, then recreational—Anna thought it would open doors for her. But it hasn't—at least not in the ways she anticipated.

For one, her criminal record has foreclosed the possibility of her ever winning a license to operate a legal dispensary. For another, what she has seen of legalization has only confirmed her suspicions about how the system of influence works in the cynical ways of the pot world. What she has witnessed is the encroachment of "corporate types—"rich white people" who have "a lot of money" to win political favor and secure licenses to operate lucrative pot shops. Sound familiar? These are some of the same claims made in Illinois by *The Chicago Tribune* and *Chicago Sun-Times.*

"Carpetbaggers" is what a friend of Anna's calls the new entrants into the legal pot field.

"The state of Michigan is the new drug dealer," he observed.

What's more he and Anna confirmed what I already suspected: the legalization of marijuana hasn't curtailed the growth of the black market, as so many pro-pot forces had promised when they were winning over voters across America.

Rather, legalization has boosted the business of illicit dealers like them.

"Legalization is expanding my sales," Anna remarked. It "pushes more people in the black market."

Anna breaks it down like this: She offers a cheaper product, selling her illicit weed at a quarter of the price of the legal stuff. An eighth of an ounce of her pot costs $20 compared to $80 for legal marijuana.

"They can't compete with my price," she said of her legal rivals.

How do you beat a discount?

While reiterating her advantage—that the supply is always available to her from those she taught to grow the product as well as from the army of legal caregivers who are illegally selling their excess pot into the black market—she revealed another surprise source. She said her suppliers also include sheriff deputies who cultivate and sell illicit pot wholesale to her on the side.

By way of defending her position, she maintains that what she sells isn't only for the down and out; it's also for a steady clientele of postal workers, real estate agents, and other regular folks who clamor for her product. The way she views it, she's simply giving people what they're asking for.

"Everybody," she said, "wants it."

But of course, how everybody is treated when caught selling it isn't always equal.

CHAPTER NINE

Perpetuating Social Injustice

Much of Anna's story reflects the life of a drug dealer thriving in a pot-legal state in the American Midwest. But what about her fellow Michigander Michael Thompson? Michael is a 68-year-old Black man from Flint who has already served 25 years—out of a possible 60—for selling pot in the same state as Anna. In Michigan, Black men are about ten times more likely to be arrested for pot than white women, yet they don't use or sell ten times the amount of marijuana.

Anna and people like Adam Bierman—the unabashed multimillionaire who made a fortune selling pot—get a free pass. Many others don't.

It's no secret that our criminal justice system promotes racist ideas and outcomes. Like so many of our institutions, it has deep roots in segregation and white supremacy. But marijuana legalization is not part of the answer.

On the contrary, legalizing and commercializing marijuana perpetuates and deepens racial injustice. It's why the head of the New Jersey Senate Black Caucus, Ron Rice of Newark, led the charge against legalizing marijuana in his state (while his white, Wall Street-bred governor led the proponents). As Senator Rice said in an op-ed, titled "Legal weed: A money grab, a hustle, and pure trickery":

> *"It's not about our economy or about social justice, as some leaders in Trenton claim. It's about enabling their friends and connections to invest in and reap profits from a virgin industry to be preposterously situated in the most densely populated state in the nation . . . . Beyond being a bad idea, it's trickery.*
>
> *. . . I hate to be suspicious of marijuana industry investors lurking as shills in the background, but I really believe this whole exercise had nothing to do with social justice or lowering property taxes."*[39]

This might also be why so many officials—from the first ever Black U.S. Magistrate Judge to the leaders of various state and city NAACP chapters—have led opposition campaigns to marijuana commercialization. They know that if pot is legal, white people will get rich while Black kids continue to be criminalized, even as they are heavily targeted by a now legal and emboldened addictive industry. The depth and pervasiveness of systemic racism in this country is such that loosening pot laws will make little difference in improving that situation. If the comparable history of the alcohol industry tells us anything, it could make things much worse. Pot shops, like liquor stores, cluster in poorer communities of color. One study of Baltimore found poor, Black neighborhoods were eight times more likely to have liquor stores than white or racially integrated areas.[40] This can mean lower property values, more crime, and more availability of an addictive substance. If this legal drug is any indication, legal pot could open even more avenues into the prison industrial complex. Few people know that today, alcohol-related nonviolent crime is the top category of drug-related arrest (in the form of DUI violations, public intoxication, and other related laws)—and that those arrests, like so many others, fall disproportionately on people of color.[41] The legal status of marijuana obscures the real issues.

Systemic racism doesn't just pervade the criminal justice system; it also pervades our capitalist economy. Big Tobacco's playbook is very revealing in this respect. David Goerlitz, the former "Winston Man," once quoted RJ Reynolds Tobacco Company executives as saying, "We don't smoke this shit, we just sell it. We reserve the right to smoke for the young, the poor, the Black, and the stupid."[42] Researchers have found up to ten times more tobacco ads in Black neighborhoods of Washington, D.C., than in white ones.[43] And a heavily financed tobacco industry lobbying effort is the reason why menthol flavors, long marketed to Black communities, have been perpetually exempt from otherwise uncontroversial legislation banning flavored tobacco products.[44]

Addiction-for-profit industries target vulnerable, underserved communities because there aren't enough resources in these areas to help consumers deal with the consequences of addiction when it occurs.[45] With a smaller safety net, people in these communities are more likely to remain trapped in the cycle of heavy use. And of course, to these companies, addiction means revenue: they reap the heavy bulk of their profits from the minority of people who use the most. Indeed, in addictive industries, 80 percent of profits come from 20 percent of users[46]. As former FDA Commissioner David Kessler has said, "... addiction is crucial to keeping smokers smoking .... Accumulating evidence suggests that cigarette manufacturers may intend this result. They may be controlling smokers' choice by controlling the levels of nicotine in their products in a manner that creates and sustains an addiction in the vast majority of smokers."[47]

Why should we expect legal marijuana companies to treat vulnerable communities any differently?

It's why so much of our work at SAM happens in collaboration with community leaders. Examples include: the large rally with Black and Latino leaders in an East Los Angeles community center protesting the pot industry's influence; the community discussion at the Hunts Point Library in The Bronx, New York, to lay out concerns residents have about that state's legalization debate; and the large gathering with the Yakama Nation and the Affiliated Tribes of Northwest Indians in Ferndale, Washington, to discuss how Indian country would be adversely affected by the normalization of today's high THC products.

At all of these meetings, several questions bring our discussion into focus. Can anyone really say legal alcohol has been a boon to poor communities? How and why would marijuana be any different from any currently legal drug? Who is getting rich now from legal weed? How will this affect the job prospects of our youth? Have you ever heard of anyone saying, "Gee, if only we had more liquor stores! Wouldn't that help our kids out?!"

There is, of course, the devastating reality that our current drug laws continue to be deeply damaging to these communities. Mandatory minimum sentences, criminal arrest records, and needless jail lockups take a heavy and unnecessary toll. We should expunge past records now and eliminate criminal sanctions for using marijuana. We can address these injustices without creating new ones through the mass commercialization of yet another harmful, addictive substance.

This is why no episode in my work has made me more profoundly sad than our recent experience in New Jersey. Senator Rice and the Black Caucus led the opposition to pot legalization in that state, joined by people including Paradise Baptist Church Bishop Jethro James (a good friend of the Democratic governor who advocates for legal weed). Because of their efforts and those of other like-minded people, the legislature could not pass a legalization bill despite many years of trying. Too many stories about the damage of today's high potency THC and the impact of legal drugs in poor communities carried the day. Nevertheless in 2019, the legislature voted to put *legalization* on the ballot for the next election, almost a year away.

And shockingly, given the social justice premise of the legalization initiative, they also refused to pass in the meantime any *decriminalization* measures in the legislature. The explanation for this move was revealing. Legalization supporters explained they didn't want to take the wind out of the sails for the upcoming ballot initiative. In other words, they wanted to ensure they could couch legalization as a social justice issue, even though the real injustices at stake could be effectively addressed with an immediate vote in the legislature. That's right: Elected leaders held hostage any hope of removing criminal penalties for low-level possession *for more than a year* because they wanted to be sure the legalization scheme went through. Having helped write the decriminalization bill in New Jersey, I was livid—but powerless. In a statewide op-ed, Senator Rice wrote:

> *"If officials in Trenton wanted all New Jerseyans to benefit from social justice reform and get poor people out of jail now to go home to their kids; if Trenton really wanted to allow people who couldn't afford good lawyers to finally have their charges reduced or their records expunged so they are free to get a better job or apartment now—the decriminalization card is still on the table. We can still point to it, pick it up and win—right here on the spot!*
>
> *Why on earth would we all just walk away and leave that card sitting there? Why would we hold so many of our residents hostage to languish in jail or to have their lives on hold because of unfair criminal records? The card we want is here! Let us win!"*[48]

The answer to Senator Rice's questions is this: decriminalization never made anyone rich. The state didn't decriminalize when it could have, even though the million-dollar legalization ballot campaign, financed substantially by for-profit corporations, presented legalization as a social justice issue. So when legalization finally prevailed *more than 14 months later*, the main winners were the almost all-white pot industry players. Even New Jersey's self-proclaimed "NJWeedman," Ed Forchion, characterized its legalization regime as "'regulated cannabis' to profit a Caucasian Cannabis Cartel when he sued his state, in December 2020."[49] Given the experience in other states, we have little reason to expect much will change now that Wall Street is in charge.

Do you know the number of states showing reductions in incarceration as a result of marijuana legalization?

None.

The number of pot legal states that have solved racial disparities in pot arrests?

Zero.

Or the number of Black or Latino multi-millionaires minted by legalization?

Zilch.

Do you see a pattern?

It was a quiet Saturday morning when William Jones and I were in the underserved northeast quadrant of Washington, D.C., a community still in contrast to its gentrified neighboring areas. Despite being located minutes away from the Capitol dome, which rises in the distance like a gleaming citadel, it seemed a world apart. Will, who recently received his master's degree from George Washington University and works as a firefighter and a community activist, was showing me around.

We turned a corner and Will nodded in the direction of a nondescript tree-lined street.

Shootings here, he noted almost perfunctorily, "happen a lot." Apparently Will was giving me the sanitized version. I later learned that a dead body was found earlier in the year on this same block, and that the murder rate in the area was almost one per day.

As he navigated his Hyundai through the streets, there was a stark, unadorned liquor store called "Big D" and then another shortly thereafter called the "Suburban." The latter had a brick, concrete, and rust façade and a window poster announcing, "Open 7 Days a Week." Just beyond that store was one called "Capital View Market Discount Liquor." Its iron gates were flung open, welcoming a line of customers well before noon.

Booze was readily available in every direction. Tobacco too. What Will fears next is the arrival of pot stores in Washington, D.C.—what he called more "addiction-for-profit companies"—preying on his neighborhood, a predominantly Black community.

As I noted already, pot shops have saturated minority neighborhoods in other cities, such as Denver. In some of that city's neighborhoods, there's one pot shop for every forty-seven people, according to a *Denver Post* investigation.[50] And that's even more dismaying when you realize that fewer than 1 in 5 pot companies have any form of minority ownership,[51] and that so-called "social equity programs," policies designed to reinvest in communities damaged by drug laws, have been relatively rare and ineffective.[52] Will does not want to see D.C. go the way of Denver. Adding to his concern is that substance misuse is already a major problem in his D.C. neighborhood. He knows this because one of his jobs is as a firefighter at Engine 30, which is just around the corner from where we were touring. Engine 30 is one of the busiest fire stations in the country.

Nearly a century ago, Will's great-grandfather, Bishop Smallwood Edmond Williams, D.D., founded Bible Way Temple, a Black Apostolic Pentecostal church with a thriving congregation on New Jersey Avenue, N.W., where the encroachment of gentrification is in evidence with Mercedes-Benzes whizzing by balding grass and misshapen fences.

Bishop Smallwood, a civil rights icon of his time, is still an epic presence. His likeness is carved in bronze on a bell tower soaring in front of the church, his right finger raised on high, a Bible open in his left hand.

His great-grandson Will knew his way around the place, entering the church through the back door, wending past a darkened cafeteria, and finding his way into the office of Bishop Ronald L. Demery Jr., who greeted him warmly. The bespectacled pastor, now in charge of the church, took a seat behind his L-shaped desk, and folded his hands in a tranquil pose, signaling that he was ready to hear what Will had to say.

Will brought a proposal with him. It was the draft of a letter intended for Mayor Muriel Browser and the city council, to be sent from scores of local faith leaders. It expressed their opposition to pot. Following a ballot initiative in 2014, Washington, D.C., legalized marijuana, but pot shops haven't been approved—not yet. Based on political rumblings he had picked up, Will believed the industry would soon push for shops, and he wanted to do something about it before it became a reality.

The pastor spoke from personal experience. One of his cousins started smoking pot as a teenager before graduating to harder drugs—cocaine and crack—until he became schizophrenic and, in his mid-fifties, died of a stroke.

"I don't want anyone else to go through it," the pastor said softly.

Will got on board with our mission about five years ago when he invited me to speak at his church about the hazards of marijuana. We hit it off so well; I enjoyed listening to him, learning from his experiences—his passion for the same issues I was dedicated to was so clear. I knew he could teach me so much, and he soon joined SAM's leadership team.

As a Black man, Will has taken some flak from people who challenge his opposition to pot because many have accepted the pot industry's false narrative—that legalizing pot is a social justice issue. As we saw in New Jersey, pro-pot forces have gained a lot of ground by spinning the notion that legalization ameliorates injustices. It's stated as fact in media reports. Pro-pot billionaires bank on this notion. But the truth is, legalizing pot has not erased racial disparities. As an ACLU study reports, for example, racial disparities persisted in states after the legalized marijuana.[53]

Another disturbing fact: In nearly every state that has legalized pot, the prison population has remained stable or *grown sharply after years of decline*, as witnessed in Colorado and Washington, D.C.[54]

Also, in some places that have legalized marijuana, official state reports have noted "legalization has had no impact on lowering racial bias in policing and in relative disparities related to particular crimes (such as selling or distributing marijuana)."[55]

Nonetheless, Will said, "I've gotten some hate."

One racist tweeted at him: 'Even the N------ at SAM want all Pot Smoking N------ in prison."

Will shrugs it off.

The pastor stated plainly what is motivating the attacks—and the push to legalize marijuana.

"The spread of pot isn't about social justice," he said. "It's about greed, control, power."

The pastor contends that the marijuana industry offers up propaganda about justice as an excuse to open the door to mass commercialization of the drug. "The bottom line is," he said, "it was about the dollar."

Not too long ago, it seemed inevitable that pot shops would arrive in Compton, the city to the south of L.A. known for being the hometown of some of the best-known rap artists, and the album and film *Straight Outta Compton*.

The marijuana machine targeted underserved Compton to be its newest conquest after state voters approved pot in 2016. Given the promise of much-needed revenue, the city seemed like a slam dunk.

Compton is a dichotomous mixture of California palm trees, vacant lots, graffitied public spaces, and pockets of homes with neatly trimmed lawns. When pot industry forces promised the city millions in tax revenue and tons of jobs, local politicians eagerly supported their plan. Local grocery store clerks were hired to go door-knocking to help activate fellow citizens to vote yes when the measure to open pot shops appeared on ballots in January 2018.

But there was only one problem.

Pro-pot forces didn't account for James and Charmaine Hays.

James is not only a scientist who founded two biomedical companies, he served on the city planning commission, worked on many political campaigns, and ran a successful campaign for a member of the City Council as well. What's more, as the son of a community activist, he was no stranger to mounting a good protest.

"I wasn't going to let them in," he told me.

For one, James didn't believe that millions of dollars would be generated in tax revenue by pot sales.

"No proof," he shrugged.

Then there was the matter of who would oversee the rules and regulations if legal pot shops came to Compton, which was already overrun by *illegal* pot shops.

"Who's going to enforce it?" he wondered.

What's more, he recognized the pot of today is nothing like the weed of his youth.

It's turbo charged.

Remembering the devastating toll of crack cocaine on L.A. decades earlier, his wife, Charmaine, raised other issues about the spread of a cheap, commoditized drug. There's addiction, its tendency to be a gateway to other drugs, mental illness, homelessness, and the destruction of lives to consider.

"The world was just a beautiful canvas," she said, before the scourge of drugs invaded Compton.

When James and Charmaine asked hard questions about marijuana and what it meant for Compton, he said, the city council and others "didn't have answers."

Even James's first cousin, Virgil Grant, was opposed to bringing pot shops to Compton—and this was saying something, because Virgil had run illegal pot shops in town going back to the early 2000s. Virgil wanted to operate legal pot shops, but not the kind that were being proposed for Compton. The measure being considered by voters lacked one essential element for Virgil: provisions to protect the community. There was nothing in the voter initiative that expressed consideration for the needs of communities of color—nothing that evidenced they would benefit from the legalization of pot shops despite the public pronouncements by the industry that they would. In a city where a third of the population is Black and the remainder is predominantly Hispanic, it's incomprehensible that they were not invited to the proverbial table.

"The social justice issue was the key factor," Virgil stated firmly.

Thus, he made an unlikely alliance with his cousin, James. The pro-pot cousin joined forces with the anti-drug cousin to take on the marijuana industry in its attempt to win over voters in Compton. James applied a simple principle to defeat the powerful industry.

There was no secret to the David vs. Goliath strategy. It took hard work. They mobilized about thirty citizens, tapping some as group captains, then they set out to knock on neighbors' doors and engage them in tough conversations about the ballot vote ahead of them.

Relying on his considerable political experience, James created "walk sheets" and "call lists," and drew on precinct maps to pinpoint voters.

During the three or so months of campaigning, James and Charmaine also planted a lot of lawn signs.

"SAY NO TO MARIJUANA DISPENSARIES IN COMPTON"

Recognizing the large Hispanic-voting bloc, they also produced a Spanish version:

"DIGA NO A DISPENSARIOS DE MARIHUANA EN COMPTON"

Altogether, James estimates his group spent a mere $500 on the campaign to stop pot shops from coming to Compton. In the face of their deep-pocketed opponent, that sum, combined with a considerable amount of grit and determination, turned out to be more than enough. In January 2018, Compton voters rejected marijuana by a landslide, with more than 70 percent opposed to the measure. James didn't even bother waiting up the night the election results were announced on local TV news.

The pot industry underestimated the resolve of James, Charmaine, and the community. This dynamic couple knew how to create coalitions and reach voters. They knew grassroots campaigning works. They knew pot was bad for individuals and neighborhoods. They knew they would win. But there was no celebration. Why? Because James and Charmaine also know the marijuana industry will be returning to Compton sooner or later.

There's just too much money at stake.

"We're ready," James vowed. "We know it's coming back."

CHAPTER TEN

A Red Herring

Marihuana.

That's what they called it in the early 1900s—not cannabis, weed, pot, or even marijuana with a "j." After the Mexican Revolution, when people began crossing our southern border, marijuana was introduced to Americans as a mind-altering "recreational" drug. The plant was originally cultivated for hemp, which was used to make rope and ship rigging. (Though it is currently making a comeback, hemp was subsequently abandoned for decades in the U.S., considered inferior to other kinds of industrial use material.)

Actually, the history of this controversial plant stems much further back, probably to ancient Egypt, though details remain uncertain. Unlike alcohol, marijuana stayed out of the mainstream. The vast majority of the world have never been regular users of the drug.

Suffice it to say, pot didn't penetrate the American consciousness until the turn of the twentieth century, and not in a favorable way. Even with low levels of THC (relative to the amount of the psychoactive ingredient in today's pot), its notoriety spread. It soon acquired the moniker "evil weed" for its intoxicating effect. Racist myths certainly played a role in our banning of the drug ("Mexicans are foisting marijuana on our perfect American kids!")—but not entirely. In fact, Mexico banned marijuana before we did because of its reported negative health effects. The U.S. soon followed suit and by the 1930s, it was outlawed in most parts of the country. This isn't to deny the racist origins of many of our laws. Instead, it acknowledges that the U.S., Mexican, and other governments highlighted the drug's health hazards more than a hundred years ago.

Flash forward to the late 1960s and early 1970s. Marijuana became more pervasive among all strata of society, reflecting the permissiveness of the counterculture whose "turn on, tune in, drop out" ethos challenged long-held assumptions about traditional sober American values. It was then that major tobacco makers—in their heyday as purveyors of cigarettes—began secretly researching the potential of pot as a lucrative new line of business.

In 1969, a University of Virginia professor supervising a Philip Morris program in chemistry wrote the following note to a research lab manager where Marlboro cigarettes were made:

> *From all I can gather from the literature, from the press, and just living among young people, I can predict that marihuana smoking will have grown to immense proportions within a decade and will probably be legalized. The company that will bring out the first marihuana smoking devices, be it a cigarette or some other form, will capture the market and be in a better position than its competitors to satisfy the legal public demand for such products. I want to suggest, therefore, that you institute immediately a research program on all phases of marihuana.*[56]

It's unclear how Philip Morris responded. What is clear, however, is that tobacco makers faced a choice: to stomp out marijuana or get into the business. As an unsigned memo distributed to Philip Morris's top management in the early 1970s declared:

> *We are in the business of relaxing people who are tense and providing a pickup for people who are bored or depressed. The human needs that*

our product fills will not go away. Thus, the only real threat to our business is that society will find other means of satisfying these needs.[57]

Philip Morris wasn't alone in this assessment. Other tobacco makers, including British American Tobacco and R.J. Reynolds, also secretly explored the idea of manufacturing pot cigarettes.

It wasn't until decades later that Stanton A. Glantz, PhD, stumbled on these secret plans.

Dr. Glantz, a professor of medicine at the University of California, San Francisco, also happens to be one of the foremost authorities in the world on Big Tobacco. He and his fellow researchers were studying how tobacco companies were trying to influence policy in the European Union when they came across a stash of old documents revealing the tobacco makers' hidden plans to capitalize on marijuana. Those plans would be actualized later.

"We were doing something totally different," Dr. Glantz said about his research when he was interviewed for this book. While he was "surprised" initially to come across these internal memos, the surprise soon faded. "Let's put it this way," he said, "when we found it, it was something that made sense."

There was, in other words, a lot of money in marijuana.

Evidently Hugh Hefner recognized the potential too. In the early 1970s, the founder of *Playboy* magazine began funding a new organization aimed at shifting public opinion toward legalizing marijuana. He must have believed in the ROI because his investment of a $100,000 a year was a princely sum for the times. The group was aptly known as NORML, standing for the National Organization for the Reform of Marijuana Laws. It's founder, Keith Stroup, is an attorney who liked to get high, which perhaps led him to say more than he meant to.

For instance, in 1979, in an interview with the *Emory Wheel*, the student newspaper at Emory University in Atlanta, Keith laid out the industry's long-term strategy to gain greater social acceptance for weed.

"We are trying to get marijuana reclassified medically," he was quoted as saying. "If we do that (we'll do it in at least 20 states this year for chemotherapy patients), we'll be using the issue as a red herring to give marijuana a good name."[58]

This is worth unpacking.

What Keith revealed was how backers of pot wanted to dress up an illicit, mind-altering product to look like something respectable—as something that could medically help people.

Lest we overlook the other part of what Keith said, a "red herring" is a ruse, a deception, subterfuge. Which is to say, his strategy to popularize pot was nothing more than a sham.

Remember the Trojan Horse strategy?

Except nowadays, Keith disavows the comment. He has been quoted denying "that we were trying to use the medical issue to lure people unsuspectingly to our larger agenda."

I reached out to Keith to speak with him for this book. He said he was busy.

It's okay. Others are quite familiar with what happened, and how the notion of marijuana as medicine would pave the way for so-called recreational pot. Dr. James Lange, a researcher at San Diego State University, said during an interview for this book that over a decade ago, a featured speaker representing the Drug Policy Alliance, a pro-marijuana group funded by George Soros, revealed the pot-as-medicine scheme during an event billed as a harm-reduction conference in Barcelona.

"He was just explicit, this is our strategy," Lange recalled of the industry speaker. "'We will get medical and then we will get general.'" Putting it all in context, Lange went on to say, "And that was a foothold to all drugs becoming legal."

Whether Keith remembers making these remarks or not, the important fact is that the industry's approach—advocating for the medical and then recreational, or the "red herring" model— worked.

The arc has been remarkable, if not disturbing.

Just two decades ago, marijuana was a drug viewed with grave concern. It was then relegated to fringe status in the era of the flower child before being cast as a medical panacea for the masses. And now, this seductive idea has been seized upon by the wolves of

Wall Street, who are doing all they can to make marijuana respectable and hip.

Let's not forget that the country's efforts against drugs were initiated by FDR and followed up by JFK (Nixon's and Reagan's campaign against drugs came later), and that those efforts were once quite effective: Pot usage fell to a low ebb by the early 1990s. That is, until 1996, when California voters approved Proposition 215, making it the first state in the nation to legalize marijuana for medical purposes. It's worth noting a few things about this initiative: it was *medicine via popular vote.* And I'm using the word "medicine" loosely here—anyone could get pot for any reason. The Food and Drug Administration had *not* said it was medical. It was simply a political declaration. But it worked, as Keith allegedly foretold, opening the way for several other states to allow so-called "medical" marijuana. Ten states did so in a mere ten years. (Note this is different than allowing non-smoked components of marijuana for true medical reasons or for end-of-life palliative care, both of which I support.)

If voting for "medical" marijuana at the ballot box cracked open the door to increased social acceptance of the drug, then the slew of ballot initiatives in recent years for "recreational pot" has blown the door wide open.

On November 8, 2016, a day after California legalized non-medical marijuana, demand for pot in that state jumped 18 percent. Every ten seconds, someone in California purchases marijuana. Use of the drug has doubled in the past two decades in the United States. Pot is legal for medical or recreational use in about three dozen states.

Have you heard of Pandora's Box?

"I'm very worried," Dr. Glantz, the tobacco researcher I mentioned earlier, remarked about this trend. He sees it as a repeat of Big Tobacco, and certainly parallels exist. There are toxins in pot smoke that pose similar dangers to those in cigarette smoke. He believes something must be done about the rapid expansion of pot before the industry hones its marketing message further and pot becomes an even bigger mass commercialized product than cigarettes.

Furthermore, Dr. Glantz believes leaders in the public health community have been too quiet. There's a need to bring what is happening in the dark recesses of the pot world to consumers' attention.

"Hopefully," he said, "people will pay attention."

CHAPTER ELEVEN

Inconvenient Truths

If there was any doubt about the avaricious impulses of pot barons, it was quickly dispelled by a New York venture capitalist who was planning to invest millions in a Caribbean pot farm. In his calculation, there was no headspace for the scientific studies indicating marijuana is linked to cancer-causing toxins, schizophrenia, birth defects, and debilitating addiction, among other ills.

For this particular venture capitalist, it was nothing personal. It was big business. Which explained why he and his team hired a high-powered lobbyist to work the halls of government in Albany, New York, seeking to influence the proposed legislation to legalize marijuana. What we learned in that fierce battle was how the New York financier and his team had zero interest in creating a legal industry that would financially benefit mom-and-pop pot shops operated by people of color, as some lawmakers hoped they would.

On the contrary, the financier's lobbyist sought to kill the language in the bill that contained provisions to encourage minority ownership of pot sold at retail. Why? For a simple reason: greed. The venture capitalist wanted to control the entire economic vertical, from cultivation to distribution to the point of sale. There was, in his estimation, no room for others.

These are the kinds of stories that make me grateful to have—along with the New York State PTA, the Medical Society of New York, and others—stopped or at least slowed the path to legal pot in the Empire State. But the corporate raiders keep trying to resurrect the bill, and it's their big target in 2021. Avarice has an unquenchable thirst.

So do the interests spinning the false promise of pot.

One particularly seductive line of reasoning they use, at least when they're appealing to cash-starved communities, is that pot produces a massive financial windfall in the form of tax revenue. It's easy money. Ballot initiatives around the country have sold marijuana on the promise that it will generate billions of dollars in state and local income to be reinvested in communities. That hasn't materialized.

The myth: In Alaska, industry forces boasted commercial pot sales would generate $55 million in 2015, the first year of legalization, and that it would soar to a walloping $106 million by 2020.[59]

The reality: Revenue was $1 million a month, a steep drop from the wild projections.[60]

The myth: In Washington, a state government estimate predicted as much as $1.9 billion in pot revenue over five years.[61]

The reality: The 2014 to 2018 numbers are a bit more than half of that prediction.[62]

The myth: That pot tax revenue pays for the increased treatment need that happens as a result of more use.

The reality: Never happened. Not once.

Here's another sobering way of looking at the vastly overstated economic impact of pot: Marijuana taxes as a percent of state budgets account for about one percent for any "legal" state.

Actually, the calculation is worse than that.

For every dollar generated in tax revenue from legalized drugs, it's estimated that ten dollars in social benefits is lost to help cover the related expenses of increased car crashes, hospitalizations, workplace productivity, criminal justice costs, and more.

Let me break that down for weed.

Regarding hospitals, one Colorado study found emergency-room admissions due to pot use alone could cost the state hundreds of thousands of dollars.[63]

A study conducted by AAA found that in the years following legalization, the number of fatal car crashes involving marijuana more than doubled.[64]

Problematic marijuana use among those aged 12 to 17 was 25 percent higher in legal states compared to states without legal recreational use.[65]

In California, emergency room admissions related to marijuana almost doubled to 236,954 instances after legalization in 2016.[66]

In Colorado, the crime rate has increased eleven times faster than the national average shortly after legalization.[67]

And in Washington State, the rate of aggravated assaults increased at a rate higher than the national average increase, from 2013 to 2017.[68]

Let's not overlook the impact on the workplace either. We're not just talking about lost productivity on the part of bewildered employees who are high; many people who've been injured or disabled in serious accidents are the victims of those who are using mind-altering drugs. We are still gathering data on the full extent of workplace costs due to pot use, including incidents resulting in liability lawsuits. We know this much, though: Financial guru Warren Buffett told me that his friends in the insurance business have said marijuana legalization has already increased the cost of insurance premiums. In effect, these companies are passing along the real cost of marijuana use to consumers. In fact, according to Quest Diagnostics, workplace weed use is up dramatically in legal states—more than 100 percent higher than past use in some places.[69]

"It's crazy," Buffett said of pot legalization at a meeting we both attended.

All of this should prove the drug's deleterious effect on society, but we haven't even touched on the many other costly effects of marijuana legalization, which have yet to be quantified but which are being felt in communities all over America. Among them are missed school days and the rapid rise of homelessness, which, if you haven't noticed, has exploded in places including Washington, Oregon, and California in recent years.[70]

But if there is anything more audacious than the claim that pot is an economic boon for communities, it's the notion that marijuana is safe.

The only ones who sanctioned pot as "medicine" when voters approved ballot initiatives for medicinal marijuana were the voters themselves. They were simply voting for the word "medicine," not medicine itself.

Only three marijuana-based medicines have been approved by the FDA:

Marinol (synthetic THC), which is used to treat nausea related to chemotherapy; Cesamet, a similar drug to Marinol; and Epidiolex, a certain formulation of cannabidiol (CBD) that is extracted from the plant and approved to treat certain kinds of seizures.

But for now, that's it.

Virtually every scientific review, including a 2016 World Health Organization report[71] and a 2017 National Academy of Sciences study,[72] makes the same point: marijuana is addictive and harmful.

Propaganda from pro-pot forces would also have you believe marijuana could lead to a way out of our opioid epidemic.

Not so.

In 2018, the *Journal of the American Medical Association* said, "The opioid crisis appears to be worsening where marijuana has been legalized."[73] According to *The Lancet*, another respected peer-reviewed medical journal, there is no evidence that marijuana reduces pain, despite the popular misconception foisted upon us by pot purveyors.[74]

Underscoring the dangers of marijuana, Surgeon General Vice Admiral Jerome M. Adams issued a stark advisory in August 2019 to the public: "There is a false perception that marijuana is not as harmful as other drugs," he said. "I want to be very clear—no amount of marijuana use during pregnancy or adolescence is known to be safe."

It was the surgeon general's first advisory on marijuana since 1982. Adams was so impassioned about the point that, a day after his strong public pronouncement, he barged onto the stage in full regalia—wearing admiral whites—to add his voice to mine while I was giving a talk in Washington, D.C., at the Oxford House World Convention, a gathering of over a thousand people in addiction recovery.

"He's right!" the surgeon general declared, echoing my message about the dangers of marijuana, as he nudged next to me at the podium in the banquet hall of the Renaissance Washington Hotel.

Given the nature of the marijuana issue, I didn't expect the surgeon general—the leading spokesperson on matters of public health in the federal government—to pop up and offer such vociferous and impromptu remarks. His decision to use the power of his office to speak out on such a controversial issue has earned my respect, and I hope he will continue to contribute to this movement.

Over the past several years, I have met with all kinds of federal officials behind closed doors—both in the Obama and Trump administrations—and virtually everyone has been supportive of my message on the dangers of marijuana.

And yet, in public, there is a dearth of strong declarations against marijuana from government officials. It was, as I understand from having been a public servant in Washington, D.C., a political reality; federal officials don't want to expend political capital when it isn't necessary, and they certainly don't want to invite pushback from pro-pot forces, which would have been a certainty, given their vehement, well-funded voice.

Being opposed to marijuana simply wasn't as popular as fighting, say, the opioid epidemic, which was understandably receiving a lot of media ink given the tremendous hazards and unprecedented overdose rates.

But here was Adams, the surgeon general, by my side, on national television (C-SPAN covered the event), sparing nothing in his withering condemnation of marijuana. In retrospect, it made sense; Adams was doing his duty as a doctor, raising red flags in his seminal advisory, including his concern about pregnant women who use pot more than any other illicit drug. By the way, the industry isn't helping on that front: 70 percent of Colorado's pot shops are pushing pot on pregnant mothers by falsely claiming it helps reduce morning sickness, and they have not received so much as a slap on the wrist for this behavior.[75]

The surgeon general also noted marijuana is the most widely used illegal drug in the nation. This is of special concern when it comes to children and young adults, whose frequent use "appears to be associated with risks for opioid use, heavy alcohol use, and major depressive episodes."

Since those remarks, the surgeon general has doubled down on the dangers of pot.

He went so far as to call it what it is: "a dangerous drug" in which "nearly one in five people who begin marijuana use during adolescence become addicted."

Addressing the exponential increase in the potency of today's commercial-grade weed, he stated, "While the perceived harm of marijuana is decreasing . . . the scary truth is that the actual potential for harm is increasing."

He warned, "This ain't your mother's marijuana." Interestingly, it was a similar message I had heard President Obama's surgeon general, Vivek Murthy, say shortly before as well:

> *". . . Public policy is outpacing science when it comes to marijuana. What we know is that marijuana is in fact addictive . . . this may come as a surprise to some people . . . marijuana is in fact addictive and we know that it has an impact on the developing brain. We don't at this point have high quality evidence that tells us that in fact marijuana is both safe and effective for use for medical purposes. And that is a standard that we use to approve any drug or medication through the FDA. So my belief is that we should hold marijuana to the same standard."*[76]

On the same day Dr. Adams joined me on stage in Washington, D.C., I had one of my semi-regular private meetings with the drug czar, the top federal official who directs drug-control policy in the United States.

These were my old stomping grounds, as I had served as a senior adviser in this office, albeit in a different building. But that was under President Obama, and there was a new drug czar now, James W. Carroll, appointed by President Trump to serve as the director of the U.S. Office of National Drug Control Policy. While we discuss policy matters quite frequently, that day's huddle was to be a deeper dive into the issue of marijuana.

Shortly after I was ushered into a spartan conference room a couple of blocks from the White House, the drug czar breezily entered wearing a dark suit and red tie. He plunked himself down in a seat at the head of the table, flanked by several of his staffers, and let his feelings be known.

"Use of marijuana in any amount is dangerous," he said right off the bat. He expressed concern about a "lot of mixed messaging out there," stressing "people are confused."

To illustrate the point, Carroll mentioned offhand how he had recently been traveling on business in Nevada where his Uber driver chatted about how people smoked "flowers."

Carroll scoffed at that mischaracterization, as if the drug were as benign as "rainbows" and "unicorns."

The reality about marijuana is quite different; drug cartels, Carroll said, were brazenly growing marijuana illegally on plots of land in California, harvesting plants that had been treated with dangerous pesticides and other hazardous contaminants. To prove the point, he produced photographs. It was startling—and persuasive. The legalization of marijuana in places such as California was not curbing the black market as pro-pot forces would have you believe; it was doing the opposite—encouraging drug cartels to expand their theater of operations.

The drug czar went further, agreeing to articulate his warnings about marijuana in an interview with me. In fact, his words were eerily similar to both of Obama's drug czars, and every other drug czar I've had the pleasure of meeting. This could be the one issue—ironically, given America's mixed views—that both Democratic and Republican drug policy officials agree on. But, alas, there were limits to Carroll's willingness. When I asked him how the U.S. government could reconcile federal law, which clearly prohibits marijuana, with states that have legalized the drug, he offered a noncommittal answer. Staff looked away. Others in the room got nervous.

Unsurprisingly, little has changed.

It is, to say the least, a nettlesome political issue.

What about the idea of marijuana as medicine? The issue is complex and charged. In reality, there are components of marijuana that do have medicinal value. If you have six months to live, you're thinking about any option available to you that can be of help, medicinal or not. But there's a sinister side to this seemingly compassionate policy.

If there is any doubt about that, just ask Helen.

When her daughter Caroline was about ten years old, she began to experience debilitating migraines multiple times a week. The headaches were so intense, Caroline threw up and missed school. Visits to pediatric neurologists throughout the New York City region revealed no cause. While certain foods seemed to trigger the migraines, anything, it seemed, could set her off: too much sleep, too little sleep, a chocolate bar, a shift in the barometric pressure. The migraines arrived without notice, including at Thanksgiving and other festive times, thus ruining family gatherings and upsetting the peace in their New York apartment.

It got to the point where just the threat of the migraines—not their actual occurrence—created a spiral of anxiety.

"You're only as happy as your unhappiest child," said Helen, speaking clinically but betraying her own personal agony when tears began to coalesce.

Nothing really helped, not a slew of prescribed medications. That's when Caroline began smoking pot. She was in the ninth grade. Helen found bits of green flakes, which she recognized as weed, on her daughter's bedroom desk and confronted Caroline about the marijuana.

"It's the only thing that helps my migraines," Caroline told her.

"I didn't know anything, I was clueless," Helen recalled.

She did what any concerned parent would do; she checked it out. First, she spoke with her daughter's therapist, who admitted, yes, marijuana wasn't a good idea, but if Helen forbade it, Caroline would just find a way to sneak it. It was so readily available in New York City anyway; you could buy a bag of weed at a bodega down the block, no questions asked.

Soon enough, Helen learned kids in middle and high school were vaping—using small handheld battery-operated devices to inhale heated weed or a concentrate of it to get high—often odorlessly and without much smoke, which means it is frequently undetected.

"They're all doing it," the therapist said.

Helen spoke with her brother, who worked on the business side of the pharmaceutical industry, and he told her, yes, people were taking marijuana as medicine.

Her brother referred her to a doctor, who in turn, referred Helen to another physician in Manhattan. This physician touted her services as "integrative cannabis for children and adults."

In October 2018, Helen took her daughter Caroline to see this doctor and ultimately pot was *recommended*. (No medical professional in this country can prescribe pot because it is not an FDA-approved medication.) Every day, Caroline took a *self-determined dose* from a MedMen vape. (There is no actual dosage given for medical marijuana recommendations for the same reason that prescriptions are not written.) Even Caroline's school allowed her to partake when needed in a room set apart from class for that purpose.

Helen took what she was being told on faith. Her daughter's therapist said everyone was doing it. Her brother in the pharmaceutical industry said it was all the rage. A physician recommended it. The school allowed it.

"I figured they knew," Helen said of those who were in a position of authority.

But something wasn't right.

Pretty soon, Caroline wanted to get high all the time—even when she wasn't suffering from migraines.

She began vaping multiple times a day—at home, at school, wherever she was.

"It took over pretty quickly," Helen recalled.

Caroline's behavior became increasingly erratic. She would wake up in the middle of the night, screaming for no apparent reason. If she ran out of pot, she would rummage through the apartment, drinking anything she could find—tequila, beer, whatever. She kicked in a full-length mirror in the bathroom, shattering it. In a rage, she flung a cup of hot tea across the room.

Early one morning, Helen arranged for two police officers to come to the apartment and escort Caroline to the hospital. Her daughter didn't put up a fight. A psychological evaluation confirmed that she was a danger to herself. She was admitted for several days. Other hospital care followed, as did a stint in a costly residential treatment program. The family hemorrhaged $50,000 for the month-long stay.

Even now, with Caroline at the age of sixteen in an outpatient program that includes drug monitoring, it's touch and go. One night, she ran away from home. Helen retained a "sober coach," who follows her daughter's every move at a cost of $1,600 a day.

More than once, Helen talked about the thought of suicide—not by her daughter but, herself.

"If I didn't have so many to take care of," she said, "I'd kill myself."

But she persists. She thinks of others. In addition to her daughter, Helen has a son and a husband to care for. She tries to hang on. "I think it's a lifetime for us," she said of her effort to cope with Caroline's affliction, which she blames on the medically recommended pot.

"The marijuana certainly put [Caroline] on a direct path to mental illness," she said.

Sadly, Helen added, "I don't have much hope."

She might find some, however, in the searing story of Anne.

CHAPTER TWELVE

Training for the Olympics

Anne Hassel was a true believer.

Marijuana was "enmeshed in my identity," she told me during an interview for this book. When she was sixteen, she felt like an "awkward" teenager. To compound matters, she grew up in what she described as a chaotic household with four siblings, raised by parents in Richmond, Virginia.

After graduating with a bachelor's degree in political science from Virginia Commonwealth University, Anne moved to Boston in 1990 and became a licensed physical therapist. But over time she found herself gravitating to the just-emerging medical marijuana industry in Massachusetts.

In 2015, she applied for a job at a pot dispensary in a countercultural hub in the western part of the state. She wanted to become a "patient service associate" (better known as a "budtender"), offering suggestions to customers about the product in the store.

"That was my dream job," Anne said.

In her application letter, she wrote, "I wholeheartedly support the use of medical marijuana as it has no harmful side effects that are present with pharmacology, and it offers significant pain relief from physical and psychological ailments."

Those words would come back to haunt her less than two years later.

On September 15, 2015, Anne was hired by the pot dispensary at $15 an hour, down from the $45 an hour she was earning as a physical therapist. But the pay decrease didn't matter to her.

Anne embraced the place, which aspired to have the same kind of sleek, funky vibe as an Apple Store, with its teakwood counters, green accents, modern dropdown lights, and big video screens of large marijuana buds captured so close up you could see the crystals and glands. She graduated rapidly from smoking weed to dabbing, which involves inhaling concentrates, also called wax and shatter, with high doses of extracts of THC, the active chemical inducing a high.

Family and friends urged Anne to quit her job. But already, as she ruefully put it, she "was in too deep."

As part of the initiation at the dispensary, Anne and the other staffers were told not to call the police even if customers got into fights. They were assured the managers would deal with it in-house. In a 2016 missive from a supervisor, staffers were also warned to be "VERY careful about who you email." The note stressed that employees should be "thinking about how your email would look on the front page of the [*Boston*] *Globe*..." The note ended, "So—always make a phone call instead of an email if possible."

Ironically, the dispensary didn't follow its own advice. This missive and others from management are on record here as they were sent via email.

Early on, one of the bosses gloated at a staff meeting that the Massachusetts Department of Health didn't know much about proper marijuana regulations and turned to dispensaries like theirs for guidance.

The medical dispensary encouraged staffers to use pot liberally and often. They made so-called "beta product" available to employees at a deep discount—a gram for $1 a pop instead of $15.

"Guinea pigs" is the way Anne described her fellow budtenders and herself.

"Feedback" is the way supervisors described it in correspondence with employees. The dispensary also called it "homework." Management wanted budtenders to review the marijuana so that they were in a better position to describe the various mind-altering experiences to potential customers.

There "ain't no such thing as a free lunch," quipped one "team leader" in an email promoting the employee discount.

"The goal is to really become familiar with our strains, and to be able to give the most dynamic and comprehensive information to our patients," this team leader wrote in a February 2016 email. "Of course, buying the gram commits you to doing your homework!"

At morning meetings, staffers lounged around on cool leather couches, talking about their experiences with various pot products. Anne recalled one saying that he "went into seizures."

Another said the marijuana sample "made my tongue go numb."

Another coworker reported, "I got really bad TMJ pain," a reference to temporomandibular joint dysfunction, which affects the jaw.

According to Anne, the supervisor leading the meeting simply laughed it off.

Other staffers and patients reported troubling symptoms from the pot they consumed too. These complaints included headaches, rashes, dizziness, wheeziness, and itchiness. Anne herself experienced headaches, a sore throat, and multiple bouts of respiratory infections.

These, too, were dismissed by her bosses.

Staffers were loopy on pot. Cuddling and hugging were rampant. So, too, was an unpleasant odor, reported by clients. It emanated from unbathed staffers too high to care about personal hygiene, even when a supervisor emailed them to "please remember to apply antiperspirants/deodorants as often as you need."

"Smoke one for the team!" a supervisor declared in an email, encouraging more usage.

Among the assignments was a review of a strain of marijuana dubbed "Rogue OG."

A staffer reported back that one of the psychoactive effects of Rogue OG was "separation of head and body."

In response, a supervisor wrote to budtenders, urging them to tell customers "this is one that hits different people in different ways."

In another review, a staffer wrote this about the "medicinal effects" of the strain, Triangle Kush x Rare Dankness #2: "Due to its potency it can be overwhelming and anxiety producing for patients with a low tolerance." Yet at the same time, the staffer professed, "This potent strain can be useful for depression, stress relief, insomnia, muscle relaxation, mood elevation, appetite stimulant, and other gastrointestinal issues."

The write-up for a strain called "Chem Dawg" said it was believed to have "derived from seeds procured at a Grateful Dead show." Also noted was that it smelled like "diesel" and "skunk" and "can exacerbate anxiety."

Yet another strain, known simply as "Goo," was purported to induce "Heavy eyes, couch lock, and the munchies," while supposedly being "helpful in treating insomnia, stress, muscle pain, arthritis, eating disorders, muscle spasms, PTSD, movement disorders, and nausea."

Forget, for the moment, that there is no basis in fact for raw—especially smoked—marijuana to be considered a wonder drug. As I have argued before and will continue to argue again, it has never been approved by the FDA and has failed in multiple attempts at proving its safety and efficacy. This isn't, of course, to say that components don't have a medical purpose—they do as I have specified elsewhere in this book. But that is different than what most states authorize today, and certainly different from what Anne's employers espouse.

Imagine if the prescription drugs you take to treat hypertension or cholesterol were never tested in a lab, but rather were taken under duress by retail workers with no medical background, who then assessed them while they were high. You wouldn't take them, right? You and countless other irate patients would be levying a class action suit to make them stop their dangerous practices. So why do we allow such lunacy in the "legal" market for pot?

Anne went on to say that the discounted samples didn't just serve as homework. There was pressure to partake. One work colleague burst into tears, relaying to Anne how upper management "contacted her daily, telling her to consume more." For her part, Anne confesses she was "so far gone in druggie world" that she remained an ardent acolyte of the place and product.

That even included when the pot shop announced, in August 2016, the unveiling of its own "Olympic Games!"

Staffers would be entered into events such as "joint rolling." The quest was to see "Who could roll the best doobie?"

The judges were enlisted from the store's "inventory specialists," "floor captains," and "security" staff.

Another Olympic challenge was aimed at seeing who could grab as close to 3.5 grams of buds just be eyeballing it rather than measuring it.

The contest also pitted staffers against one another in a different kind of guessing game. Competitors had to successfully identify the strain of marijuana in each of several unlabeled vials of buds. Anne boasted, "I easily won the gold medal and selected a bong as my prize."

She was elated that day but over time she began noticing something was awry.

Ceiling tiles were missing in the dispensary, and dust dropped onto the workstations where client orders were filled. Some of the marijuana buds for sale, she observed, were covered in mold.

"I could see wispy gray on the bud stalk," Anne recalled.

Upon telling management about it, she said, "I was told to sell the moldy marijuana." The directive didn't sit right with her, but Anne had signed a nondisclosure agreement as part of her employment. She was afraid to speak out, and went along with it, not sure what else to do.

Later she was dispatched to a nearby cultivation center to harvest the plant. There Anne noticed more mold. When she brought her concerns to the attention of higher-ups, they told her that she should trim around the mold. "It wasn't right," she said, as her sense of unease continued to mount.

Two problems existed: Even by trimming the mold, Anne could tell the plant still retained some of it; the mold couldn't be completely excised. What's more, she was trimming away mold for eight hours a day—without a mask—potentially exposing herself to contaminants.

It got worse. A coworker observed other staffers dipping full stalks of marijuana into a barrel of caustic hydrogen peroxide, a technique used to mask the mold. When she asked a boss about this, she was told, "Hydrogen peroxide is the industry standard."

It wasn't.

Everywhere she looked, she saw cause for alarm. Clients returned products, including vape cartridges, which were then resold to other clients as new. Marijuana-infused products, such as nuggets and lozenges, expired, only to be relabeled with new expiration dates.

Staffers, herself included, were getting so high on a daily basis—before, during, and after work—that they were also giving the wrong measurements of marijuana to clients or including inaccurate information on product labels regarding the content of THC, the psychoactive ingredient in pot.

For instance, a batch of pot might be labeled to contain 4 percent THC when it actually contained 25 percent.

Or a bin of edible marijuana—nuggets that look similar to some of our age-old, favorite chewy chocolate snacks—might be labeled as containing 10 milligrams when they really had 100 milligrams.

A huge difference.

Faulty vapes inexplicably caught fire and blew up.

"We made so many mistakes because we were all high," she admitted.

Workers were vaping in the bathroom. A supervisor told Anne where the recording blind spots were so she could easily elude security cameras, which were behind the sliding doors of a "patient consulting room."

Anne was consuming so much marijuana—especially high-potency THC concentrates such as wax and shatter—that she began to slide, almost imperceptibly at first, into an abyss of vivid daydreams about vandalizing cars. She started fantasizing about beating a person with a baseball bat, or stabbing someone with a knife, or shooting and killing people.

After vaping, Anne's eyes would roll up in the back of her head and she would pass out. Her friends told her she would remain unconscious for extended periods, then awaken and consume more pot. Anne said she wasn't aware she had ever lost consciousness.

What she became increasingly aware of was the voice in her head growing louder, telling her to kill herself.

Feeling out of control, empty, and in despair, Anne would spend her days contemplating ways to end it all.

Before long, she began noticing physical symptoms, such as abdominal bloating, nausea, cramps in her gastrointestinal tract, and difficulty sleeping. Those gave way to numbness in her toes and the ball of her right foot. Then came the spasms of escalating pain and intensity in her calves.

Eventually Anne was medically diagnosed with heavy lead poisoning—three times the normal level. Her medical records showed that she also suffered from high levels of cadmium and nickel, and an elevated presence of thallium. All of this is likely from the pot itself and the vape pen she occasionally used.

On March 10, 2017, Anne quit her job—and she quit marijuana.

She's mostly recovered. Once she stopped consuming shatter and wax, the debilitating symptoms dissipated. If she suffers from any residue, it's from a persistent bout of cynicism about the business from which she extricated herself.

"This industry has nothing to do with public health, just profits," she said.

"I never thought marijuana could do this to me," she confessed. "That's what scares me."

Anne referred to marijuana products loaded with nearly 100 percent THC as hooking an unsuspecting audience. "It's not Woodstock," she said. "It's Wall Street."

When she tried to report her concerns to the Occupational Safety and Health Administration, she was told that it was not in OSHA's "jurisdiction."

Today the former pot diehard has become a fierce opponent of the product. She has relayed her experience to state regulators and the U.S. Food and Drug Administration. She wants people to know the truth.

"The industry is really dangerous," Anne now insists. "I never knew it was all about a commodity. I thought it was a plant. I was wrong."

As it happens, other former pot acolytes are speaking out, including Gregg Padula, who worked at a pot cultivation center. "The two most common fungi found in medical cannabis produced in Massachusetts grow facilities are powdery mildew and gray mold (*Botrytis cinerea*)," he wrote, echoing Anne's troubling account of contaminated product.

And that's not all. Several firms in Massachusetts have been fined for repeatedly using pesticides even after they were warned multiple times by state authorities. But warnings, verbal scoldings, and fines seem to do nothing to deter them from doing it again.[77]

The problem isn't limited to Massachusetts. Marijuana products with high levels of contaminants, such as pesticides, fungus, heavy metals, and solvents, have been reported in states that legally regulate the market, including Alaska, Colorado, California, Michigan, Oregon, and Washington.

The latter state *doesn't even pretend* to test at all for heavy metals and pesticides, and efforts to change that have been met by the industry with major resistance. Industry players worry it will drive up costs and force them to offer fewer products, hurting their bottom line.[78]

Given Anne's personal experience on the inside, this former budtender reached a visceral conclusion similar to that of the Gentleman Toker.

"I'm disgusted by this industry," she swore. And she has not looked back. Anne now tells her story to whoever will listen.

Bob Troyer, the fellow Obama appointee I mentioned earlier, shared this same sentiment.

By August 2016, Bob had ascended to the position of acting U.S. Attorney for Colorado. He was now the state's top federal prosecutor and could attest firsthand how much legalized marijuana had spread—or to use his terms, "how invasive this species was."

Commercialization did what pro-pot forces assured it wouldn't; it served as a magnet for what Bob described as "investment criminals, fraudsters, money launderers, high-end foreign national financial criminals," and of course, drug cartels from Mexico, Cuba, and Asia.

Over time, their main theater of operations became the suburbs. Organized criminal syndicates bought quaint houses on quiet cul-de-sacs to create anonymous marijuana growhouses. They gutted the wiring to install industrial hydroponic lighting, dug up main water lines to draw from new unmetered piping, and installed commercial-grade heating, ventilation, and air conditioning equipment.

This was a different kind of criminal. These weren't the Crips or any of the other gangs with which Bob and his law enforcement associates were all too familiar. This new entrant in the illicit field tended to lurk under the radar. Yes, they carried firearms—handguns, 9 millimeters mostly—but they didn't walk around shooting people, unless prompted.

What gave them away to observant people such as Bob was when you happened to be driving by a nice little suburban development—places with adorable street names and kids playing with their Big Wheels—and you happened to smell a fair amount of a skunk stench or detect an unusual clatter of ventilation equipment.

Occasionally, a house would catch fire—or explode—the result of a lab explosion, electrical overload, or, as Bob so aptly put it, when "morons learned how to extract THC using butane."

On other occasions, a gunfight would break out. Cartels sometimes sent crews to steal shipments from their rivals, and shootouts would occur, possibly resulting in a homicide. These events were commonly referred to as "rips" since one party was there to rip the other party off.

Bob had enough. If the industry was taking a different approach than usual, he knew he had to as well. By 2018 he was no longer "acting"—he was the confirmed U.S. Attorney. In his newly elevated position, he set out to learn even more about marijuana and his options to control its proliferation. A U.S. Justice Department official involved in checking drug trafficking recommended that he speak with me.

"Who's he?" Bob asked.

That's when the two of us finally met.

At about the time that Anne, the budtender, was calling it quits, Bob convened a conference in downtown Denver that was comprised of about fifteen U.S. Attorneys from California, Oregon, Washington, Nevada, West Virginia, Vermont, and Hawaii—an extraordinary gathering of federal prosecutors. There was no media. No security, either. And not much in the way of adornments except for a single window that provided a view of a guy lighting up a joint on the sidewalk.

Even food was sparse—sandwiches, water, and cookies—courtesy of Bob, who spent about a thousand dollars *out of his own pocket* to host the event.

That's when I stepped in, addressing the group of prosecutors who were seated around a rectangular table. My PowerPoint presentation went over the basics—what the pot industry was up to and how history was repeating itself with marijuana borrowing from the Big Tobacco playbook.

I also put in a plug for prosecutors to pay special attention to the investments that would inundate the industry, warning that they'd fuel the next wave of expansion.

Bob sat there, eyeing me throughout the entire talk. He shared his impressions with me later. He said he was thinking, "This dude, his brain is overheating his body. This guy is seated, talking a mile a minute, [his] eyes are lit up from the inside, he's plugging in, he's talking, he's learning as he's talking to two people. His laptop accidentally converted his PowerPoint slides into Thai . . . he's talking to me, he's getting a muffin, he's fixing his slides, five things at once, and he just goes for an hour."

When I was done and gone, Bob said he and his colleagues looked at one another, dazed at the enormity of the problem that the rapid commercialization of pot presented.

"Everyone," he recalled, "was left there thinking, 'Oh, f - - k.'"

CHAPTER THIRTEEN

The Whistleblowers

Someone told me I had to talk to Jan. Or, rather, Jan had to talk to me. Probably both. They promised she had something explosive to reveal.

Jan is an army veteran who used to work for the sheriff's department in Los Angeles County as a station clerk, checking records, assisting detectives, and fingerprinting bad guys.

When she and her husband, Dan, moved to Denver in 2008, she marveled at the awe-inspiring snow-draped mountains. The couple bought a two-story house in the 'burbs, with a big beautiful spruce tree in the front yard, which they decorated every Christmas with multicolored lights. Jan thought this is where she and Dan would die.

But then legalized marijuana arrived in 2014, and Jan was none too pleased. "I've not ingested marijuana and any other drug that was not prescribed for me—and that was cautiously, because I don't like to be out of control," she said.

So it made sense the following year when Jan made use of her law-enforcement background and went to work for the Marijuana Enforcement Division—otherwise known as MED—the Colorado agency that oversees the state's legal foray into pot. "I wanted to make a difference," she said. She even hoped this might be her forever job.

It wasn't.

For a while, things seemed normal. She moved up quickly from a temp worker to become a compliance investigator. In that position, Jan thought her job was to thoroughly vet those who applied for marijuana licenses to operate in Colorado, so she checked that they paid their taxes, ensured that their property leases were correct, and searched for any hidden ownership issues.

This kind of work was right up Jan's alley. She prided herself on her thoroughness and diligence. "My boss . . . called me 'The Bulldog.' I won't let go of anything. He knew if he gave me a job to do, I would do it, and do it right."

That, as it turned out, was the problem.

"I was hamstrung," she said in an exclusive interview for this book. "Our hands were tied behind our backs."

As Jan began denying applications, she said she encountered resistance from within her own agency. In one instance, while vetting a marijuana business license, she discovered the applicant had been arrested in another state decades earlier for what she described as "running a drug organization internationally."

This seemed pretty straightforward. She noted the agency rules have all sorts of reasons for denying an application, which, as she cited, included the lack of "a personal history that demonstrates honesty, fairness, and respect for the rights of others and for the law." This applicant was a felon who had served prison time. Jan promptly denied the application. But her decision was reversed because his felony conviction occurred over ten years earlier.

Jan was perplexed and raised another reason for denying the applicant. "He forged his daughter's signature" on a related document, she said.

This didn't move the agency either.

Ultimately, the head of the agency signed off on the application, which she believes is still being processed as of this writing.

Jan began to come to the uneasy realization that marijuana applicants were not getting proper vetting. "They weren't looking at them in-depth—the applications and the applicants," she said.

If she had any doubts about her assessment of the situation at the agency, they were put to rest when she investigated an applicant who, she discovered, owned property in Pueblo upon which a murder had occurred. He insisted he wasn't present when it happened. As if that weren't disturbing enough, Jan also found out that the property was the site of an illegal grow; marijuana was being cultivated even though the state hadn't approved it. The applicant insisted he didn't know about this either. But when the Drug Enforcement Administration raided the site, they found equipment for marijuana cultivation—and a water bill, several other receipts, and a copy of an out-of-state driver's license, all in the applicant's name.

"I was going to deny him, but the MED wouldn't let me deny him, because there was no official charge brought against him," she said of the state agency.

The upshot: the Marijuana Enforcement Division approved the applicant, and he is now a state-sanctioned business, cultivating marijuana.

This is about the time when Jan started thinking about leaving the agency. But not quite. In early 2018, she kept at it, compiling a four-inch-thick binder of worrisome information about another application, this one from a husband-and-wife team who were being investigated by the U.S. Securities and Exchange Commission for alleged securities fraud.

Jan also pulled documents showing that the couple was being sued for real estate fraud.

Ever the bulldog, she found inconsistencies between what the couple said in SEC depositions and what they wrote in their marijuana business application. When Jan brought all of this damning information to her bosses, asking, "Do we want this person in our industry?"she was shrugged off.

Jan decided to try to take matters into her own hands.

One Friday, she and her husband happened to be driving from Denver to Durango for a quick weekend getaway, when Jan asked him to take a little detour to Huerfano County.

That's where Jan suspected a different applicant was already in the pot business before actually being approved. She had reviewed a year's worth of this applicant's bank statements. The applicant had already purchased lights and other equipment to cultivate marijuana. Jan's husband wasn't particularly happy when he parked their Dodge truck outside of this suspected grow location.

What she saw confirmed her suspicions. She took pictures of a greenhouse as evidence. Zooming in, she managed to capture images of pot plants. Jan sent the photos in and asked, "What can we do? Can we deny him on this?" She was told they would talk about it the following Monday. When that day came, Jan said, "I got a verbal reprimand."

She was castigated for working off duty. She was scolded for placing herself in harm's way. She was told she should have brought someone with a badge along. Jan's stunned reaction was, "I'm like, 'Are you serious? I'm doing my job. I'm going above and beyond.'"

Feeling disillusioned, Jan mentioned to a fellow investigator in her office that her bosses weren't letting her investigate. Her colleague echoed the sentiment, saying, "We're substitute teachers correcting homework."

When Jan spoke to a friend who also worked as an investigator in the field, she asked him how often he checked marijuana businesses to ensure they were in compliance with the state.

"Well, we do it when we can," he said. "But most of the time, we're putting out fires, doing paperwork."

Jan grasped his meaning. "So there are a lot of licenses that have never seen an investigator," she said.

That, she came to learn, was especially true the farther west you went in Colorado, where there were fewer investigators to cover wide swaths of territory. The state, she told me, was approving licenses left and right—over 3,500 for shops and grows—but without the requisite number of investigators to keep an eye on what they were doing.

In the span of just six months, between January to June 2018, Jan enumerated a dizzying array of violations uncovered at marijuana businesses, including: incorrect labeling on products; inventory that didn't match records; outdated business documents; unlicensed or unapproved visitors working on the premises; identification of pesticides and solvents; incorrect and missing surveillance cameras; receipt of marijuana from unapproved sources; expired business licenses; the sale of medical marijuana to individuals without medical cards; the sale of marijuana containing mold; the hidden ownership of marijuana businesses; improper advertising; giving away free marijuana; the sale of marijuana to minors; improperly tagged pot plants; undisclosed investors possibly laundering money; refusal to show business records to investigators; the sale of marijuana online by employees; and the sale of more marijuana than is allowed to an individual—a technique so common, it's garnered its own term of "looping."

And that's only what state investigators caught.

Things were getting so out of hand that at 5:30 one morning, Jan was awoken by a loud noise. She rose to take a look. A SWAT team had broken in her neighbor's front door.

They were nabbing renters who were cultivating marijuana in their garage. "*Two* doors from me," she said. "From *me*. My neighborhood was perfect."

Jan quit in May 2019. She moved to Tennessee because, in her words, "I don't want to smell marijuana."

She had come to the final conclusion that the Colorado state agency tasked with ensuring the proper administration of licenses for marijuana stores and cultivation was nothing more than an illusion.

"There's no oversight," she said of the applicant review process, adding, "Now they're not investigating. They're just checking basically that they're breathing. If you're breathing, come on in. They don't do the deep investigations."

The threshold to get into legalized marijuana in Colorado was reduced to this: "All we care about is, they have money, it's from a legitimate source, they're a U.S. citizen, and they have no current criminal history," Jan said. That leaves the way open for "a robber, a murderer, as long as they served their time," she said. Five years after a felony, ten for a drug felony, and, she said, "They get a license."

Prior drug offenses were beside the point, and she noted about 15 percent of all applicants for a license to operate a marijuana business in Colorado had some kind of drug conviction.

It could be for "meth," she said. "It could be anything. Heroin, whatever. It's like selling candy."

Lest Jan be dismissed as an isolated example of a renegade former state investigator, let me introduce you to another whistleblower, Kati, who also worked in the Colorado Marijuana Enforcement Division before quitting in similar fashion, out of sheer disgust.

There's one major difference between the two investigators though: Kati isn't opposed to pot as Jan was. With a background in environmental sciences, Kati identifies herself as "pro-smart regulation." Her problem, however, is there has been little that has been smart about what is being done to ensure the health and safety of the citizens of Colorado—ground zero for pot in the United States as the state leading the pack in the legalization of marijuana.

In an exclusive interview for this book, Kati told her startling story and how it had ended with her resignation in December 2018 as a state investigator. She began by expressing her disagreement with a lot of the way things were handled. "It isn't how I believe investigations should be done," she said. "The people who want to do things by the book, who want to follow the law, are targeted."

Kati was one of those who wanted to do things by the book. At a minimum, she wanted to use her expertise in pesticides and molds to ensure the safety of her state employee colleagues when they ventured out into the field to inspect marijuana cultivation facilities. It was there that they could be exposed to toxic chemicals.

Such was the case when, in the fall of 2018, a state inspector was about to check out a Denver warehouse full of growing pot plants.

Kati offered to join her on the inspection, but a supervisor ordered Kati not to interfere. "It's not your job," she was told.

Kati felt it *was* her obligation. Pesticides can be acutely toxic. Inhalation or dermal exposure could lead to pesticide poisoning, or worse, cancer in the long run. So Kati texted her colleague to ensure she took proper steps to protect herself.

"Glad I did," Kati said.

From experience, she knew marijuana cultivators frequently used improper pesticides. "That happens all the time," she attested. It was a slipshod way of doing business; cultivators often lacked proper training and looked to use whatever pesticides worked best to keep the marijuana plants growing faster, bigger, and better. "A lot of growers don't have an ag [agricultural] background, so they'll use whatever . . . works," she explained.

Illegal pesticides are being used "left and right," Kati noted. Many samples of marijuana tested "positive for all kinds of illegal pesticides." She explained that oils and other marijuana concentrates used in edibles and various infused products sometimes eluded inspections to the extent that they contained "upwards of a hundred times the contamination levels" of pesticides found in other forms of pot. "The public is usually unaware," she added pointedly. The message gleaned from this: If you are consuming pot anywhere in Colorado, you have to know the risks. "You're relying on the honesty of growers about what they're using on the plants," she said.

One of Kati's big concerns is the use of sulfur pellets, which if burned, can turn into sulfur dioxide. It's acutely toxic. "If you inhale it," she said, "you will probably die."

It's not just that some marijuana growers are using such pesticides; it's also that some of those cultivators are unaware of the dangers. Kati is worried that many don't know what they're doing.

The same goes for those in charge of marijuana enforcement. "It's a circus," she said.

What the public doesn't know, according to Kati, is that the state agency regulating marijuana hasn't been regulating it with any consistency. "For a while," she told me, "everyone was kind of doing their own thing." One manager would tell an inspector to examine an applicant's financial transactions dating back two years; another manager would ask inspectors to check for three years.

"Arbitrary" was the way Kati described marching orders. What's more, investigators weren't receiving what she called "formal training." Kati herself was among those whose training amounted to being handed a checklist of what to investigate and being advised to ask questions if she had any. Missing from the checklist were instructions to be scrupulous. "If you did too thorough a job, it was frowned upon," she said.

So how hard was it to conduct pot inspections by the rules she was provided? "A trained monkey could basically do it," Kati quipped.

Things, not surprisingly, fell through the cracks. Some cultivation employees were diverting "clones"—tiny marijuana plants that haven't been tagged and placed in a tracking system—for sale in other countries. Only God knows where and to whom they'd be going.

Some growers also knowingly used minute amounts of illegal pesticides in the hopes they would go undetected by state inspectors.

A black market flourished in plain sight of legalized markets "because it can hide among licensed grows," Kati said. "There are ways to beat the system." Especially when the system is lax.

And if you can't beat 'em, as the saying goes, join 'em. That is precisely what happened, per Kati's account, with marijuana enforcement higher-ups abandoning the state agency to work for the other side, the pot purveyors.

In a 2018 meeting in a plain conference room with a window overlooking a parking lot, Kati witnessed firsthand the symbiotic—if not parasitic—relationship between the regulators and regulated.

The investigators and supervisors gathered there were considering an applicant who was planning a major Colorado pot shop. He was called a "shepherd," a wheeler-dealer who not only had lots of money but, access to other investors with lots of money. Turned out, the shepherd was also a liar. The inspectors caught him making false statements on his applications, which, by all rights, should have disqualified him automatically.

But it didn't.

"The overall feeling of upper management to us was, he's investing enough money, we're going to look the other way," Kati said.

It was simply about cash flow. " 'This guy was investing a lot of money,' " Kati was told. " 'We want him in the industry.' "

Not one to sit idly by, she spoke up, telling the gathering that this was wrong, that they shouldn't be doing this. If the state agency let in one bad actor like this applicant, it would have to let in all of them. Jan, the other inspector, chimed in as well, expressing her concerns.

The state approved his application anyway.

Kati is now in private practice, running her own consulting firm, American Custom Environmental & Safety. She remains committed to ensuring health and safety when it comes to pesticides, even if the state agency has failed in its job. "Whose responsibility is it to protect the public?" she asked rhetorically.

What is happening—or not happening—in the regulation of Colorado's burgeoning marijuana business is of grave concern to Kati—and should be for all the states following suit.

"I think it's a public health crisis," she said. "It exists, and nobody's paying attention to it."

If there's any question about Kati's conclusions, talk with Sarah, a toxicologist and chemist, who for many years owned and operated a well-respected lab in Boulder, Colorado. Like Kati, Sarah isn't opposed to pot. Actually, she's not only pro-regulation; she's fully in favor of legal pot. Which makes her story all the more remarkable.

In an exclusive interview for this book, Sarah, yet another whistleblower, revealed how alarmed she is by what she sees in the marijuana market.

In 2008, Sarah went into the lab business to test blood and other bodily fluids for cases involving drunk-driving, murder, and other law-enforcement matters. "I wanted to bring accurate, reliable, accessible science to a community where people's lives were on the line," she said of her early days when idealism reigned. "That's what I wanted to do."

As a lab operator registered with the Drug Enforcement Agency, based in a sprawling 9,000-square-foot operation, Sarah couldn't test a federally illegal drug, such as marijuana.

But the lab community is small, and Sarah was startled by what she was learning about other labs, which were not registered with the DEA. Such labs were suddenly popping up overnight all over the place, offering cheap, quick turnaround services for this new market in legal pot.

These new labs are supposed to be testing for THC, pesticides, and heavy metals, but many are "doing junk science," she explained. "They give you a piece of paper, saying whatever you want, literally making sh-t up."

Just to be sure she's being utterly clear, Sarah repeated, "They are literally making up results. That's exactly what I'm saying."

Sarah noted these new "marijuana labs are certified through MED," the state's pot enforcement agency, quickly adding, "for what that's worth, which is nothing."

Part of the problem, as she described it, is that in Colorado's haste to develop regulations to grapple with this newfangled pot industry, the state borrowed snippets of regulations from other types of testing protocols, which were "not at all relevant or related" to marijuana. The first time she reviewed the new pot regulations, "I almost fell out of my chair," she recalled. "They did nothing. They just winged it."

The other part of the problem, Sarah said, was the Marijuana Enforcement Division was not qualified to do the testing itself, or, as a result, to properly monitor what labs were testing.

Sarah took it upon herself to visit various marijuana labs to see what they were up to. They didn't like her questions. She was banned from some. She also talked with friends in the business who were either cultivating marijuana or testing it. What she learned was, in some instances, the same marijuana bud samples yielded different results at different labs. For instance, the level of the psychoactive ingredient THC could vary widely from 15 percent to 25 percent to 45 percent—a variance that could significantly impact a user's mind-altering experience.

In other words, people who are consuming marijuana have no idea what they're consuming.

"The blind leading the blind, that is what we have here," she remarked. "Think Wild West. The whole industry is built on this sh--ty lab model. It's a crap shoot." Sarah characterized the test results of the marijuana receiving the state's stamp of approval and being sold legally in authorized stores as "unreliable at best and potentially fictitious."

Even a pro-legal pot supporter such as Sarah can't help but reach the conclusion that what is unfolding in Colorado is a concern for citizens living in that state. But she adds that it also "should be extremely alarming to anyone who doesn't live here."

Similar concerns extend to other states that have opened the door to legal marijuana.

In more muted language, a 2019 audit by California's Department of Finance found a disturbing lack of proper regulation of the marijuana industry, stating that the California Bureau of Cannabis Control's "current status and location of personnel is not sustainable to provide effective and comprehensive oversight of cannabis activities."

Later that year, Nevada regulators reached much the same conclusion about their own state; when they investigated marijuana testing labs, they found pot with high levels of yeast and mold were making their way to legal store shelves.

Sarah recently got out of the lab business in Colorado. But she remains concerned about the level—or lack—of oversight that exists as mass commercialization of marijuana takes over.

"This is bad," she said. "We took a situation where we expected a state to implement FDA-level testing with no resources. How we thought this wouldn't jeopardize the general population boggles the mind."

PART THREE
Addressing the Consequences

CHAPTER FOURTEEN

Public Health Crisis

On August 17, 2019, the U.S. Centers for Disease Control and Prevention announced the disturbing emergence of a mysterious illness in Wisconsin, Illinois, California, Indiana, and Minnesota, which the CDC characterized as a "cluster of pulmonary illnesses linked to e-cigarette product use, or 'vaping,' primarily among adolescents and young adults."

Perhaps even more alarming, the CDC said further information was needed to determine exactly what was causing the illnesses—ninety-four of which had so far been reported in the span of less than two months.

But federal officials vowed they'd "get to the bottom of this issue."

Within days, the Illinois Department of Public Health said a person who "recently vaped and was hospitalized with severe respiratory illness" had died. This was believed to be the first fatality linked to what was quickly emerging as a full-fledged vaping crisis.

A week later, the CDC took the unusual step of recommending that, "Anyone who uses e-cigarette products should not buy these products." That, the federal agency announced, included those laced with THC, the psychoactive ingredient found in marijuana.

The fast-unfolding national scandal grew with another death—an unidentified victim who had been hospitalized after vaping THC with a product acquired at a pot shop in Oregon.

Public health officials there said the middle-aged victim had used an electronic cigarette containing marijuana oil from a legal dispensary—a startling admission. A death was linked to a state-regulated pot shop. The officials didn't know, however, whether the pot product had been contaminated, or whether the victim had added something to the device.

"Our investigation has not yielded exactly what it is in this product," said Dr. Ann Thomas of the Oregon Health Authority.

By early September, federal officials had identified about four hundred and fifty people afflicted with the mysterious lung illness in thirty-three states. The CDC acknowledged that many patients had reported using products with THC. Others, though, said they only vaped nicotine. Meanwhile, the total number of illnesses continued to rise to eight hundred and five, including a dozen known deaths, by late September.

The median age of the afflicted: twenty-three years old.

As troubling as that trend was, pro-pot forces sought to turn it to their advantage. By late September, in the midst of the unfolding carnage, the powerful National Cannabis Industry Association argued that the vaping crisis was reason enough for authorities to remove marijuana from the list of drugs that are federally illegal.

"As the leading trade organization, representing nearly 2,000 cannabis-related businesses, we are circulating a sign-on letter, asking the Speaker of the House to deschedule cannabis and provide federal regulators with oversight of cannabis and related compounds," the pot association stated in a mass email to its members. "It's a commonsense solution to a complex and serious problem."

In other words, by the logic of the pot association, marijuana could only be made safer if it was made even more widely and legally available. But we know regulation didn't work for tobacco; the mass availability of tobacco made smoking much more harmful by legitimizing a deceitful industry. How could it work for marijuana?

On the face of it, it was outrageous that pro-pot forces wanted to unleash marijuana as federally legal in the wake of a vaping crisis that was killing people and causing illnesses across the country. That marijuana was closely linked to many of the cases was, incredibly, overlooked.

Not by federal authorities though. In October, the CDC announced the death toll had risen to at least thirty-three across twenty-four states. The lung injuries had spread to every state except Alaska, afflicting nearly fifteen hundred people. And, not lost in the troubling disclosures, most of the illnesses were linked to vaping products containing THC.

In other words, marijuana was in the middle of the mess.

Weighing in, I issued a public statement in October, saying, "We are witnessing a marijuana vaping crisis. We have allowed this industry to run too far ahead of the science, and now we're experiencing the tragic consequences."

Blaring headlines, panic among state regulators, and a spate of investigations and lawsuits ensued.

"If you or a loved one is vaping, please stop," said Dr. Lee Norman, secretary for the Kansas Department of Health and Environment. "The recent deaths across the country, combined with hundreds of reported lung injury cases continue to intensify."

Massachusetts Governor Charlie Baker announced, "I'm declaring this a public health emergency because medical and disease control experts have been tracking a rapidly increasing number of vaping-related illnesses that in some cases have led to death."

New York Governor Andrew Cuomo declared a ban on flavored e-cigarettes, stating, "These are obviously targeted to young people and highly effective at targeting young people."

The Trump administration entered the fray with Alex Azar, the U.S. Secretary of Health and Human services, saying, "The Trump administration is making it clear that we intend to clear the market of flavored e-cigarettes to reverse the deeply concerning epidemic of youth e-cigarette use that is impacting children, families, schools and communities."

Over a hundred and forty staffers were assigned to the emergency response at the CDC. That number quickly grew to over two hundred and eighty. Others were brought in from the Food and Drug Administration, along with a slew of state-level public health officials.

Federal and state officials were rushing to find the culprit, working around the clock—literally twenty-four hours a day, seven days a week—in labs, obtaining vaping products, testing samples, sifting through biological and clinical data, examining historical trends, crunching numbers on laptops at cubicles. By late October, they still didn't know what was causing the health crisis, but they had figured out at least one thing: whatever it was had been triggered over the summer just before the injuries came to light.

"Something new happened in June and July," said Dr. Brian King, the senior official with the CDC's lung injury response team, in an interview for this book. "Something new definitely happened. What that factor was, we're not sure."

Investigators, though, were beginning to sense they were inching toward a breakthrough.

"We're definitely closer than the first week of August," the senior CDC official said.

More people continued to die throughout the United States—with the count reaching thirty-nine by early November. Finally, on November 8, federal health officials reported that tests among twenty-nine ill patients showed the presence of vitamin E acetate, an additive used in THC products. Not surprisingly, the CDC continued to urge people not to use e-cigarettes or to vape products containing THC.

Lost in the chaotic din of the vaping crisis were these startling facts:

- 80+ percent of all cases were marijuana related.[79]
- At least three deaths were linked to pot vapes purchased from legal dispensaries.[80]
- A study also found one in six cases were from vapes and oils sold by legal commercial shops, indicating the legal marijuana industry was selling a sizable portion of the products causing illness and death.[81]

- Seeking clarity, SAM submitted a Freedom of Information Act request to the state of Massachusetts, which compelled the state to reveal six EVALI cases linked to the Massachusetts "legal" marijuana market.[82]
- In Michigan, the state's regulatory agency was forced to issue a recall of tens of thousands of vaping products sold at state-licensed dispensaries after it was revealed that they contained vitamin E acetate.[83] Remarkably, the state said medical marijuana legalization laws disallowed them from tracing the outbreak of these products back to its source.[84]

Also lost was this remarkable fact: innumerable people had been vaping THC for years without any idea what they were putting in their bodies.

That included seventeen-year-old Jordan Davidson.

It started for Jordan in 2015 with nicotine. He was then a freshman in high school. He thought vaping e-cigarettes was a safer alternative to smoking traditional cigarettes. That, at least, was how vaping was touted. But by the spring of 2018, when Jordan was a junior at Phillips Exeter Academy, the prestigious boarding school in New Hampshire, he was vaping THC.

"We didn't know what was going on," said his mother, Tiffany. "We knew he had vaped Juul, smoked pot a couple of times. Honestly, I thought it was the pot that I smoked in high school."

It wasn't.

One weekend, when Jordan came home from school, he broke down, sobbing to his mother.

"What is going on?" Tiffany tried to get him to talk. "I finally asked him, 'Do you have an addiction?'"

Jordan said he did. "He was so upset," his mother recalled. "He had heard it wasn't addictive."

All that Jordan wanted to know was, "What am I going to do?"

The first thing his mother told him was that he wasn't alone. She immediately took him to a Narcotics Anonymous meeting, followed by an intensive outpatient drug treatment program. That's when Tiffany learned the extent of Jordan's vaping and its devastating effects.

"I had no idea this stuff existed," she recalled. "I asked the psychiatrist at outpatient, 'What the hell is my son smoking?' The psychiatrist replied, 'The crack cocaine of marijuana.'"

Then Tiffany's jaw dropped. The psychiatrist laughed. "Why are you laughing?" Tiffany asked. 'You don't know how many people I sit across from who ask that,' " Tiffany recalled him saying.

It all started to make sense: the devolvement, the paraphernalia, the Juul charger, the dab pen, the friends at school who told Jordan he had a problem, his anger, the denial. At one point, Jordan had contracted pneumonia. He suffered from a history of upper respiratory infections, and yet, through it all, he kept vaping.

He's been sober for more than two years since the acknowledgement of his marijuana addiction. His parents still drug test him at home. "Addiction is something you deal with every day," Tiffany said. Though Jordan has moved on to attend college at American University in Washington, D.C., his mother remains vigilant, especially in light of the vaping crisis gripping America, killing scores of users.

Jordan has taken note.

"He's seeing people actually getting sick from this," Tiffany said. "People are dying."

For Tiffany, the realization led her to found the organization Moms Against Marijuana Addiction.

She also came to understand a hard truth that her son Jordan had told her when he came to her for help with his addiction. "I realized," he said, "I was no better than a junkie in a back alley."

Jordan might have avoided his ordeal had he known what happened to another teenager like him.

CHAPTER FIFTEEN

An Intolerable Habit

By all indications, Annika was a picture-perfect teenager. She maintained a 4.0 grade point average in high school in a small seaside town on the coast of California. She took a slew of AP classes and was named captain of her basketball team. Annika had an easy smile and a mature way about her. The only hint that something was amiss was perhaps a subtle scar above her right eyebrow. Call it the remnants of a marijuana nightmare.

It didn't take a national vaping crisis to awaken Annika to the dangers of pot. In her case, it took a deeply personal experience.

Annika grew up in a comfortable home within a gated-community, the child of two engineers—one, chemical and the other, civil. She was your typical active kid who played soccer and liked to hike and bike. Things, though, began to fray at the edges of her youth when, in middle school, Annika started to feel isolated. By the time she turned 15 years old in 2015, things got worse. One night, Annika snuck out of her home with a friend, and they paid a visit to a neighborhood boy. He was older. He also smoked marijuana.

A lot.

His father was a successful builder who smoked too. They lived in a big, beautiful home, and Annika marveled at the surroundings. "I was thinking, *Man, this successful grownup is smoking pot*," she recalled. "*It can't be that destructive to your life.*"

What's more, this older boy began proselytizing about the false promise of pot. "I remember this kid telling me how much he hated high school before he started smoking," she said in an interview for this book. That struck home for Annika, who continued to feel isolated as a sophomore in high school. Smoking, she was given to believe, "made things more tolerable."

The next time Annika snuck out of the house with her friend, it was close to midnight, and they went again to the home of the older boy. It was late and his folks were asleep.

"He said his parents knew he smoked a ton and didn't care and didn't do anything about it," Annika said.

What's more, the older boy told her he had a stash of "dispensary-quality weed." "My dad got it for me," he added. So the teenagers went into a bathroom, opened a window, and smoked a joint. It wasn't the experience Annika expected. "I was dying, coughing, hacking up," she said.

The next time Annika smoked pot, it was with two of her basketball teammates, and they were struck with a fit of laughter. "Super giggling," she called it. They also had a bout of the munchies, devouring a bag of popcorn. For a fleeting moment, Annika thought it was cool. It was, she told herself, a way to keep up with the older kids in school.

"I was trying to show that I was, like, part of the game." Besides, she said, "I knew we had a ton of fun when we were doing it."

It didn't last. The giggles went away "pretty quickly."

The social acceptance of marijuana was reinforced by the normalization of pot—a legal drug in California. Annika's mother, Linda, became aware of her daughter's occasional dalliance with pot but, like many other parents, she remained unaware of the dangers.

"She did talk to me about marijuana using initially," Linda recalled. "I was not the parent who said, 'Zero tolerance.'"

Linda viewed marijuana as a substance on a level with alcohol—not condoned but not something to be terribly worried about. What Linda didn't know, however, was about all the newfangled options—concentrates, or vapes, or how the turbo-charged marijuana of today is nothing like the mild marijuana of her own youth. And Linda certainly had no idea that Annika, feeling depressed, would soon turn occasional smoking into frequent use.

"I had no idea," she said.

What began for Annika as a weekend-only thing progressed into something more: a habit. She bought her own bong. She quickly graduated from smoking weed to inhaling more powerful dabs and vaping concentrates. It resembled nothing like its weak predecessors.

"You don't call it weed," she said. That was too tame.

By her junior year of high school, Annika said she was getting "high morning to night."

She would order marijuana from an app on her phone. A dealer would show up in a Walmart parking lot. He'd pop the trunk of his car and show Annika an array of pot products—with discounts to boot. Buy five, get one free. Buy enough and get a bonus, a cookie infused with THC.

"It's like a store," she said, "with bargains and flavors."

The habit turned into an obsession. Annika would plan it all out. Where to buy. How to use—five times a day. She'd smoke in her car during lunch break. She'd inhale in the school bathroom. She'd even toke in the hallways between classes, hiding the vape cartridge in her sleeve. It was virtually smokeless *and* virtually odorless. "No one would know," she said. "It was super accessible and easy." Whatever money she had—from allowance or for food and clothing—she'd use to buy pot. "My brain," she said, "I could not think of anything else."

As Annika got deeper into pot, she also sank into a deeper depression, though she discounted the connection between the two. All she knew was, she didn't care about things, whether it was the weekend or dances. She went through the motions of attending classes, but she felt nothing. Pot, she said, "made me not feel all the feelings all the time."

Meanwhile, Annika hid her rampant use from her family. "I wanted to have a relationship with my parents and not get caught," she said. "But I wanted to keep using. What they didn't know wouldn't hurt them."

Linda thought her daughter was experiencing the trials of being a teenager—that she was struggling with unhappiness when she came home from school and immediately withdrew into a nap.

"We just didn't have all the information," Linda explained. "I thought she was depressed." But she still worried there must have been something else troubling her daughter.

This, she told herself, *is not normal.*

For Annika, it became increasingly difficult to hide all the unusual things that were happening—not just her catatonic behavior, but the couple of fender benders she had too. When the police pulled her over, she would be stoned and driving without her headlights on. Somehow she'd talk her way out of a ticket each time. But she couldn't talk her way out of what happened on July 11, 2017.

On the beach, in the middle of a summer day with her then-boyfriend, she was using a butane torch to heat up a dab of marijuana. When she stood up, she suddenly felt weird and woozy. Within seconds, she fainted. She doesn't remember what happened next.

Annika fell and struck her head on a rock. There was a big bloody gash, and she was unconscious. Her boyfriend dragged her body to the car. She was wet and sandy.

"What happened?" she asked him when she roused again.

"It's really bad," he said in a panic. "We need to call your mom."

"No, don't call my mom," she pleaded.

With his smartphone, he took a photo of the blood dripping from her head and showed it to Annika.

"Okay," she agreed, startled when she peered at her wound, "Call my mom."

At the ER, it took about 12 stitches to suture the cut. Doctors asked Annika if she had been using drugs. She said no.

It was, as it turned out, the first of many ER visits in the coming months.

The gash in her head didn't serve as the wake-up call you'd expect. Annika simply kept "smoking a ton."

In the fall of her senior year of high school, Annika started vomiting practically every Friday—a few random times in the morning just after her first smoke of the day. She'd pull into the school parking lot, open the door and throw up right on the spot. She didn't know why. Maybe, she thought, it was something she ate. Maybe she caught a bug. Her mother thought the strange illness was caused by anxiety. Neither blamed the pot—at first.

But then one Saturday, Annika started vomiting multiple times an hour. When Sunday rolled around, she was still vomiting. Lying in bed, feeling nauseated, Annika struggled with intense stomach pain. By Monday, she was back in the ER, taking in IV fluids to treat her dehydration. A nurse asked Annika whether she was frequently smoking pot. Annika denied it. She was sent home, but she couldn't stop throwing up. "When I say nonstop, I mean *nonstop*," she said. For days, she couldn't stomach any food.

Once again, Annika was admitted to the hospital, but doctors still didn't know what was causing her mysterious illness. Frantically, they sought to identify the culprit, taking abdominal X-rays, administering ultrasounds of all her organs, examining her brain with an MRI. Maybe, they thought, she had a tumor. Several days passed in the hospital, and Annika was quickly losing an enormous amount of weight. More tests followed: an upper-gastrointestinal scope, blood work, urine analysis. Hospital bills mounted into the tens of thousands of dollars. Through it all—over twenty-eight days of hospitalization and a 24-pound weight loss—Annika still didn't know what was afflicting her. That is, until she took a scalding hot shower, which temporarily brought Annika some relief. It also got her thinking. She googled her symptoms.

A hot shower is known to briefly ease the burden of something called cannabinoid hyperemesis syndrome—or CHS. It's a condition marked by repeated and severe bouts of vomiting. And it's caused by daily, long-term use of marijuana, though experts don't know why for sure some heavy users get the syndrome while others don't.

The syndrome, if untreated, can lead to kidney failure, seizures, brain swelling and even death.

Annika was done lying.

"It was finally time to be honest about it," she said. She told her mom she had been using marijuana every day. She also told her mom she might have CHS.

A drug test confirmed what Annika suspected: her THC levels were stratospherically high. It would take weeks to clean out her system. She worried she might not finish school. Her mother worried Annika might have brain damage. She was dangerously thin, sipping only Pedialyte, a drink to rehydrate children. Annika was so weak that she could barely walk to the car. She'd take about ten steps and stop, shivering in her older brother's big, dark blue down coat that made her seem even smaller than she had become.

It got to the point where Annika heard things in her head. "What's that bell?" she'd ask.

"It's nothing, sweetie," her mother would say.

That October, a feeding tube was inserted through her nose into her stomach. Days passed. Annika was sedated. Still, she suffered through what she described as major withdrawal. "I was having crazy dreams where I would smoke, like, crave it in my dreams," she remembered.

Annika would wake up crying.

Finally, by late November, she tested marijuana-negative.

Now, two years later, the yearning is gone. "I go weeks without think[ing] about it," she said.

In a sense, for young people like Jordan and Annika, the seeds of their marijuana problems were planted decades before they were born. That's when another addictive industry—Big Tobacco—wrote the playbook on youth drug use. And it's a playbook Big Marijuana has studied very carefully.

Decades ago, the tobacco industry was publicly claiming to be against teen smoking. They were working hard, tobacco executives told the public, to keep cigarettes only in the hands of adults. In reality, they were doing the exact opposite. We know this for sure because a treasure trove of documents was forcibly released to the public by a large lawsuit against Big Tobacco some twenty years ago. It shows these companies were engaged in willful deceit:[85]

> *"[T]he base of our business is the high school student,"* one document from Lorillard Tobacco read.
>
> *"[W]e must get our share of the youth market.... The fragile, developing self-image of the young person needs all of the support and enhancement it can get. Smoking may appear to enhance that self-image...."* RJ Reynolds (RJR) proclaimed. *"[T]he 14-18 year old group is an increasing segment.... RJR must soon establish a successful new brand in this market if our position in the industry is to be maintained over the long-term. [Young people are] the only source of replacement smokers..."*
>
> Brown & Williamson Tobacco wrote: *"[In] an attempt to reach young smokers, starters should be based, among others, on the following major parameters: Present the cigarette as one of a few initiations into the adult world.... Don't communicate health or health-related points."*

The documents go on and on. These tobacco executives, of course, knew exactly what they were doing. Since adolescent brains are developing until at least age 25, they are much more susceptible to addiction. In fact, if someone doesn't try a drug before the age of 18, *they are highly unlikely ever to do so*.[86] Ninety percent of people with a substance use disorder started using drugs before age 18. This is why tobacco products were marketed by cartoons: Joe Camel, yes, but also Fred Flintstone, whose character was actually a paid spokesman for Winston cigarettes. It's also why tobacco products came in all kinds of flavors. Getting lifelong customers means you have to start them young.

People are often shocked when I show them the kinds of products the marijuana industry is producing: "treats" such as "Stoner Patch Dummies," "Fruity Pebbles Magic Cereal Bars," and "Medicated Sour Skittles." While we may not have the smoking gun documents from Big Marijuana just yet, it's hard to imagine we won't be reporting on them in a few decades. Meanwhile, more kids will be lured by the flavored vapes, candies, and waxes that make today's marijuana so appealing to their susceptible brains. I fear that, sadly, in the years to come, we will learn of many more Annikas and Jordans.

Annika is now 19, waiting on tables and working hard in college. She's majoring in agricultural business. She gets good grades. She's not quite sure what she wants to do with the rest of her life. But she is certain about one thing: She wants people to know about the dangers of marijuana and what it did to her.

"It was just unlike anything I've ever experienced," she said.

Her mother feels the same. "You're not going to know when it's a problem until it's a problem," Linda warned.

Some of Annika's friends still smoke pot. So does her ex-boyfriend. Marijuana, though, is in her past. "I need a whole new life," she declared. What lies ahead for her is "starting over."

CHAPTER SIXTEEN

Breaking from Reality

Back to Phoenix.

Community activists Andrea Kadar and her husband, Dwight, had attended my talk in the Arizona desert. We didn't meet then, but our paths would soon cross.

Some months after my talk, marijuana legalization would qualify for the 2020 ballot, and, after a $5.5 million effort, sail to victory in November.

And though these determined citizens couldn't compete with the big money machine driving pot in Arizona, Andrea and Dwight put up a good fight as they were all too aware of what was at stake.

In 2015, when recreational marijuana first appeared on the Arizona ballot, Andrea and her husband immediately recognized the threat. Reading the fine print of the proposed measure—known as Proposition 205—they were alarmed at the idea that a marijuana store could open just feet from a school. It appeared that kids were being targeted. "We didn't want to be lying on our deathbed rationalizing to our grandchildren why they didn't have the opportunities we had," Dwight said. So they mobilized. With almost equal amounts spent for and against, Prop. 205 would fail, but the issue wouldn't go away.

As it turned out, the threat they were fighting hit close to home, though it was a relative who was in his 30s who was affected, not their grandchildren. The retired couple tried to warn this young man about the dangers of marijuana. He was, they knew, already smoking pot and vaping.

They told him how today's marijuana was highly potent.

"Not any worse than alcohol," their relative shot back.

"At first, he was incredulous," Andrea recalled. "We were fuddy-duddies."

"What was the big deal?" he asked.

He was about to find out.

The way this young man put it, he had always been a "straight-edged" kid. He was also something of a savant with a yo-yo. And he liked to swing dance, roller skate, and play tennis. He did all these things incredibly well—throwing himself into them with fervor.

He also threw himself into something else with abandon: marijuana.

It would ultimately lead him to a sudden—and devastating—break with reality.

Not at first though. It was the summer of 2001, just before he went off to college. He took a trip to Amsterdam, and that's when a friend, a smoker, introduced him to pot. "I wanted to see what the experience was like," he said. They rolled a joint and he took a drag, but he didn't feel much of the sensation of being high. Over the following two weeks, while still traveling overseas, he tried again. For someone whose mind always seemed to be racing at hyper speed, he began to feel what he described as "euphoria."

Seeking that sense of well-being quickly became a pattern and then a habit. "Through most of college," he said, "I was pretty much a daily user." But pot didn't just slow down his mind, it lowered his grades from As and Bs to Cs and also led him to drop courses. He simply stopped going to classes.

Whenever he had enough money on him, he'd buy more marijuana. It was a yearning.

"You want that feeling again," he explained.

When his dad found out he was using, he made him sign a contract promising to stop. It specified that if he broke the agreement, his father would cease paying for college. They both signed the one-page document. "I broke the contract," the son confessed, yet his dad continued to write the tuition checks. "He didn't know," the young man said. The son had kept his continued use a secret from his father.

Marijuana kept its grip on him after college, when he went to work at a financial firm, sitting behind a computer all day, handling the daily operations of mutual funds.

The lure of pot grew over the years, as he gathered an array of paraphernalia, such as pipes, bongs, and papers, and transitioned from "flower" (the term for smoked weed) to newly developed products with increasingly high levels of THC—drinks, tinctures, concentrates, and shatter. All the while, he viewed marijuana as no more harmful than, say, alcohol.

His love, though, was for the flower, which he always returned to. "I'd smoke probably half a gram a day," he said. "It was like having a beer after work. That's how I'd enjoy it."

He'd tell himself marijuana didn't affect his job. He'd assure himself it was a safe alternative.

"It was my way of relaxing," he told me.

That is, until December 2016—just a month after his relatives, Andrea and Dwight, helped defeat Prop. 205 in Arizona.

He'd been smoking pot as usual. But thoughts began to swirl in his head. Something about Bitcoin, the digital currency. For reasons he can't account for now, he found himself incredibly preoccupied by it. He said, "I became absolutely convinced it's evil and will ruin the planet." He proceeded to obsessively research Bitcoin online, staying up late at night, googling the decentralized currency, fearful of its environmental impact, and growing evermore anxious it was exploiting youth.

"I was on a tear," he said.

When he was at work, he became equally convinced he was surrounded by evil people.

The paranoia got to the point where "I'm just walking in the parking lot, freaking myself out, thinking people are after me," he recalled.

There was a military installation nearby. He got it in his head that armed forces were trying to protect him, that he had closely guarded information, and it was of great importance.

Late one night, he collected all his valuables from his apartment—his passport, birth certificate, and his cat—and loaded them all in his car, driving around aimlessly for hours.

The next morning, when he got to work, he marched to into the human resources department, lured an HR representative he didn't know into a conference room where he tried to explain the dangers of Bitcoin, drawing frantically on a white board. He demanded this evil be brought to the attention of higher ups at their financial firm. As he continued to talk a blue streak and gesticulate wildly, the HR person grew uncomfortable and made a quick call.

"I'm being insane," he says as he recounts the situation. "I'm a crazy person."

Minutes later, when a security officer arrived, he resumed his rant about Bitcoin. More security staff had to be called in. The room was locked down until EMTs arrived. They asked what was going on. Again, he launched into his diatribe about Bitcoin. Then he started introducing himself in Japanese. The next thing he knew, he was body slammed onto a conference table and restrained while his clothes were being cut off to check for visible signs of why he might be behaving this way. He was screaming at the top of his lungs, "Help me! Save me!" Still flailing about, he was finally sedated, cuffed, and dragged out of the office.

A stint in a hospital psychiatric ward followed. He was diagnosed with bipolar disorder and medicated for it. The disorder is associated with wild mood swings, ranging from depressive lows to manic highs. The marijuana was the trigger. "It helped ramp up the anxiety, the paranoia," he explained. "It totally helped set me on the path."

Numerous and powerfully delineated studies, including compendia by the independent National Academy of Sciences, have indeed shown a link between psychotic breaks and marijuana usage.

This young man's relatives, Andrea and Dwight, gave him a copy of one such study, which he read. He hasn't smoked since his break from reality. Nor has he had another episode since then. He began to listen to his relatives' warnings about the hazards of pot.

"I don't think he fully understood how dangerous high-potency marijuana was," Andrea said.

Not until his hospitalization. Finally, he admitted, "Marijuana usage had exacerbated my problems to a critical point."

And yet, despite the harrowing experience that led to his hospitalization, he still misses marijuana.

"Oh, yeah," he said when asked about it. The way his mind races ahead of itself makes it difficult for him to turn it off. He's almost "too alert, which is really annoying," he bemoaned. Some three years later, he hasn't found a calming substitute. He's a teetotaler.

He yearns for the high, the fix that is gone. "I've got to have some sort of something" is the way he describes the lacking—the absence of marijuana. He sees pot shops popping up everywhere around him, and after the legalization victory in November it's gotten much worse. But all he's left with, at the age of 36, is his own effort and discipline to find another way. He calls it his "force of will."

CHAPTER SEVENTEEN

No Stopping for COVID

I'd venture to say that each of the young people who shared their stories of addiction in the preceding three chapters would tell you that at the height of their struggle, they thought of marijuana as vital to their survival—perhaps even as necessary as sleep, air, food, and water. Or so it felt. What does it say about the marijuana industry that during the COVID-19 pandemic, not just dispensaries, but recreational pot shops sought status as an *essential* service? Could it be an admission of the substance's addictive qualities? Another sickening display of the industry's unchecked greed? Or both?

To contain the coronavirus in its initial months, governments scaled down public services to the bare bones—only those that literally meant *life or death* were permitted to operate. Hospitals, pharmacies, grocery stores, and take-out restaurants could remain open. Getting high wasn't atop the list of priorities . . . yet. But within weeks, the governors of several marijuana-legal states had succumbed to Big Weed's pressure. Colorado's Governor Jared Polis, for instance, caved to lobbyists and allowed curbside pot pick-up and take out. When that wasn't enough, he agreed to indoor weed sales as well. Had he and other governors been persuaded to believe that marijuana, like liquor, is recession proof? In the face of a potential global economic meltdown, was this their golden ticket? It begs the question: to whom exactly is marijuana essential?

Governor Charlie Baker of Massachusetts and the state's Cannabis Control Commission held out under the pressure longer than many others. They halted the sale of marijuana for fear of increased sales to out-of-state-buyers. Not only is selling pot to people crossing state lines a violation of federal law but doing so during a pandemic can also increase the spread of the virus. Baker agreed to let medical cannabis stores stay open just as pharmacies remained open, but recreational cannabis stores were ordered to remain closed. Big Weed soon decided to exert its own force of will. The industry levied a suit against Baker hoping to use the long arm of the law to get him to meet their demands. Baker ultimately reversed course and gave the industry what they wanted.

But let's not single out just one or two parties here. The public had a hand in this too. In many legal states, the run on pot was almost as crazed as the run on toilet paper! People were hoarding. And not just those who were concerned their monthly recommendations might not be filled. Others, who expected marijuana to be the cure-all for the stress they were already feeling—or at the least, a welcome relief from the boredom they anticipated—were stocking supplies too. The public outcry and panic caused Denver Mayor Michael Hancock to reopen recreational marijuana retail stores immediately after his initial instincts led him to close them. On March 23, 2020, that city saw a 392 percent increase in sales over the same day in the prior week, which was just before the stay-at-home order went into effect.[87] California raked in an incredible $778 million in tax revenue on marijuana through September 2020, more than all of the revenue they made the year prior.[88]

Delivery services were also booming. One such service in Reno saw a 400 percent increase in business the week before in-person retail operations were told by the state to close.

Throughout all of this, I remained flummoxed. COVID-19 is, after all, primarily a viral respiratory infection and a deadly one at that. The memory of the EVALI crisis several months earlier was still fresh in my mind. Didn't it linger in users' minds too? This was not an insignificant event. EVALI had seriously damaged the lungs of many people and killed many too. But as we're seeing in public behavior throughout the COVID-19 pandemic, the invincibility effect is at play. A considerable number of people evidently think that this horror will not strike them partly because some messaging says so, and partly because the counter messaging may feel too restrictive, or even too grim.

A new study in Canada helped fuel this behavior. It—or rather, the headlines reporting on the research—promoted the possibility that marijuana could help prevent COVID-19. According to this study, twelve different CBD-prominent strains may keep the virus from forming in the mouth. Research indicates that some of them may alter enzymes previously linked to COVID-19 infections, while others may reduce the number of virus receptors in the mouth, potentially decreasing the chance of getting infected.

I, like everyone else, would eagerly welcome effective ways to prevent this dreaded illness. But we should be cautious: during the Egyptian plague of the 1830s and the cholera epidemic in France of the mid 1800s, marijuana was touted as a cure—it didn't work, and thousands died from these diseases. In the case of COVID-19, more research is needed to know what exactly (and in what form and dose) could be helpful. These twelve CBD-related strains were made for the first time in a lab by experienced researchers. It doesn't mean all kinds of pot will help with the coronavirus.

Pot promoters are, however, less cautious. The study promises a sales bonanza for marijuana companies—whether further research proves its claims to be true or not. And don't count on these companies to distinguish between the very specific CBD-dominant strains of marijuana identified in the study, and the millions of other varieties of pot in their marketing. In fact, promises of a marijuana miracle became so widespread that in April 2020, *The Washington Post* published an op-ed titled "No, cannabis is not a miracle cure for covid-19." In it, author David Guba, Jr. warned, ". . . while cannabis purveyors may want to use this pandemic as an opportunity to promote the medicinal qualities of their products, they would be wise to measure their claims of the drug's curative power so as to avoid a second obsolescence," referring to the blowback the drug received after the false curative claims in the 19th century.

My go-to sources for information on best health practices during the pandemic are the National Institutes of Health (the organization from which corona czar Dr. Anthony Fauci hails), the World Health Organization, and the American Lung Association. All have identified certain groups of people more susceptible to developing a severe case of COVID-19, and unsurprisingly, those who smoke marijuana or tobacco are among them. This virus targets the lungs and the immune system, so users of edibles are not in the clear either, as studies have shown THC to be an immunosuppressant.

At the end of the day, how Big Weed was able to manipulate the system to be declared essential is no big mystery. Like the liquor and firearms industries, they took advantage of the widespread misinformation that was afloat in the early days of the pandemic. Most state governments—pot-legal states among them—were functioning with incomplete procedural and scientific information. There was conflicting advice coming from national and international sources. Although a preparedness plan for a pandemic had been prepared in 2005 and updated three subsequent times between then and 2017, COVID-19 was looking different than prior influenza and virus outbreaks. In fact, it was looking unpredictable. Developing an effective strategy was left to individual states. Amidst these conditions, the expression of concern over the security of our economy in the wake of the stay-at-home orders created openings for lobbyists in all industries. Big Weed naturally inserted itself into the conversation.

Not only has it managed to declare marijuana essential, but it has used the pandemic to push for a telemedicine platform and for banking access, both of which had previously been widely denied.

The marijuana industry has always had an end game in mind. COVID-19 accelerated that plan.

CHAPTER EIGHTEEN

Waging A Federal Fight

"I have to show you this," SAM's executive vice president messaged me through Slack as I opened my computer one day to start working.

When Luke Niforatos—who almost always starts our day with a cheery "Good morning!"—begins like this, I know it has to be important.

The words, "Watch this," appeared on my computer screen, accompanied by a video. When I opened the file and pressed play, I could hardly believe my eyes. A SAM volunteer had gone to a handful of marijuana shops in Denver—the belly of the beast—credit card in hand and asked if he could pay with his Visa card. Almost all of the shops said yes.

Big deal, you might be thinking.

Well, it actually is.

Stay with me.

A key contention of the marijuana industry is that state-legal marijuana establishments should have access to banking services—a means of doing business that is off limits to them because, while pot may be legal in their state, federal law still classifies it as a Schedule 1 drug—in other words, as illegal. If banks were to do business with these establishments, they'd risk being charged with aiding and abetting a federal crime or of laundering money—no small matter, by the way. But the marijuana industry argues that being a cash-only business makes them prime targets for crime. It is only fair, industry leaders insist, that pot businesses get access to the U.S. financial system of credit and banking like any other tax revenue generating company. (Yes, federally illegal businesses technically still have to pay the IRS!)

When I first heard this argument, part of me sympathized with them: Cash-only businesses are risky, and I guess I could see the merit of them taking credit. I thought, heck, maybe we could even trace people who buy inordinate amounts of pot to sell on the black market this way.

But this video, and the testimony of dozens of people I have spoken with in and outside of the business, convinced me that the banking argument was faulty, if not fraudulent. As the video I was looking at illustrated, most pot shops already take credit cards. It seemed to me that the cash thing is not the reason why they are magnets for robbery. After all, jewelry stores take credit cards and yet they are still vulnerable to thieves.

It's the product that's the lure.

And the product in this case—high potency marijuana—is extremely valuable.

So if pot shops take credit cards, why would they want banking access? Moving huge sums of cash through the banking system would only evidence how much profit they're really making, versus what they may be reporting to the IRS in less traceable sales. (No one wants to pay taxes that badly.) And then it dawned on me: It's really about attracting flush institutional investors, such as big banks, who all want a piece of the pie.

Perhaps it's this hunger for pie, so to speak, that has led the American Bankers Association and other related groups to spend millions of dollars lobbying for federal bills like the SAFE Banking Act, which would shield financial institutions from penalties for working with the pot business.

After seeing what some of these banks are capable of—many are guilty of moving billions of dollars around among foreign drug cartels—I can't fathom why we'd sanction their involvement in the pot business. In some instances, legal pot purveyors and drug cartel members have formed an unholy alliance, with the cartels buying excess product from legal sources when there has been a particularly high yield of marijuana that remains unsold.

These concerns were serious enough for former officials from the Carter, Reagan, H.W. Bush, Clinton, W. Bush, and Obama administrations to sign a group letter in 2019 to the Senate urging Congress to oppose marijuana industry banking access. In the letter, they wrote the bill would make it "extremely difficult for banks to know whether large bundles of cash presented for deposit were made from the sale of marijuana, rather than from the sale of heroin, fentanyl, or methamphetamine." That ultimately could give cartels the cover of legitimacy, enabling them to deposit bags of cash made from the sale of illicit drugs that are killing tens of thousands of Americans every year.

Luke's video made the rounds on Capitol Hill. But the SAFE Banking Act was being pushed hard by the banking and pot industries—with encouragement from one of Colorado's sitting U.S. senators, who for a time had the ear of President Trump on the issue. I sat squarely across a small lunch table one afternoon with that very same senator. When I began talking about the video—and more generally, about today's high potency marijuana—the senator smiled and nodded in agreement. "I know," he said. "The cartels surely haven't gone away." He went on to mention an elaborate story about drug gangs in his state. I was perplexed. Here was the senior pro-pot Republican in the Senate, smiling and agreeing with me as I stood on my soapbox.

It's a position I've often found myself in. Politicians say one thing in public—and a different thing in private. When I fortuitously met with Bernie Sanders at a Christmas party in Washington and explained that the big banks wanted in on marijuana and that today's pot was leading to mental illness, issues he cared about, he also nodded in agreement. His wife chimed in, implying she knew of my work: "I thought you were going to come here and say this. Thank you." And when I met another sitting U.S. senator (who later claimed to favor legalization when she ran for president), she looked at me and loudly gasped, "Where have you people been? You are making so much sense. Thank you! I am going to use this."

On another occasion, I was taking a shortcut between meetings and ran into Marco Rubio, the senior senator from Florida. He looked wary as I took the seat next to him on the underground people-mover that connects Capitol buildings. I launched into a quick description of SAM. In this case, I was able to thank him for supporting our position on marijuana. Rubio offered a terse response, saying, "The last thing this country needs is another intoxicant."

But beyond favorable reactions like Rubio's, or the mixed signals I've sometimes gotten from others, the most frequent responses I receive from members of Congress reveal a considerable lack of awareness—whether about the basics of marijuana as a drug, or about where we're headed now that pro-pot forces are seeking banking access and federal legislation to make their drug legal nationwide.

In every meeting we attend with legislators, we come prepared with visuals.

"Not sure you've ever seen modern pot products," a fellow coworker usually says as she presents a handout with images of the seemingly countless new marijuana offerings on the market.

We point out the rising prevalence of high-potency concentrates and THC-laden gummies.

The bewildered looks we get indicate that many are seeing the new generation of marijuana products for the first time.

Luke, my second-in-command at SAM, will often speak to his experiences as a father in Colorado, where legalization has set precedents for other states. We generally find these legislators can't eat up this information fast enough.

Luke does well on Capitol Hill. He is charismatic, earnest, and—most importantly to me—a man of integrity and faith. He, too, is a father of a little girl. We met while I was on a fact-finding trip in Colorado. After being introduced by a mutual friend, we became fast partners in this work.

We are both pragmatic idealists. We will speak to as many people as it takes to get them to see the need to stop and reassess the legalization train we are on—to evaluate industry motives and practices and their impact on individual and community health. And as we gear up for meetings to address this latest challenge, we know that stopping the Big Banks on their quest to get into the pot business is going to be a tough sell—a longshot.

As it happens, Luke, who is more steadfast and determined to do right than almost anyone I know, is familiar with long shots. It's a family thing. He grew up hearing the story of how his grandmother was riddled with cancer until she was miraculously healed. Luke's father, then in medical school, instantly dropped out to become a pastor, as did his mother. Luke's family traveled all over the world as part of their ministry. As a young boy, he saw searing cases of suffering in Asia and Africa—places such as Thailand, Malaysia, Kenya, and Uganda. He witnessed abject poverty, malnourished children with distended bellies, families torn apart both by health and economic woes. He helped set up clinics in remote outposts, where there was a dearth of medical supplies, no electricity, and no running water.

When Luke ended up at college in Denver—the epicenter of marijuana mania—he just couldn't fathom the acceptance of the drug in the face of clear evidence about its health harms, not after everything he had witnessed worldwide in the way of sickness, and damage to the human body and soul. After graduating, he gravitated to the healthcare field, working as a project manager for community clinics, before joining a major healthcare system in Colorado, and then starting his own company.

It was then that Luke and a buddy created a phone app for doctors so they could better manage patient documentation and care. He sold the company and did well. But he wanted to do more in the world. Soon after his success, a mutual friend introduced us at a local breakfast place, The Egg and I, and we forged an instant kinship. I sensed his infectious energy, his eternal optimism, and his dynamic ability to see beyond the odds to a greater truth.

"I wanted to do something that had a meaningful impact on the world," Luke would tell me later.

Those words could've just as easily come out of my own mouth.

Luke divested himself of his business and joined SAM in 2017. Now here he was, two years later, looking more like a polished member of Congress than the son of preachers. Actually, he'd fit in very well in Congress—if only Congress had more of a conscience.

I tell you all of this because I feel grateful to have people who possess such strong, clear, and unwavering convictions on my team. I've been fortunate to meet and work with some extraordinary people on this journey. Never could I have imagined that the organization I founded with no budget would grow as much as it has in less than six years, commanding a budget north of a few million dollars, and commanding the attentions of people with the power to make meaningful changes. It's sometimes still hard to believe that Luke, Will, other members of our crew, and our devoted volunteers, sacrifice so much for this cause—missing family meals, school open houses, and so many things we all take for granted. It's also sometimes hard to believe that our intense work in the halls of the Capitol led *The New York Times* to call us "well-coordinated coalition of (legalization) opponents."[89]

Admittedly, it's not at all reassuring that some politicians have said one thing to me privately and done an entirely different thing publicly. But in a sense, it shows me they know what is right—they just may not have the courage yet to talk about their views more openly in a system that skews incentives in all the wrong ways.

In that regard, I am grateful for a few people who could have easily remained silent on the issue, or even expressed some enthusiasm for legal pot, but in fact, did the opposite. When the Obama administration released the Cole Memo through the Department of Justice in 2013, I almost felt betrayed. While I was no longer working for the administration and therefore was not present in those meetings, I just knew the president knew better. But then the public comments—from the president himself, not his Justice Department—came, and his support for pot didn't seem strong at all. If anything, he seemed to discourage marijuana use when he told *The New Yorker* in 2014 that the drug is "a bad habit and a vice," and said he told his children, Sasha and Malia, that using marijuana is "a bad idea, a waste of time, not very healthy." He continued, "(T)hose who argue that legalizing marijuana is a panacea and it solves all these social problems I think are probably overstating the case. There is a lot of hair on that policy."[90]

In fact, during a visit to Jamaica in 2015, I thought for a moment that he may have read our website, when he said criminalization was not the right move, but equally that legalization was not a "silver bullet." His exact words were, "A lot of folks think, 'You know what? If we just legalize marijuana, then it will reduce the money flowing into the transnational drug trade—there are more revenues and jobs created.' I have to tell you that it's not a silver bullet."[91] He doubled down on this antipathy when he told *VICE News* in 2015: "So let's put it in perspective, young people. I understand this is important to you, but you should be thinking about climate change, the economy, jobs, war and peace—maybe way at the bottom you should be thinking about marijuana." (By the way, this was a sentiment echoed that same year by U.S. Supreme Court Justice Sonia Sotomayor, who, at a lecture at Amherst College, implied marijuana was not something worth being passionate about.) Obama continued, "I'd separate out the issue of criminalization of marijuana from encouraging its use . . . . I always say to folks, you know legalization or decriminalization is not a panacea. Do we feel the same way about meth? Do we feel the same way about coke? How about crack? How about heroin? And there is a legitimate, I think, concern about the overall effects this has on society, particularly vulnerable parts of our society."[92]

He was fairly consistent in his remarks during a town hall meeting he conducted on CNN in 2009:

"I have to say, there was one question that was voted on that ranked fairly high, and that was whether legalizing marijuana would improve the economy and job creation. I don't know what this says about the

online audience . . . but . . . this was a fairly popular question. We want to make sure it's answered. The answer is no, I don't think that's a good strategy to grow our economy."[93]

Was Obama perfect on pot policy? Most certainly not. With a stroke of a pen, he could have probably prevented the pot industry from growing the way it did, both in 2009 under Ogden and in 2013 under Cole. He could have written a letter telling governors they could allow the decriminalization of possession and use, but because federal law was clear, the states could not sanction pot production, sales, and commercialization. But he didn't. And the industry thrived in this gray area. But the fact that he continued to chide the pot movement even after leaving office says something. In his celebrated memoir, *A Promised Land*, the former president talks almost derogatorily about the subject: "Truthfully, just the act of negotiating with Republicans served as a handy excuse to deflect some of the less orthodox ideas that occasionally surfaced from our side of the aisle ('I'm sorry, Congressman, but legalizing marijuana isn't the kind of stimulus we're talking about here . . .')."[94]

Whether it's the discussions I've had with more liberal icons such as Jimmy Carter, or centrists such as Mike Bloomberg, or financial wizards such as Warren Buffett, our dialogues have all had one thing in common: They've pushed me to do more to prevent the rising tide of drug commercialization and acceptance. They've urged me to elevate the conversation, and to keep going, despite the odds. These are things Luke and I, and all of our colleagues, try to do every day.

CHAPTER NINETEEN

What More Is in Pandora's Box?

At first blush, this could have been any industry conference. An info desk situated up front, just in case you got lost. Bad snacks, including cookies and tepid coffee. Breakout sessions on arcane subjects with a panel of international experts opining on matters of import. Even the setting was as establishment as could be—the Union Station Hotel in downtown St. Louis, a limestone structure with the air of Victorian repression and a looming tower, an ornate vestige of its 1894 origins. It was a chilly winter day in 2019, and people were milling about, wearing name tags on lanyards indicating their titles and affiliations.

But then, hints that this was something different began to surface. Naloxone, a medication for narcotic overdoses, was available if needed. Phrases such as "the right to use drugs" echoed everywhere. The message did more than just hang in the air; like a heat-seeking missile, it hit its targeted audience every time.

Which made sense; this was the much-anticipated event staged once-every-two-years by the Drug Policy Alliance (DPA)—the powerful Soros-backed initiative behind the move to legalize marijuana along with all other drugs. Dubbed the International Drug

Policy Reform Conference, the gathering drew more than 1,500 ardent attendees from over 50 countries—drug aficionados, professors, public health officials, and assorted others.

Despite how much time had passed, it was reminiscent of the first legalization conference I'd attended twenty years earlier. The same theme kept popping up. "Use an incremental approach," a speaker proclaimed at the present-day conference, "because most Americans will agree with you if you frame it just right."

This was the exact approach prescribed at a similar conference back in 2000 by Bill Zimmerman—the man who organized the 1967 March on the Pentagon and later became a sought-after political consultant in the fight to legalize pot. In his talk back then, he acknowledged, "The people are not out there demanding what we in this room have come together in the last couple of days to demand. Quite the contrary." He proceeded to break down the reality of the challenges pro-pot legalization forces were facing as follows:

> *"Eighty/twenty people think the drug war is a failure. Seventy/thirty . . . think it can never work, no matter how many resources you put—society puts into enforcing it.*
>
> *"How many are for total drug legalization in the face of this inevitable failure? Twenty percent. That's a complete flip, so you can't work that level. You have to go down and look at what makes up that opinion at lower levels."*[95]

The opinion that people were most conflicted about, according to Zimmerman, was whether jail or treatment was more appropriate for users. Appealing to folks on that issue alone was how he proposed pro-legalization advocates win the public over to their side of the argument, even though the majority of people disagreed with their stance on the larger issues. The lesson he was conveying: couch your view in the nicest terms and public opinion will follow.

George Soros agreed. Before giving millions to the DPA, he told its founder, as reported in a 1994 issue of *Rolling Stone*, the organization should ". . . come up with an approach that emphasizes 'treatment and humanitarian endeavors' . . . hire someone with the political savvy to sit down and negotiate with government officials, and target a few winnable issues, like medical marijuana and the repeal of mandatory minimums."[96]

There was no mention of legalizing drugs. The focus was squarely placed on the issue most people could get behind. It's clear from the origins and writings of these groups—including from such pieces as "Should We Legalize Drugs? History Answers: Yes" by DPA's founder, Ethan Nadelmann— what this is all about.[97]

The "incremental approach," Zimmerman assured the crowd at his speech, "is the fastest way to get to the goal we all want to reach."

That goal? The legalization of all drugs.

Back to the 2019 conference in St. Louis, where, like at all large conferences, all kinds of reports and handouts were floating around. One popular pamphlet contained a mission statement from a group called "Doctors for Cannabis Regulation." As its name indicates, this group believes that "cannabis prohibition has failed." (Statements such as these from the medical community are reminiscent of the tobacco-paid doctors, who at one time flagrantly recommended cigarettes. Yet no major medical association was represented at the conference.) At another table, refrigerator magnet tiles were available from the Drug Policy Alliance. It offered a string of words juxtaposed to each other: "now" "more" "safer" "psychedelics." Students for Sensible Drug Policy, another DPA-backed initiative, distributed a one-pager, stating, "Due to the illegal status of psychedelics, the public lacks knowledge about how to use these promising substances safely or therapeutically." Yet another group offered a flyer about its film *Psychedelia*, purported to be about "psychedelic drugs and their ability to induce mystical or religious experiences."

None of this talked about legalizing methamphetamine or crack specifically. It seemed that everyone understood what they could freely say, and, as is so important in politics, *when* they could say it. Interestingly, Nadelmann, the poster boy for legalization, had told the *Harvard Law Review* in 2005 that, "With regard to decriminalizing other drugs, such as heroin, cocaine and methamphetamines . . . .

We basically don't support that."[98] And yet, here we are fifteen years later, looking at ballot measures written and funded by the DPA that, indeed, propose to relax laws on all drugs.

What they did outwardly support in 2005 were ballot initiatives to legalize marijuana for any purpose. After a few failed attempts in different states, they prevailed for the first time in 2012, with Colorado and Washington voting to legalize. During the 2020 election cycle, four more states legalized marijuana sales, bringing the total to fifteen. All but two of these states had done it via well-funded ballot initiatives with large cash infusions from the likes of Miracle-Gro, Peter Lewis (the billionaire founder of Progressive Insurance), Weedmaps (a marijuana company found to be noncompliant with California's own pot regulations), Dr. Bronner's Soaps (which used some of its sizable profits from the COVID-19 crisis) and several other pot companies. For these moguls, funding a legalization campaign is an investment that yields dividends in marijuana sales. But nobody makes money funding an anti-legalization campaign. So opponents, when they lost, were always vastly outspent—65 to 1 in one state alone in the 2020 election cycle. This is typical of ballot initiatives: whoever has the most money wins. In this case, the financing was jaw-droppingly lopsided. As Sasha Issenberg said in a *Washington Post* op-ed shortly after the election:

> *"In the five states that passed pro-marijuana initiatives this month—from authorizing its medical use in Mississippi to full legalization in Arizona, Montana and South Dakota—supporters spent a total of $19.8 million, compared with just $1.3 million by opponents, according to campaign finance summaries by the website Ballotpedia . . . . These multiples are unimaginable in the world of people running for office.*
>
> *". . . We should resist the desire to imagine them as an idealized counterfactual election, in which citizens can choose the best policies without having to worry about flawed candidates. Instead, think of ballot measures as more like lobbying campaigns, but with a target audience of voters rather than legislators. The real factor in victory*

is not which policy citizens would support in a vacuum but which interest groups you can get on your side."[99]

When marijuana policy is rationally and calmly discussed in the legislature, by contrast, with months or even years of debate from experts on all sides, pot proponents almost always lose. I can't tell you how many Democratic lawmakers have called me from their personal cellphones to say thank you for helping their state dodge the bullet, even though publicly, they had to be a bit quieter. In fact, the pot industry's success rate of legalizing marijuana via the legislature stands roughly at a mere 5 percent. It's why a state like Colorado legalized several years before many more liberal states—a frenzied ballot initiative leads much more easily to legalization than does a reasoned, expert-led debate in the legislature. (For more on legal pot outcomes, see the Appendix.)

What began with only the legalization of medical marijuana has morphed into the approval of so-called recreational weed—but now the movement wants more.

Their latest ambition? Psychedelic mushrooms.

Excuse me. I mean, "medical" mushrooms.

Denver, the epicenter of legal marijuana, recently became the first city in the nation to take this leap, decriminalizing hallucinogenic mushrooms. For so-called drug reformers, psychedelics are considered the next frontier after the loosening of laws related to marijuana. Washington, D.C., the nation's capital, followed suit in 2020, as did the state of Oregon.

How commercialized psychedelics will look is still too early to tell, though in Denver, profiteers are beginning to emerge in the shadows, as should be expected when there's money to be made. Attorneys, lobbyists, therapists, and yogi masters have begun to offer their services to fungal users who are under the impression they may need guidance, spiritual or otherwise, during their psychedelic 'shroom trips. Even the "Shark" everyone loves to hate—Kevin O'Leary—is getting in the business. As one of his famous phrases goes, "Show me the sales."

Putting political deception and greed aside, are there legitimate uses of psychedelics in medicine? Maybe. Some early research has emerged, in small, extremely well controlled trials that show promise. But this use has nothing to do with a ballot initiative written to allow mushroom use *en masse*. The subject requires much more dispassionate research, not ballot initiatives where money and special interests prevail.

What about decriminalization when it comes to all drugs? Even President Biden, who was the only 2020 Democratic presidential candidate to oppose marijuana legalization, has said things like, "No one should be going to jail because they have a drug problem." (I've been lucky enough to confirm these positions on drug policy with senior Biden administration officials.) And to again be clear, decriminalization and legalization are not the same thing: one keeps people out of jail, the other encourages commercial sales.

Not going to jail because you have a drug problem makes sense. But the devil in the law is most certainly in the details. In Oregon in 2020, in addition to the measure focused on "medical mushrooms," voters also passed something called Measure 110, which decriminalized all drugs. Funded by the Drug Policy Alliance and touted as "treatment over incarceration," it promised a path to a public health-oriented drug policy. Sounds pretty good, I thought when I first heard of it. But then I read the fine print. There's certainly more to the initiative than meets the eye. Bill Zimmerman must have been smiling somewhere.

Measure 110 made the possession of heroin, methamphetamine, crack—all of it—a "violation," requiring the payment of a $100 fine or a phone call. The phone call would be to a newly established "recovery center," which would provide treatment resources. When I first heard about this, I remember thinking, *maybe* this could be a good thing.

But then I took a closer look. I also spoke with people who did not think it was a great idea. "Treatment resources" did not mean treatment. In fact, the initiative didn't provide a penny to pay for people's rehabilitation. Participants in organizations such as Oregon Recovers, the largest state group of people in recovery of addiction, did not approve. Nor did others, including John Kitzhaber, Oregon's longest-serving governor, who happened to be both a Democrat and a medical doctor. They were horrified by the implications of Measure 110. Dr. Kitzhaber said,

> *"I understand that a central motivation behind this ballot measure is to help reverse the disaster caused by the War on Drugs, which incarcerated people suffering from addiction and had a disproportionate impact on Black and Indigenous people and other communities of color. I agree with this goal, but Measure 110, as written, makes it more difficult to treat the underlying addiction that leads to drug use in the first place."*[100]

The ex-governor is probably right. Measure 110 will take away the ability to send people who use drugs to drug courts, an incredibly effective mechanism to reduce crime and promote recovery, because drug offenses would now simply be violations (ineligible for drug court, a specialized court where offenders are given treatment options and motivated to succeed). This has downstream implications; it means that those who used to get in the front of the line for treatment because they were *referred there by a judge* would now have to wait in the back of the line. And the treatment wouldn't be paid for. Measure 110 doesn't create one new bed. Instead it tells users to pay $100 or call a hotline.

What happens if they don't call? No one really knows. There is also talk that teens who get caught with drugs won't have their parents notified of the offense. They can just pay the $100 or call the number and move on.

This does not sound like a promising approach. Especially since so many people rely on that little extra push—the carrot-and-stick method—to get help. I can't tell you how many people have told me they would be dead if it wasn't for a judge mandating them to get help. You don't always have to want it at first; in fact, the disease of addiction is one of denial.

There is no doubt we need to overhaul how we treat addiction in this country. People should not be jailed for their substance use disorders. But because many kinds of crimes are often associated with addiction—65 percent of prison inmates suffer from a substance use disorder (SUD) and another 20 percent did not meet SUD criteria but still were under the influence at the time of their crime[101]—we need to better marry public health with the criminal justice system, not separate them entirely. Drug courts, HOPE Probation (a program proven to reduce incarceration, crime, and drug use by holding probationers accountable via drug testing and light, but reliable, sanctions), LEAD (a program that diverts people away from the criminal justice system), 24/7 (a testing and sanctions program for repeat offenders who drive under the influence), and the Drug Market Initiative (a way to help low-level drug sellers who want to get their life in order) are effective programs that introduce public health principles into criminal justice settings. And they are funded by people from across the political spectrum. We should be scaling these programs up, not pushing them aside.

But I don't think these details really concern the legalizers. It's hard to take at face value that these groups only want the *decriminalization* of drugs. It's plainly obvious that they want more.

A few weeks after the conference in St. Louis, everything crystalized when a DPA tweet announced a "closed-door" meeting they would be hosting for people "who can think creatively about proposals for the *legal regulation* of illicit drugs." The meeting's first goal wasn't social justice or criminal law reform. Instead, it was to "develop preliminary proposals for the legal regulation of psychedelics, stimulants, and opioids."

And now? Oregon's pair of ballot initiatives, the "medical mushrooms" measure and the decriminalization of all drugs measure, passed easily. November 2020 also saw the legalization of marijuana succeed in New Jersey, Montana, South Dakota, and Arizona. I'm not sure voters yet see the connections between these initiatives—the legalization of marijuana and the relaxing of laws on other drugs. But the media is starting to understand what we've been saying all along: *Politico Pro's Morning Cannabis Newsletter* of December 8, 2020, contained the headline "The movement to change drug laws for psychedelic substances is following the pot playbook."[102]

For those of you who are still with me, keep your eye on the ball. This is a Ponzi-like scheme being perpetrated on America by the marijuana industry. You are likely opposed to marijuana with THC concentrations from 55 to 99 percent falling into the hands of young people, or those predisposed to addiction. But the industry has distracted you by placing the emphasis on how marijuana can be useful in managing the pain of those suffering from serious medical conditions and by stressing how the tax revenue generated by sales of the drug can make quality-of-life improvements in your own community. This is the so-called incremental approach at work.

While you are likely opposed to banks legitimizing the activities of cartels, whether inadvertently or not, the marijuana industry has led you to believe that banking access for the pot industry will help stimulate the economy after the devastating effects of COVID-19. This, too, is the incremental approach at work.

While you are likely opposed to the legalization of other illicit drugs, the marijuana industry, like all addiction-for-profit businesses, will try to sway you by framing it as freedom of choice.

Do you see how the incremental approach works?

There are things you are *not* okay with, but the industry has used a smokescreen to get you to think only about the things you *are* okay with.

Even when you're in sync with them on certain issues, they tend to do more on these fronts than you may be aware of.

While you are likely okay with adults smoking a joint in the privacy of their own home, you'd be horrified if Big Tobacco and Big Pharma took the marijuana industry over and started to fund your local politicians. But this is happening now, and it's part of the incremental approach too.

While you may shrug your shoulders at the modest increases in school dropouts or may not be focused at the moment on the few thousand deaths a year currently tied to pot (via driving under the influence or suicides, for example), you may find them disturbing over the next thirty years as the costs in lives mount. We never could have fathomed five years after the advent of Big Tobacco in the early 20th century that one hundred years later, tobacco would kill 400,000 people annually and become a leading cause of global mortality. Such realities emerge slowly, over a long time. Studies take a while to complete. The full picture is not seen for a while. The incremental approach counts on us not noticing the disturbing realities that commercial marijuana could usher in.

Most of us know plenty of people who occasionally smoke pot without a problem, but what you may not know is that the marijuana industry doesn't make its money from casual users—it relies instead on those who use the drug early and often. Like alcohol and tobacco, marijuana makes most of its money from the 27 percent of people who consume 82 percent of the product, according to a state of Colorado study.[103] All of this is to say that you may look around and think of marijuana as benign now, but as the marketing machine grows, so, too, will the targeted consumer base the industry feeds off of. This too is the incremental approach at work.

With several more states legalizing marijuana in 2020, we are getting closer and closer to federally legalized pot (and as you can now see we are also getting closer to the legalization of so much more). In fact, in the waning days of the 2020 Congressional session, the House of Representatives passed the MORE Act—or the "Marijuana Opportunity Reinvestment and Expungement Act"—which, as it turns out, has very little to do with reinvesting in communities or expunging records. It's touted by many, in fact, as "decriminalization" (that's the term used by most of the media covering it, to my great consternation), even though it calls for the full legalization of marijuana—releasing marijuana use, sales, and production entirely from its illegal status. To be sure, passing something in the lame duck session of Congress is sort of like winning an exhibition baseball game. It means little (the Senate did not take it up, so the bill died), except to signal that more prominent people have bought into the marijuana myth. And when public officials, or those very close to them, start taking money from any big industry (don't forget what John Boehner has to gain, or even Nancy Pelosi's son, who is on the board of a medical marijuana company), you have to be concerned that public health will take a back seat to private profit.

Consider yourself warned. Always pursue the deeper truth. Do your own research (*Wikipedia* shouldn't be your only source).

And cast your votes responsibly, as if your life depends on it.

Because it just might.

Epilogue

In this third decade of the 21st century, sometimes I feel like we are where we were in the 1950s with cigarettes: mass normalization, celebrity endorsements, huge political support, and a large and growing industry with no intention of backing down. It took decades before Big Tobacco was unmasked for what it truly was—an addiction-for-profit business preying on the most vulnerable. Today no one would dream of showing off their Marlboro endorsement or standing proudly on the Senate floor defending that industry.

It took us a while to get here.

My earnest hope is it won't take as long for people to realize that the marijuana industry, already in bed with tobacco and alcohol companies, is making the same play, exploiting our youth, endangering people with a mind-altering product that indisputably threatens our health and lives.

I will never forget Sally Schindel and the loss of her son, Andy. Helen and her daughter Caroline's suffering remain with me too. As does the harrowing experience of Anne the "budtender" before she got out of the business.

And there are so many others who've been damaged by weed and killed in the wake of the vaping crisis, lost in the spiral of addiction.

I'm thankful for the whistleblowers whom I met along the way—Jan, Kati, Sarah, and the others—who shed light on the shocking realities of regulators asleep at the switch. Their accounts evidence a commercialized industry with little oversight.

The story of Compton isn't simply an inspiration. It's also a roadmap. There's a way to beat back the well-funded marijuana machine. Despite the well-financed idea that there is nothing we can do to stop this voracious industry, there is time to fight back, to stop this profit model from encroaching on all of our communities. What it will take is initiative, a grassroots mindset, and a commitment to the truth. It's early still. The industry is commercializing at a rapid pace, but it hasn't overtaken us. There is still time. Our voices must be heard.

To say that Big Marijuana can yet be stopped is not to suggest that our heads are in the sand. America has made grave mistakes before, and if legal pot should ever become the law of the land, we will have to work overtime—but we won't quit. We will have to ensure kids—and parents—are even more aware of the dangers of today's high THC marijuana. We will have to hold today's weed industry—and the decision-makers they support—accountable to the people. And we will have to ensure that *how* we "regulate" marijuana is based on sound public health principles.

My north star in this work is education. Education toward a society where decisions are shaped by independent investigation and truth, not mass manipulation and money spent. For the sake of drug policy—and all the other staggering challenges we face—I hope we can learn to follow this star closely.

APPENDIX

SAM Lessons Learned from State Legalization Impact Report

Contrary to federal law[104], under which the use and sale of marijuana for any purpose is illegal, fifteen states legalized the commercial sale of marijuana from 2012–2020. Despite this, dozens of other states (as of January 2021)—including Florida, New York, Connecticut, Texas, Maryland, New Mexico, Minnesota, North Dakota, Delaware, Ohio, and New Hampshire—have continued to reject marijuana legalization, as have the vast majority of localities in "legal" states that continue to ban marijuana production and retail sales.

Compiled below are publicly available state-level data, reports, and investigatory findings, peer-reviewed studies, and government health surveys to assemble this report.

In 2013, the U.S. Department of Justice (DOJ) decided to take a hands-off approach toward legalization at the state level. Officially, the DOJ stated it would only get involved if any of eight requirements laid out in the "Cole Memo" (e.g., sales to minors, increased drugged driving) were violated. Unfortunately, according to the

COLORADO TRAFFIC FATALITIES WHERE THE DRIVER TESTED POSITIVE FOR MARIJUANA

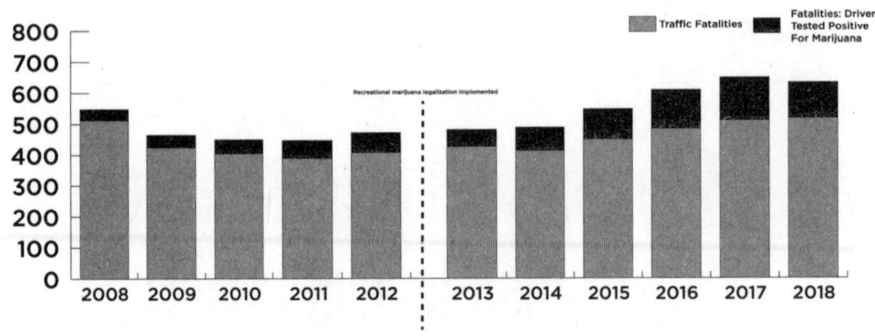

(Colorado Department of Transportation, 2019)

STATE REGULATORY FRAMEWORKS STRUGGLE TO KEEP UP WITH THE NUMBER OF LICENSED SHOPS.

(Oregon Liquor Control Commission, 2019)

MARIJUANA HOSPITALIZATIONS INCREASES SINCE LEGALIZATION

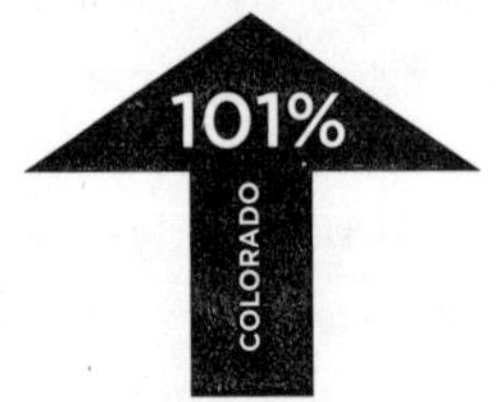

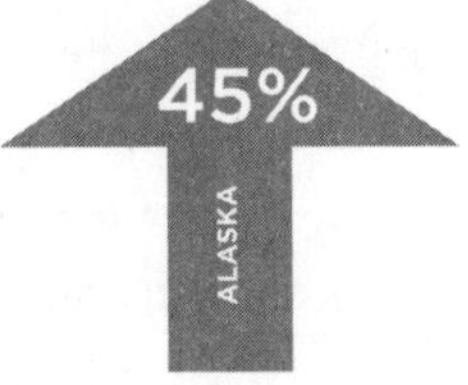

(Colorado Department of Public Health and Environment, 2013-2017; Alaska Department of Health and Social Services, 2020).

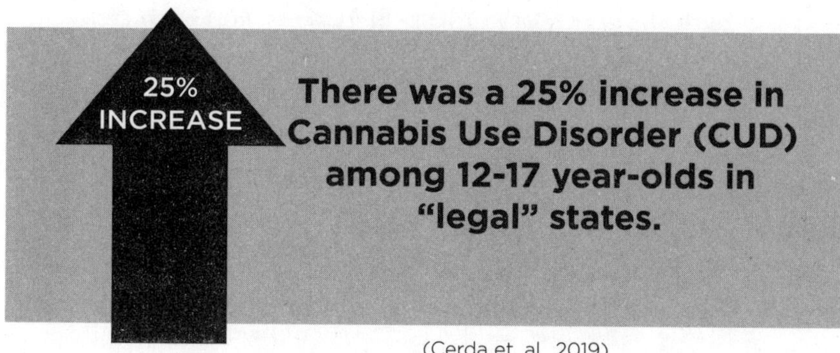

(Cerda et. al., 2019)

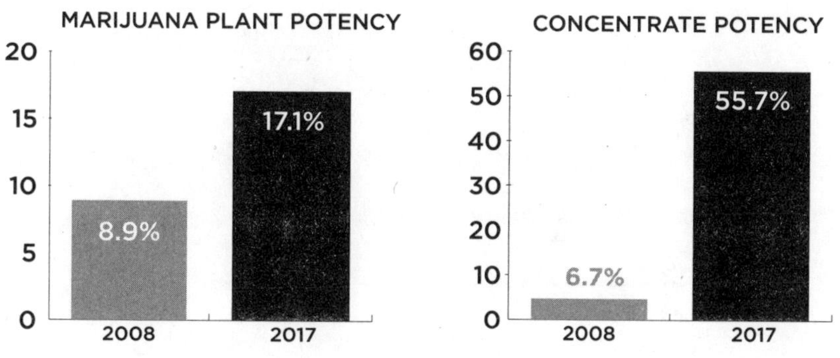

(Chandra et. al., 2019)

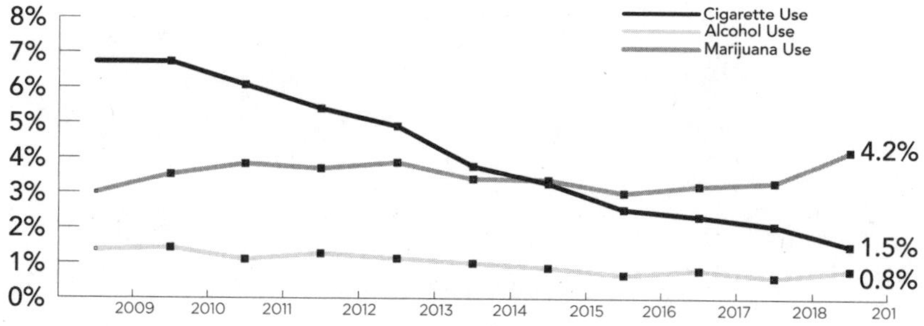

(Miech et al., 2019)

PAST MONTH AND PAST YEAR YOUTH USE IN "LEGAL" STATES OUTPACES SUCH USE IN NON-LEGAL STATES.

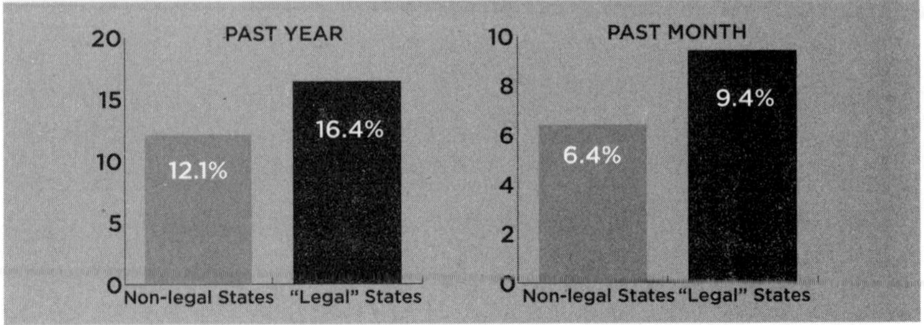

(NSDUH State Comparisons, 2019)

ILLICIT MARIJUANA PLANTS SEIZED OFF OF COLORADO PUBLIC LANDS

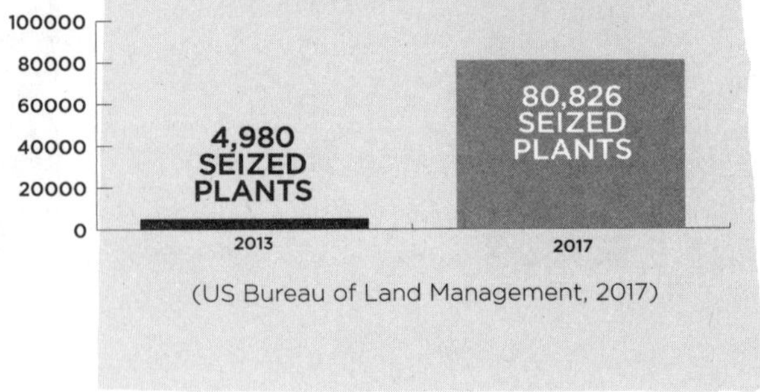

(US Bureau of Land Management, 2017)

2019 DEA DOMESTIC CANNABIS ERADICATION/SUPPRESSION PROGRAM

3,232,722
outdoor marijuana plants eradicated

3,210
weapons seized

4,718
arrests made

770,472
indoor marijuana plants eradicated

>29M
cultivator assets seized

(Drug Enforcement Administration, 2020)

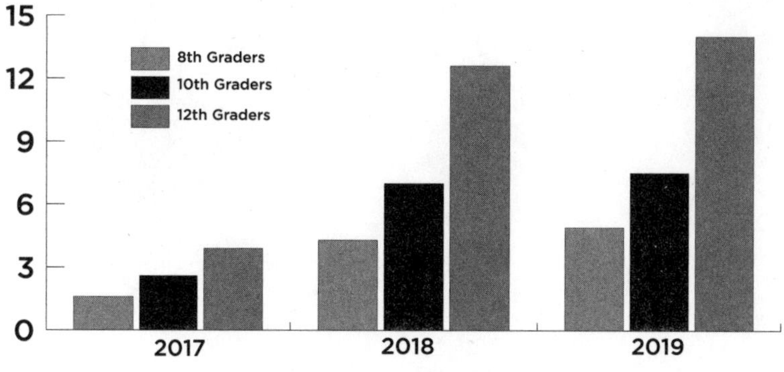

(MONITORING THE FUTURE, 2019)

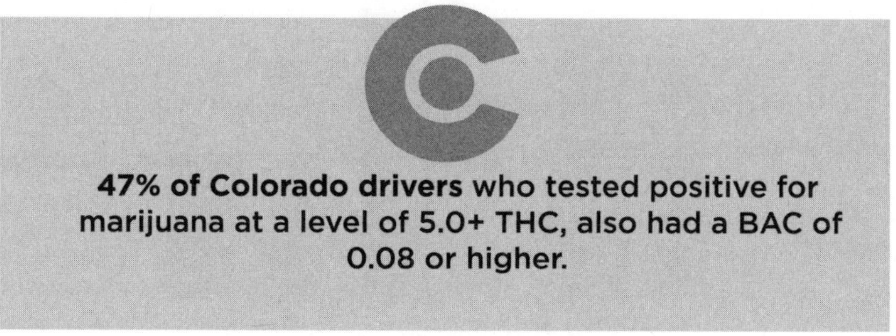

(Colorado Division of Criminal Justice, 2019)

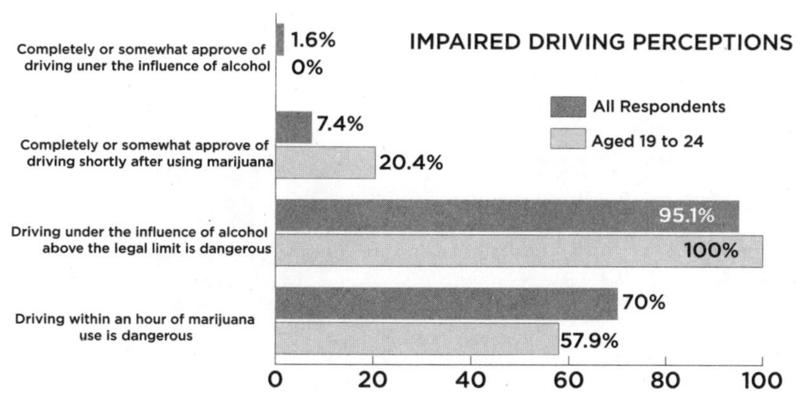

(AAA Foundation for Traffic Safety, 2019)

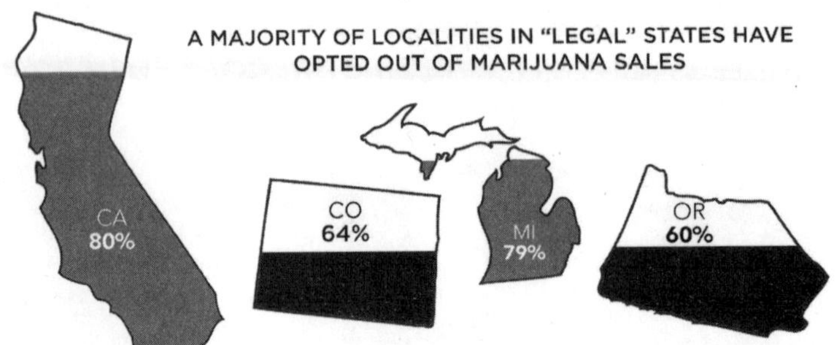

(Alfonsi, 2019; Colorado Department of Revenue, 2019; Walsh, 2019; Oregon Liquor Control Commission, 2019)

PERCENT OF YOUTH REPORTING PAST 30-DAY USE WHO DABBED*

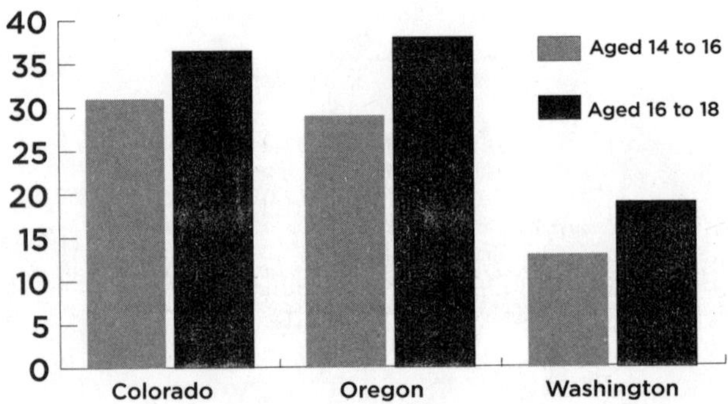

(Colorado Department of Public Health and Environment, 2019; Oregon Healthy Teens, 2019; Washington State Healthy Youth Survey, 2018)

* Taken from most recent data available, ages are an average based on an age range

The indoor cultivation of one kilogram of marijuana requires **5.2 megawatt hours** of electricity and releases **4.5 metric tons** of carbon dioxide emissions

(OREGON-IDAHO HIGH INTENSITY DRUG TRAFFICKING AREA, 2018; US ENVIRONMENTAL PROTECTION AGENCY, 2015)

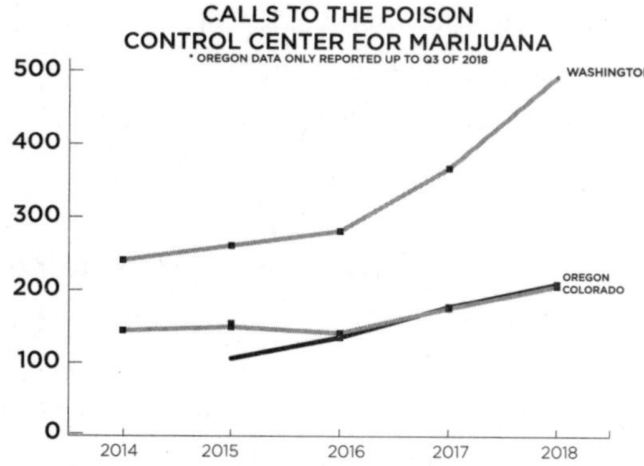

(Rocky Mountain Poison and Drug Center, 2019; Washington Poison Center, 2019; Oregon Poison Center, 2019; Massachusetts & Rhode Island Poison Center, 2019)

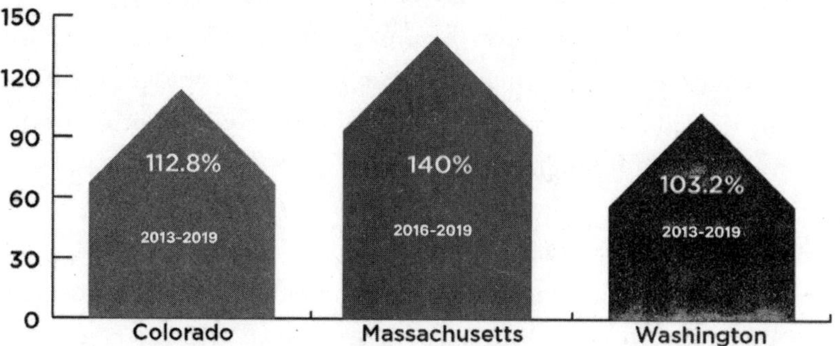

(Rocky Mountain HIDTA, 2019; Whitehill et al., 2019; Washington Poison Center, 2018)

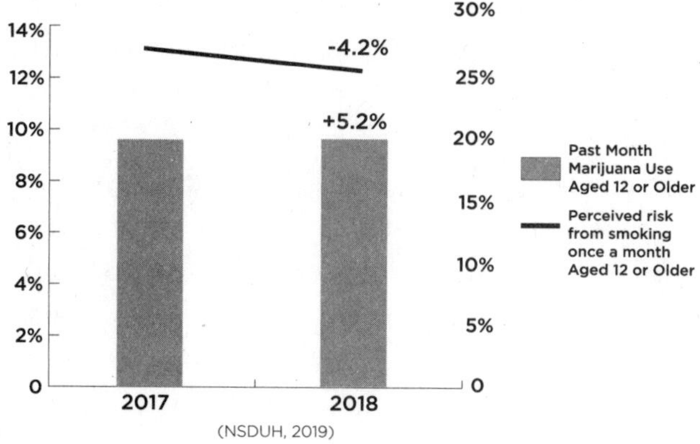

(NSDUH, 2019)

U.S. Government Accountability Office (GAO), the DOJ took no meaningful action even as states routinely violated the "Cole Memo." However, public health and safety departments and law enforcement agencies in states where legalization has been in place for the longest time have produced primary data and impact reports that shine a light on how current marijuana policies are failing to protect the health and safety of the general population.[105]

In 2018, the DOJ rescinded the Cole Memo policies, signaling an uncertain future for the marijuana industry. One thing is certain: by legalizing marijuana, states continue to violate federal laws.

We now have eight years of data to show how these marijuana policy changes—and the industry they created—affect families and communities. This industry is chiefly driven by higher use rates and increased normalization, seeking to convert casual and nonusers into life-long customers. As we are only now beginning to address the far-reaching and devastating consequences of the addiction epidemic—driven largely by opioids—the rise of additional corporate promotion of drug use comes at an inopportune time.

Research on Marijuana Harms

Scientific literature on the harms of marijuana use exists in abundance and is discussed in this report. There are over 20,000 peer-reviewed research articles linking marijuana use to severe mental health outcomes, ranging from depression to psychosis, as well as to consequences for physical health, and even negative outcomes for neonates exposed in utero, including inhibited cognitive development. The connections between marijuana use and consequences to mental and physical health and brain development, among other risks, are often lost in conversations on legalization.

The distinction between medical and recreational marijuana has been deliberately blurred by an industry with a heavy hand in both markets. A recent study found that in spite of evidence that lower THC dosage is more appropriate for medical purposes, the medical marijuana products advertised in retail stores contain around the same amount of THC as recreational marijuana products—and generally contain upwards of 15 percent THC.[106] Though there is potential for the medical use of certain components found within the marijuana plant, these components should be researched through well-designed clinical studies and under the guidance of the FDA.

These are just some examples of the conflict between data-driven research and marijuana normalization. The science is clear. Yet legalization proponents march forward, eyeing profits.

Key Outcomes

As with the tobacco industry, it will take decades for the consequences of marijuana commercialization to become fully evident. However, we do not need to wait that long to understand some key outcomes. For example, the data in this report—and many others—show states that legalized marijuana have among the highest rates of marijuana use in the country, and use is sharply increasing in such vulnerable demographics as youth and young adults, whose brains are still developing.

These states also have:

- Higher rates of marijuana-related driving fatalities.
- Issues with "legally" sold, but contaminated, marijuana vapes.
- More marijuana-related emergency department visits, hospitalizations, and accidental exposures.
- Expansive and lucrative criminal markets.
- Exacerbated racial disparities in marijuana industry participation and criminal justice enforcement.
- Increases in workplace problems, including labor shortages and accidents.

Commercialization: A Growing Concern

The commercialization of marijuana results in negative consequences for public health, social justice, and public safety. Medical marijuana legalization gave way to recreational marijuana legalization in states across the country and both industries are heavily capitalized. The result is the creation of a new and powerful addiction-for-profit industry.

More and more people are using marijuana while remaining largely ignorant of its negative consequences and use rates are surging across the United States after years of declines. More than 43.4 million people reported past year marijuana use in the U.S. in 2018, a more than 6 percent increase from the previous year. The alarming increase in use among young people, as well as pregnant women, in particular, prompted now former U.S. Surgeon General Dr. Jerome Adams to issue a first-of-its-kind advisory on marijuana use.[107]

Though his advisory specifically addressed significant increases in use among youth and pregnant women, he does not shy away from cautioning against marijuana use more generally. At one congressional hearing, he told senators, "I don't want anyone to mistake what I'm saying as implying that these products are considered safe for general adult usage."[108]

Dr. Adams continued to warn senators at the hearing of the "massive public health experiment," telling them, "We need to learn from our mistakes and be careful of normalization of behavior."[109] The commercialization of marijuana exemplifies just what Dr. Adams cautions against.

The sudden emergence in all 50 states and some U.S. territories of mysterious lung illnesses tied to vaping represents a unique case study on the impact of marijuana legalization. New technology and rapid commercialization drove an increase in the popularity of marijuana consumption through vaping devices. As demand increased subsequent use increased—and with it an epidemic resulting in over 2,700 hospitalizations (and more than 60 deaths) at the time of this report's publication, along with a double-lung transplant.[110]

In states where marijuana is "legal," retail and medical licenses outnumber popular food chains. For example, in Colorado, marijuana retail locations outnumber all McDonald's and Starbucks locations in the state combined.[111] In 2019, there were a total of 1,016 registered marijuana retail and medical locations within the state[112] compared with 392 Starbucks and 208 McDonald's (as of 2018). The sheer commonplace numbers of these stores promote and normalize marijuana use.

Adding to the danger of marijuana commercialization is the increasing market demand for high-potency products created by the combination of aggressive promotion and ever-increasing tolerance by heavy users. With innovation, the industry responded to meet the demand it had created, modifying marijuana to increase its potency. The commonly conceived "Woodstock weed" had only 1–3 percent THC, the psychoactive intoxicant responsible for the high. According to recent studies, today's average marijuana flower—touted by industry advocates as a harmless plant—contains around 17.1 percent THC, though independent studies in "legal" states found the percentage to be even higher. Concentrates and edibles pack a more potent punch, containing an average of 55.7 percent THC.[113] But these products can be even more potent than that. Many marijuana retailers promote, and profit from, products containing up to 95–99 percent THC.[114]

One significant problem with high-potency products is the lack of regulation. Numerous studies have found that product regulation in "legal" states is limited[115] and internal audits conducted by state governments have exposed gaping holes in regulatory frameworks. In Oregon, for example, the Oregon Liquor Control Commission found that there is one state inspector per every 83 marijuana licenses.[116] Perhaps more concerning, no state has limited the potency of these products—and attempts have been quickly blocked by the industry.

The mislabeling of products also plagues the "legal" market. Studies have found that labeling of active ingredients in concentrates and edibles often misrepresents the actual ingredients in those products.[117] Unsuspecting consumers often have no idea what exactly they are smoking or ingesting.

Furthermore, the adaptability of marijuana gives way to mass-marketed products modeled after popular consumer goods. Marijuana-infused "edibles" come in the form of cookies, candy, ice cream, sodas, and other sweet treats that are particularly appealing to children.[118] Marketing tactics make use of bright colors and catchy names, replicating images or appropriating the names of well-known commercial food products. For example, the brand recognition of "Pop-Tarts," a widely consumed kid-friendly breakfast product, was seized upon by one marijuana producer to market "Pot Tarts." Unfortunately, these products are thought to be contributing to the increased accidental marijuana exposures among children and others.

These kinds of growth tactics by industry are not new. They largely mirror the boom of Big Tobacco in the early 1900s—and not by accident.[119] Though marijuana proponents operate under the guise of up-and-comers, they are now well financed and advised by professionals from the tobacco industry. For example, the corporate owner of the Marlboro brand, Altria, purchased a 35 percent stake in Juul shortly after acquiring a 45 percent stake in Cronos, one of the largest international distributors of marijuana.[120] The UK-based Imperial Brands invested around $123 million CAD (~$94M USD) in Auxly, a Canadian marijuana company. This partnership, which entitles Imperial Brands to a 20 percent stake in the company, will focus on utilizing Imperial Brand's vaping technology to develop marijuana vaping products.

The marijuana industry has also caught the attention of Big Pharma and Big Alcohol.

Former Purdue Pharma executive John Stewart left the pharmaceutical industry to create his own marijuana company.[121] Teva Pharmaceuticals signed an agreement to become a medical marijuana distributor in Israel.[122] And Sandoz, a subsidiary of Novartis, signed an agreement with Tilray to distribute marijuana products.[123]

Constellation Brands, maker of Corona, purchased a 9.9 percent stake in Canopy Growth for $191 million, then upped the stake to 38 percent for $4 billion in 2018. The company has the option to increase their investment and purchase up to 139.7 million new shares at a price of up to $5 billion more.[124] Anheuser-Busch InBev announced an upcoming partnership with marijuana giant, Tilray, to explore the potential for marijuana-infused beverages. Molson Coors and Blue Moon also made substantial investments in the marijuana industry.[125]

The investments of these big industry players coincide with more covert action taken to push legalization forward. In an investigative report, journalist Jonathan Gornall linked several commercial organizations with vested interests in the creation of a recreational marijuana market with individuals and activists pushing for more access to medical marijuana. What's more, he found that several tobacco companies were funding studies on medical marijuana, an activity that calls for some questioning into the validity of that research.[126]

These connections are unsurprising. Marijuana commercialization presents addiction-for-profit industries, long under public scrutiny, with a new and innovative pathway to profits.

Adverse Health Effects of Marijuana

Contrary to popular belief, marijuana is a harmful drug. The main psychoactive ingredient in marijuana, THC, causes many different types of mental and physiological health problems—especially in children, young adults, and pregnant women. Its potency has skyrocketed in recent years and its addictive properties exacerbate its potential harms as marijuana users become dependent on it.

Researchers found that marijuana is an addictive drug.[127] Brain scans of marijuana users show changes in the structure of the brain's reward center to be consistent with addiction[128] and up to 47 percent of regular users experience withdrawal symptoms when they cease use.[129] The National Institute on Drug Abuse reports that around 30 percent of marijuana users have some form of marijuana use disorder and that people who begin using marijuana before the age of 18 are four to seven times more likely to develop a marijuana use disorder compared with those who start later.[130] One recent study on rats found that marijuana vaping may support "conditioned drug-seeking behavior," a cause for concern as vaporized marijuana gains popularity.[131]

Studies found marijuana use can cause severe consequences for mental health. Marijuana is increasingly linked to the onset of psychosis and schizophrenia[132] and shows a more modest association with depression and anxiety.[133] In one of the most comprehensive studies to date on marijuana and psychosis, Di Forti et al found that daily marijuana use is associated with an increased likelihood of developing psychosis. What's more, researchers reported a more than four-times odds of daily users of potent marijuana to develop psychosis.[134]

Chronic marijuana use increases the likelihood of anxiety in adults in their late twenties and older, and those who met the criteria for cannabis use disorder (CUD) had a high risk of all mental health symptoms across all ages.[135]

These studies are worth noting, particularly as marijuana is increasingly marketed as a solution for anxiety and other mental health ailments.

Frequency of marijuana use, as well as higher THC potency, is associated with the most severe impact on mental health, which is evidenced by psychosis, suicidality, reshaping of brain matter, and addiction.[136] The increasing demand for high-potency marijuana products and the coinciding prevalence of marijuana use disorder are indicative of a future maelstrom with unknown consequences for public health, especially as the industry engages in a concerted effort to undermine scientifically proven risks of marijuana use.

The legalization of marijuana coincides with a nationwide increase in marijuana use disorder. According to the Substance Abuse and Mental Health Services Administration's (SAMHSA) National Survey on Drug Use and Health (NSDUH), 4.4 million Americans reported marijuana use disorder in 2018, up from just over 4 million the previous year.[137] One study comparing marijuana use of respondents before and after legalization in their home state found a near 25 percent increase in people aged 12 to 17 who reported marijuana use disorder.[138]

In addition to this alarming trend, more Americans who report any, or serious, mental illness issues also reported past-year marijuana use. Co-occurring mental illness and substance use disorder was higher among past-year marijuana users than past-year opioid users.[139]

Marijuana is also linked to significant physical ailments. Researchers have found a connection between marijuana use and lung damage, as well as serious cardiovascular problems, including hypertension, myocardial infarction, cardiomyopathy, arrhythmias, stroke, and cardiac arrest.[140]

Studies find marijuana to be linked to certain types of cancer,[141] including testicular cancer.[142]

Researchers at Boston University found that marijuana use among men may double the risk of partner miscarriage—regardless of the woman's use.[143] Additionally, marijuana use during pregnancy is accompanied by a host of risks for the baby. Use during pregnancy may affect cognitive development by increasing the risk of hyperactivity, impulsivity, and inability to focus.[144] Prenatal exposure to marijuana also predisposes offspring to neuropsychiatric disorders.[145] A mother's marijuana use during pregnancy may also increase the risk of low birth weight and small for gestational age births, preterm births, and may also increase the risk of neonatal intensive care unit placement and developmental problems.[146] Low birth weight and preterm birth increase the risk of short- and long-term complications for the child.[147]

Increasingly, government officials sound alarms on marijuana use during pregnancy after research and reports have revealed that more pregnant women are using the drug. In Alaska, for example, 9 percent of women who delivered a baby in 2017 reportedly used marijuana during their pregnancy.[148] In fact, in Colorado, researchers found that seven in ten dispensaries recommended marijuana to women posing as pregnant women.[149] Dr. Nora Volkow, the director of the National Institute of Health's National Institute on Drug Abuse, published a report in response to this alarming trend of increased marijuana use during pregnancy developing across the country and warned of the detrimental health risks of in utero marijuana exposure.[150] In 2019, the U.S. Surgeon General issued an advisory on marijuana use during pregnancy.[151] In 2019, a newborn whose mother reportedly used marijuana while pregnant was found dead at just 11 days old and doctors believed the cause was acute marijuana toxicity.[152] The trend in marijuana use during pregnancy even prompted the U.S. Surgeon General to issue an advisory that warned women not to use marijuana to alleviate nausea during pregnancy.[153]

Commercialization advocates have also suggested that marijuana may help PTSD sufferers, a claim with important implications for veterans in particular. This may be a dangerous assumption. Two studies conducted on military personnel suffering from PTSD found an elevated risk for suicidal thoughts and behaviors among those using marijuana.[154]

Marijuana commercialization, normalization, and misinformation pose a significant risk to public health as the science continues to be downplayed or dismissed. Numerous Department of Health and Human Services officials—from every single modern U.S. presidential administration, regardless of party—have repeatedly asserted the dangers posed by marijuana are settled science, yet pushback from the industry inhibits wider acceptance of that fact.

Marijuana and Co-Use with Other Substances

Some industry proponents claimed that legalizing marijuana would have a positive impact on other substance use in the United States, such as alcohol and opioid use. Common industry rhetoric holds that former alcohol users will switch to marijuana if it is made legal. They also suggest that legalization will be "the exit to the opioid crisis,"[155] and cite a since debunked and severely flawed study that seemed to show a decrease in opioid overdoses in states that legalized medical marijuana.

Amid the third wave of the decades-long opioid crisis[156] and in a population in which nearly 14.5 million people are impacted by alcohol use disorder,[157] the false assertions by the marijuana industry are harmful and not backed by science.

A 2014 study[158] suggested medical marijuana legalization was associated with a decrease in opioid-related deaths until 2010. However, a more recent study of that data showed the opposite. This 2019 study, which now includes more years of data, found instead that marijuana legalization coincided with a 23 percent increase in opioid-related deaths after 2010.[159] (However, the study notes that medical marijuana legalization, more likely than not, had no impact on opioid-related deaths.) Medical marijuana users, according to findings from this study, represent 2.5 percent of the U.S. population and consequently medical marijuana legalization is likely incapable of exerting a demonstrable impact on opioid overdose deaths. Other studies have backed the finding.[160] The positive correlation found in this study is still worth further examination, given the previously discussed relationship between marijuana use and opioid misuse.

Studies have found a link between marijuana and opioid use as well as marijuana and future use of other drugs. Marijuana exposure in adolescence in particular seems to impact future opioid use.[161] A large proportion (44.7 percent) of lifetime marijuana users go on to use other drugs.[162] A study by Azagba and colleagues[163] found marijuana users were more likely than nonusers to report prescription opioid misuse, echoing an earlier study demonstrating that participants who reported marijuana use in the previous year were 2.6 times more likely to abuse nonprescription opioids.[164]

A body of research shows early marijuana use is associated with more than doubling the likelihood of non-marijuana drug use later in life.[165] In fact, according to the National Survey on Drug Use and Health, 95–97 percent of people who used cocaine or heroin started with marijuana.[166] The scientifically validated relationship between substance abuse and marijuana use is difficult to ignore.

Marijuana is often lauded as a plausible substitute for opioids in the treatment of pain. But there is evidence to suggest that marijuana use—particularly chronic use—is associated with poor pain control.[167] A recent study found adults with pain are vulnerable to adverse marijuana use outcomes, a finding that calls into question the prescribing of marijuana as pain relief.[168] Considering that severe pain continues to be one of the most common reasons for obtaining a medical marijuana card—93 percent of registered cardholders in Colorado reported severe pain as the reason for marijuana use[169]—current state policies should be reconsidered.

A four-year prospective study in the highly respected journal The Lancet Public Health followed patients with chronic noncancer pain and found no evidence marijuana-use mitigated pain severity or interference or that marijuana affected rates of opioid prescribing or opioid discontinuation.[170]

Rising alcohol use is also an issue. According to a 2018 report, Washington State saw a 9 percent increase in gallons of beer consumed since legalization.[171] Since legalization in Colorado, state officials recorded a 7 percent increase in gallons of alcohol consumed.[172] Other studies showed no meaningful decrease in alcohol use since legalization.[173] Further analysis found that, "Allowing for changes in the adult population over the period 2005–2017, the data show a continuing increase in wine servings alongside . . . legalization."[174]

Rather than discouraging polysubstance use (the use of multiple drugs), marijuana legalization is associated with further use, misuse, and dependence on other drugs. While the "gateway" effect of marijuana is sometimes considered outdated, the association between use of marijuana and other drugs is supported by the science. Marijuana use often predicts future drug use—ranging from tobacco and alcohol use, to opioid use.

Marijuana use itself may be forecast by other, seemingly less harmful drugs, such as tobacco and alcohol. Among high schoolers who first initiated alcohol use by 12th grade, subsequent marijuana use was more likely. Marijuana seems to both impact—and be impacted by—tobacco use in younger age groups.[175] The relationship that these drugs have on use of each other is important to note.

A 2018 study published in the Journal of Studies on Alcohol and Drugs found that, similar to tobacco and alcohol co-users, marijuana and alcohol co-users were more likely than non-marijuana alcohol users to overvalue alcohol, signaling a dependence on both drugs.[176] Marijuana use is also associated with an increased likelihood of alcohol use disorder.[177]

The commercialization of marijuana perpetuates an understatement of dangerous consequences of marijuana use as the United States continues to grapple with the fallout of not only the opioid epidemic but also widespread tobacco and alcohol addiction.

The Vaping Epidemic

The vaping epidemic is the first national, marijuana-driven crisis in this country and is a direct result of marijuana commercialization. The vaping of marijuana in THC oil pods or cartridges is a relatively new marijuana industry innovation. Vaping quickly delivers 70–90 percent THC concentrates to users by heating extracted oils so that they can be inhaled as vapor. No studies on consumer safety were conducted prior to the mass marketing of vaporizers, which are also popular among tobacco users.

The ensuing crisis, dubbed EVALI (e-cigarette or vaping product use-associated lung injury) by the Centers for Disease Control and Prevention (CDC), has left nearly 70 dead and resulted in the hospitalizations of 2,739 as of the publishing of this report.[178] Many of these victims suffered lung damage that their bodies will never recover from. One hospitalization resulted in the double-lung transplant of a 17-year-old.[179]

Of EVALI cases, 52 percent of affected patients are under the age of 24. Victims killed by the vape-related lung illness ranged in age from 15 to 75. Cases of vaping illnesses have appeared in all 50 states as well as several U.S. territories.[180] Fifteen percent of EVALI victims are under the age of 18—and therefore under the legal age limit to buy a marijuana vape. This is in keeping with the unfortunate and fast-moving upward trend in youth marijuana vaping.[181]

Eighty-two percent of the vape cases investigated in connection with EVALI were found to contain marijuana. One in six of these cases were from vapes and oils sold by commercial shops. Yet when the CDC determined that THC was a common contaminant, the marijuana industry immediately pointed to the underground market and used the epidemic to suggest that legalizing marijuana was the only solution to the public health crisis. The CDC, meanwhile, advised people to stop using THC vapes altogether, as scientists struggled to discern what could cause the kind of intense lung damage that was apparent in EVALI cases.

Various studies of lung biopsies point to different causes. One Mayo Clinic study revealed what researchers defined as a chemical burn[182]—a potential consequence associated with inhaling heated metal toxins from vape devices. Others pointed to vitamin E acetate, which is a chemical not meant to be inhaled. While the CDC continued to advise users not to use any THC vape products, because they could not definitively say that vitamin E acetate was the cause of illness, the marijuana industry continued to point to vitamin E acetate in order to assert that only illicit vapes were complicit in the disease—even as vitamin E acetate was found in some "legal" vapes.

Many victims obtained vapes initially purchased from "legal" dispensaries in "legal" states. In Oregon, two deaths were linked to marijuana products purchased at state-licensed dispensaries.[183] A death in Tennessee was linked to a vape purchased at a dispensary in Colorado.[184] Cases in Delaware, Maryland, California, Washington, Michigan, and Massachusetts were linked to "legal" marijuana.[185]

This tragic epidemic, which impacts users across the country, came about because of widespread legalization and relaxed attitudes towards marijuana.

High Potency Marijuana

In the 1970s, "Woodstock Weed" contained roughly 1–3 percent THC,[186] the psychoactive component of marijuana. Since then, products became increasingly potent, driven in large part by market demand as well as a shift in consumption methods. THC concentrates such as shatter, budder, and waxes—as well as gummies and edibles—are packed with more THC than joints ever were. Now even the plant itself is genetically engineered to contain a greater percentage of THC. One study found that the average potency of the marijuana plant increased from 8.9 percent THC in 2008, to 17.1 percent THC in 2017. Concentrates, which contained an average potency of 6.7 percent THC in 2008, contained an average potency of 55.7 percent in 2017.[187]

The market for marijuana flower hybrids and concentrates continues to rise with the increase in demand for products with higher THC potency levels. In Washington State, market share for flower products with 10–15 percent THC declined by 60.4 percent between 2014 and 2017, while the market share for flower products with more than 20 percent THC increased by 48.8 percent during that same period.[188]

In Oregon, concentrates and extracts easily surpassed flower marijuana in sales and comprise an increasingly large proportion of all marijuana sales. In the month of December 2019 alone, nearly 1 million units of concentrates and extracts were sold in the state and the number of units of edibles sold exceeded the pounds of flower marijuana sold.[189] Retailers increasingly promote higher potency marijuana in order to drive profits—high potency marijuana sells.

The demand for stronger marijuana is dangerous. High potency marijuana exacerbates many of the consequences of marijuana use. Frequent marijuana users and users of higher potency marijuana are more likely than regular users to develop schizophrenia and psychosis.[190] Users of Butane Hash Oil (BHO), a marijuana concentrate that yields a potency of between 70–99 percent THC, are more likely to have lifetime diagnoses of depression and anxiety while being more likely to report other substance use.[191]

The lucrative cash potential of high potency marijuana also emboldens illegal producers of BHO. Its production involves forcing raw marijuana and butane into a reaction chamber, which creates a highly combustible liquid that can easily explode when introduced to an ignition source. This has implications not only for public health but public safety as well.

From 2012 to 2018, over 100 marijuana extraction labs were seized in Oregon. Over 30 fires and explosions related to the production of this kind of marijuana were reported in the state in that time period.[192] The number of labs seized in the area reached a new high of 37 in 2017.[193]

In addition to these concerns, BHO explosions led to an increasing number of BHO burn victims. The Oregon-Idaho High Intensity Drug Trafficking Area report found that 87 marijuana extraction burn victims were treated from 2015 to 2017. Since 2013, treatment costs for marijuana extraction burn victims totaled $15 million.[194]

Products with high amounts of THC proliferate with market demand and, as such, consequences associated with highly potent marijuana become more apparent.

Emergency and Hospital Admissions

The widespread availability and accessibility of high potency marijuana due to legalization has resulted in an increasing number of marijuana-related poison control calls, hospitalizations, and ER visits.

A 2020 study found that recreational marijuana commercialization is associated with between 66–77 percent increase in marijuana exposures. State-specific data shed greater light on this phenomenon.[195] As drug policy scholars Wayne Hall and Daniel Stjepanović write,

"Shi & Laing's analysis of poison center calls adds to evidence from emergency department presentations that legalization of retail cannabis sales has increased the rate of acute adverse effects of cannabis. These effects include: increased accidental ingestion of cannabis products (gummies and extracts) by children; unpleasant psychological experiences in adults receiving larger than intended doses of tetrahydrocannabinol (THC); and a new syndrome, cannabis hyperemesis syndrome, in heavy daily cannabis users."[196]

In Colorado, the number of marijuana-related emergency department visits increased 54 percent from 2013 to 2017.[197] Yearly marijuana-related hospitalizations increased 101 percent in that same period.[198] Calls to the poison control center for marijuana exposures also increased. In 2013, 125 calls were made for marijuana-related exposures. By 2018, that number jumped to 266, representing a 112.8 percent increase. Youth cases (instances of marijuana-related exposures of children aged 8 or younger) increased 126.2 percent from 2013 to 2018. In 2018, youth cases represented over half of all marijuana-related exposure calls.[199]

A study by the Colorado Department of Public Health and Environment found that in 2018, over 23,000 homes in the state with children aged one to 14 years had marijuana products stored unsafely.[200] In 2018, 60 percent of youth marijuana exposures involved edibles, compared with just 18 percent in 2016.[201] Even when packaging is compliant with Colorado's regulatory requirements, it fails to discourage or prevent children from accessing potent and dangerous marijuana.

Researchers who studied the impact of medical marijuana legalization also found many pediatric marijuana exposure cases in the state, despite childproof packaging and warning labels.[202] During the eight-year period studied, the Regional Center for Poison Control and Prevention (RPC) recorded a 140 percent increase in single-substance (marijuana) exposures, with 81.7 percent of these calls regarding marijuana exposures of 15- to 19-year-olds.

A study conducted in Washington State found that the rate of pediatric exposures to marijuana (children aged 9 or under) was 2.3 times higher following "legal" retail sales than before legalization.[203] Poison control center cases in Washington State have increased 103.2 percent. Cases for children aged 5 and younger increased in 176.5 percent. In 2018, there were 497 calls—compared with 245 when legalization in the state began.[204]

In Alaska, in 2017 there were a total of 3,296 inpatient discharges and 6,639 outpatient discharges related to marijuana.[205] In Illinois, just several days after legalization, doctors reported a surge in emergency room visits and hospitalizations for marijuana, including several cases of marijuana-induced psychosis.[206]

Though it is true that marijuana misuse does not result in the same kind of immediate overdose that other drugs may cause, cases of Cannabis Hyperemesis Syndrome (CHS)—or sometimes CVS (Cannabis Vomiting Syndrome)—have increased significantly since legalization. CHS is a disease that presents as episodes of screaming and vomiting, dubbed "scromiting," and the only effective treatment is immediately stopping marijuana use. The disease appears to mainly affect heavy, daily users of marijuana.

From 2010 to 2014, researchers recorded a 46 percent increase in CHS cases in Colorado.[207] Another study of CHS in Colorado found at least two deaths that were caused by CHS and recorded a third death that CHS is believed to have contributed to.[208] This is an entirely new phenomenon; the first case of CHS was recorded in 2004.

The dramatic increases in emergency cases related to marijuana exposure highlight the danger of commercialization. In many instances, the danger impacts unwitting children or people who mistakenly consume marijuana. Innocent and unwilling citizens are subjected to consequences of a situation that they did not create.

Impact on Youth

The legalization of marijuana has had a profound impact on young people's use of the drug as well as perceptions of its harms.

Years of playing catch-up to alcohol and tobacco normalization have resulted in important downward trends in youth alcohol and cigarette use. But a new wave of substance use among children is rising. Given the relationship between marijuana use, alcohol, and cigarette use, it is important to note that use rates of all substances among youth may rise if the dangers of youth marijuana use go ignored.

While some marijuana industry proponents have suggested that a strict legal marijuana market would limit youth use, marijuana use among youth is rapidly increasing along with legalization—while perceptions of risk associated with use are decreasing. Compounding this problem are the increasing use rates of adults. A 2019 study found that parental marijuana use increases the likelihood of marijuana use among children in the household, as well as increases their risk of tobacco use and opioid misuse.[209]

In part, the ease of obtaining marijuana has contributed to youth use in "legal" states. Restrictions on selling to minors have not stopped state-sanctioned sellers from selling the drug to underage consumers in "legal" states. In 2018, 46 percent of young people nationwide aged 12 to 17 reported that they perceived marijuana to be easy or fairly easy to obtain.[210] In Washington State, where marijuana is "legal," this number is much higher, with 49 percent of 10th graders and 61 percent of 12th graders believing that marijuana was easy to obtain.[211]

In Washington State, marijuana violations have remained high since legalization in 2014. As of December 2019, 3,220 violations have been documented. Violations pertaining to the sale or service of marijuana to a minor, or for allowing a minor to frequent a restricted area, comprised 16.3 percent of all of these violations.[212]

Among Oregon's 11th graders who currently use marijuana, 67 percent reported obtaining marijuana from a friend.[213] Furthermore, 37.2 percent of 8th and 49.5 percent of 11th graders reported being exposed to online marijuana advertisements in the past 30 days.[214] A recent study found that one in three youth living in a state where marijuana is "legal" engaged with marijuana promotions on social media. The same study found that youth who engaged with marijuana promotions were five times as likely to use marijuana.[215]

In Washington State, 22 percent of 6th and 8th graders believed there to be no or low risk from regular marijuana use, while 40 percent of 10th and 12th graders reported no or low risk from regular marijuana use. Sixty-seven percent of 10th and 12th graders in the state reported no or low risk of trying marijuana once or twice.[216]

At the national level, the normalization of marijuana has resulted in an increase in marijuana use among young people across the country.[217] NSDUH (National Survey on Drug Use and Health) data show that among young people aged 12 to 17, lifetime, past-year, and past-month marijuana use increased from 2017 to 2018. More than 3.1 million youth used marijuana in the past year, a moderate 0.5 percent increase from 2017 use rates; and almost 1.7 million used marijuana in the past month in 2018, up nearly 3 percent from 2017. Furthermore, past-year initiates of marijuana use among 12- to 17-year-olds increased in 2018—after dropping off in prior years.

Additionally, near daily marijuana use—as reported by the University of Michigan's Monitoring the Future (MTF) survey—increased dramatically from 2018 to 2019 with 6.4 percent of 12th graders, 4.8 percent of 10th graders, and 1.3 percent of 8th graders reporting near daily marijuana use in 2019. The increase in near-daily marijuana use among 8th graders is particularly concerning: 2019 near-daily use rates jumped 85.7 percent from 2018 to 2019.[218]

Youth marijuana vaping has added to the already-alarming trend of increasingly prevalent marijuana use among young people amid widespread commercialization. Trends in youth vaping have given way to a countrywide epidemic[219] that present implications for youth marijuana use. Youth vaping of any kind (tobacco or flavors) has been shown in several studies to increase the likelihood of subsequent marijuana vaping or marijuana use generally.[220] As youth vaping of any kind has increased, so, too, has youth marijuana vaping.

Past-year youth vaping of marijuana has increased dramatically since the MTF survey began recording data on the subject in 2017. As reported by this survey,[221] lifetime, annual, and past-month marijuana vaping among 8th, 10th, and 12th graders have all dramatically increased in just one year. Past month use among teenagers increased over 72 percent from 2018 to 2019. An average of 10 percent of teens reported past-month marijuana vaping in 2019. In 2019, MTF first recorded data on near-daily marijuana vaping and found that 2.4 percent of this age group vaped marijuana almost every day. That number exceeds near-daily cigarette and near-daily alcohol use among this group.

As marijuana legalization advocates have argued that youth marijuana use falls in conjunction with legalization, it is important to note trends in use in states that have legalized the drug. More young people are using marijuana in "legal" states—and they are using it more frequently. These trends are driven by the decreased perception of risk as well as the increased availability of marijuana that accompanies legalization.

Nationally, fewer people, especially youth, perceive a risk from smoking marijuana. This downward trend is driven by the relaxed approach to marijuana in states where it's "legal." The perception of risk associated with smoking marijuana once a month fell over 7 percent from 2016/2017 to 2017/2018 in "legal" states.[222] Only 17.4 percent of youth aged 12 to 17 in "legal" states reported perceiving a risk from smoking marijuana, a dramatically lower percentage compared with the national rate of over 27 percent. Consequently, marijuana use among this age group is up in those states.

Past-year as well as past-month marijuana use among 12- to 17-year-olds in "legal" states increased from 2016/2017 to 2017/2018.[223] An average of 16.4 percent of 12- to 17-year-olds in "legal" states reported past-year use in 2017/2018, and an average of 9.4 percent reported past-month use. In California, Colorado, Massachusetts, and Nevada, past-month marijuana use among young people jumped over 4 percent in each state from 2016/2017 to 2017/2018. In Washington State, use increased even more dramatically: 9.9 percent of young people reported past-month marijuana use, marking a near 11 percent increase in past-month use from 2016/2017. An independent report in Alaska found that 22 percent of high schoolers in the state reported past-30-day use in 2017.[224]

These increases far exceed marijuana use rates among youth aged 12 to 17 in states where marijuana remains illegal.[225] According to 2017/2018 NSDUH state-specific data, 12.1 percent of youth in non-legal states reported past-year marijuana use and 6.4 percent of young people in those states reported past-month use. Use rates in "marijuana-legal" states sit around three percentage points higher.

The issue of marijuana use among youth in "legal" states is further elucidated by data taken on first-use rates—the percentage of young people initiating marijuana use in the past year.[226] The average rate of first use in "marijuana-legal" states was 7.4 percent in 2017/2018, up from 6.8 percent the previous year. In California, first-use rates have increased 10 percent from 2016/2017 to 2017/2018. In states where marijuana remains illegal, first-use rate among 12- to 17-year-olds in 2017/2018 was 5.4 percent.

Marijuana commercialization—and the subsequent normalization of marijuana use—play an important role in the increased marijuana use of young people. A 2017 study found that the longer duration of legalization and higher dispensary density was associated with increased use of vaping (inhaling vaporized marijuana oils) and consumption of edibles by 14- to 18-year-olds.[227] Marijuana dispensary density has been linked to more use among youth, with 16 percent of 11th graders reporting marijuana use in areas with less dispensary density compared to 24.3 percent of the same age group reporting use in more retail-dense areas.[228]

The commercialization of marijuana has also adversely impacted schools and youth academic performance. According to Joe Zawodny, director of secondary education for the Anchorage [Alaska] School District, "Because it's legal in the community, I think, the stigma around marijuana use is decreasing. The data would seem to say there is increasing use."[229] In Washington State, high schoolers reporting marijuana use also reported lower grades (more Cs, Ds, and Fs) than those of their peers who did not smoke marijuana.[230]

Marijuana was cited in 23 percent of Colorado school suspensions, the highest of all documented school offenses. Further, between 2012 and 2014, the percentage of 10- to 14-year-olds who once or twice tested positive for THC increased from 19 percent to 23 percent; those who tested positive three or more times increased from 18 percent to 25 percent.[231] In Alaska, the number of youth referred for marijuana-related crimes jumped to a high of 302.[232]

Marijuana use among youth in "legal" states also coincides with marijuana misuse and substance disorder. A 2019 study[233] found that recreational marijuana legalization was followed by a 25 percent increase in adolescent cannabis use disorder (CUD). This trend speaks to the higher potency of marijuana products. In Washington State, a 2018 youth survey showed that 13 percent of 8th and 10th graders, and 19 percent of 12th graders, reported dabbing marijuana.[234] Dabbing involves heating marijuana concentrate, often of unspecified potency that can reach up to 99 percent THC, and inhaling the vapor. One study on dabbing found that the process may deliver significant amounts of additional toxins, such as methacrolein and benzene.[235]

There are intense ramifications to marijuana use by youth. Young, developing brains are especially susceptible to the negative effects of marijuana use and young users have demonstrated changes in gray matter volume, indicating negative consequences for brain development.[236] Young users are also at a greater risk for mental health problems, dependence on marijuana, and future substance abuse of other drugs.[237] Chronic adolescent marijuana use has been correlated with cognitive impairment and worsened academic or work performance.[238]

Youth marijuana use poses a significant risk for depression and suicide.[239] In Colorado, where teen suicides have become the cause of one in five adolescent deaths,[240] youth suicide toxicology reports have demonstrated this devastating effect. In 2013, marijuana was present in 12.5 percent of suicide toxicology reports for young people aged 15 to 19 years; in 2018, marijuana was present in over 36 percent—representing an almost 300 percent increase.[241]

The efforts to legalize marijuana are playing out with devastating effects on youth across the country while public health agencies are ill-equipped to mitigate the consequences. But youth are not the only group at risk.

Impact on Young Adults

Though the legal age for marijuana consumption in "legal" states is 21, marijuana use during young adulthood carries a host of adverse effects. Marijuana has a particularly strong impact on developing brains, which continue to develop through a person's late twenties. Still, marijuana use in this age group is higher than that of any other. The low perception of risk associated with marijuana use, as well as the highest use rates of all age categories, make marijuana an unexamined issue for many young adults.

According to data recorded by SAMHSA's national NSDUH survey,[242] in 2018 young adults across the country had the lowest percentages of perception of risk associated with marijuana use. Only 12 percent of young adults believed that smoking marijuana once a month was risky and only 15.4 percent perceived a great risk from smoking marijuana once or twice a week. This is far lower than the perception of risk of people aged 12 or older, 25 percent of whom perceive great risk from smoking once a month, and 30.6 percent of whom perceive great risk from smoking once or twice a week.

Young adult marijuana use outpaces other age groups in the United States. Young adults aged 18 to 25 reported lifetime, past-year, and past-month use in much higher numbers compared to other age groups at 51.1 percent, 34.8 percent, and 22.1 percent, respectively. Use reported among people aged 12 or older sits at 45.3 percent, 15.9 percent, and 10.1 percent, respectively.[243]

Higher instances of marijuana use disorder have been reported by people aged 18 to 25, coinciding with higher rates of marijuana use. In 2018, after years of decreases, 5.9 percent of people aged 18 to 25 reported marijuana use disorder, marking an 11 percent increase from 2017.[244]

These trends in use are most dramatic in states that have legalized marijuana.[245] The percentage of young adults, aged 18 to 25, reporting past-year and past-month use have increased significantly from 2016/2017 to 2017/2018. An average of 46.3 percent of young adults in these states reported past-year use in 2017/2018 and 31.6 percent reported past-month use in 2017/2018. In Nevada, for example, past-year and past-month young adult use jumped by 18.9 percent and 24.1 percent, respectively, from 2016/2017 to 2017/2018.

Use rates among this age group in "legal" states far exceed those of states where marijuana is illegal,[246] with 32.7 percent and 20.7 percent of 18- to 25-year-olds reporting past-year and past-month use in states where marijuana is not legal: a difference of more than 10 percentage points compared with "legal" state-use rates. Legalization has not reduced use; it has encouraged and accelerated it.

Given what we know about marijuana's effects on the developing brain, young adults should be discouraged from using it, yet the commercialization of marijuana heavily promotes its use instead—with no warnings about the risks. The same health risks faced by teen marijuana users affect young adult users. For example, marijuana use during young adulthood carries a higher risk of developing psychosis.[247]

Co-use also presents a compounded harm to young-adult users. As this age group goes off to college, where drinking, drug use, and other kinds of experimentation are prevalent, marijuana may be used in conjunction with a host of other drugs, presenting a risk for future substance use disorder. Researchers from Oregon State University found that college students who were binge drinkers before the age of 21 saw relatively large increases in marijuana use after legalization.[248]

Impact on Communities of Color and Low-Income Populations

Marijuana legalization poses a significant threat to low-income and minority communities. Though industry proponents suggest that marijuana legalization will alleviate injustices against socioeconomically disadvantaged populations, disparities in use and criminal offense rates have persisted in states that legalized marijuana.

While it is important to evaluate the impact of incarceration within certain communities, it is also important to understand the impact of marijuana legalization on those same communities. It is inappropriate to suggest that only through marijuana legalization will social justice be achieved or criminal justice inequity remedied. In fact, no such effect has been demonstrated in the states where marijuana was made "legal."

Although arrests for marijuana-related offenses have generally fallen across all racial demographics in Colorado since legalization, marijuana-related arrest rates of people of color have held steady and arrest rates among African Americans are nearly double that of Caucasians.[249] In addition, 39 percent of African American marijuana-related arrests in 2017 were made without a warrant, while only 18 percent of Caucasians were arrested without one.[250]

Law enforcement contacts with young people of color in Colorado also remain high. During the 2016–2017 school year, 23 percent of all law enforcement contacts with Hispanic youth and 15 percent of all law enforcement contacts with African American youth were related to marijuana.[251]

In Washington, D.C., between 2015 to 2017 (the years immediately following legalization), while total marijuana-related arrests decreased, distribution and public consumption arrests more than tripled. In 2017, 89.7 percent of all marijuana-related arrestees were African American.[252] Additionally, in 2017 marijuana-related arrests comprised an increasing percentage of all arrests across racial demographics in D.C. but, was especially pronounced among African Americans. While marijuana arrest rates were roughly even among racial demographics for years preceding legalization, arrest rates of African Americans far outpaced Caucasians in 2017.[253]

Instead of fixing social justice disparities in one fell swoop, legalization merely changes the nature of the arrest in lower income and minority communities. What's more, the marijuana industry has recognized an important new consumer base.

An early study of medical marijuana implementation in California found that marijuana dispensaries were disproportionately located within areas where the demand for marijuana was greater—where there were higher rates of poverty as well as a higher number of alcohol outlets.[254] In other words, when choosing where to locate dispensaries, owners followed the data to low-income communities. Further studies of Los Angeles marijuana dispensaries found that the majority of dispensaries have opened primarily in African American communities.[255] And an overlay of socioeconomic data with the geographic location of pot shops in Denver shows marijuana stores are disproportionately located in disadvantaged neighborhoods.[256] In Oregon, the state conducted an analysis on the distribution of state-sanctioned dispensaries and found that sites were concentrated among low-income and historically disenfranchised communities.[257]

As a result, the harms associated with marijuana dispensary locations (such as increased use and substance misuse, normalization, hospitalizations, and so on) are disproportionately concentrated within particularly vulnerable communities.

The importance of this cannot be overstated. Historically, disadvantaged communities lack many of the resources to combat this kind of targeting by industry and also often lack adequate access to proper drug treatment facilities, thereby exposing community members to an increased likelihood of substance abuse with limited resources to combat the consequences.[258] What the country has seen in the fallout of the opioid epidemic and the expansion of Big Tobacco[259] is being replicated by Big Marijuana.

Perceptions of risks associated with marijuana use among young people of color fall well below the national rates.[260] Nationally, 34.9 percent of youth aged 12 to 17 perceived a great risk from using marijuana once or twice a week. Only 31.9 percent of African American youth, and 28.9 percent of American-Indian Alaska-Native (AIAN) youth perceive a great risk from using marijuana once or twice a week. As stated previously, frequent marijuana use among young people exacerbates the damaging health consequences associated with it.

The decreased perceptions of risk translate to increases in use. In 2018, past-year and past-month use among minority young people was higher than the average, as reported by SAMHSA.[261] Past-month and past-year marijuana use among youth aged 12 to 17 years was more prevalent among African Americans and AIAN youth. For example, nationally, 6.7 percent of young people aged 12 to 17 reported past-month marijuana use, with 6.8 percent of Caucasian youth using in the past month. Comparatively, 7.5 percent of African American youth and 9.4 percent of AIAN youth reported past-month marijuana use. Young people of color face enormous risks.

The decreased perception of risk associated with marijuana use during pregnancy has a particularly damaging impact on socioeconomically disadvantaged communities. A study by the American College of Obstetricians and Gynecologists reported that young, urban women from lower income levels have a 15–28 percent rate of marijuana use during pregnancy.[262] As previously stated, marijuana use during pregnancy has a host of dangerous consequences for neonates.

From an economic standpoint, advocates of the marijuana industry often argue that any detrimental effects of marijuana will be offset by the cash potential of the drug. Proponents of legalization suggest that the new industry presents previously disenfranchised groups with new economic opportunities. In reality, though some states have attempted to use legislation to protect and provide for minority marijuana business owners, the industry is largely bereft of diversity. Nationally, fewer than 20 percent of all marijuana businesses are owned by minorities.[263]

Massachusetts serves as a case study for this phenomenon. The state requires all "Marijuana Agents," persons who work at marijuana businesses, to register with the state. Demographic analysis revealed that of 1,306 agents who applied in the city of Boston, 6 percent were Hispanic and 4 percent African American. This is unrepresentative of the city's population.[264] Indeed, an exposé by The Boston Globe revealed that a handful of out-of-state marijuana corporations had locked-in almost all of the licenses through shell companies.[265]

In Chicago, Illinois, where not one of the eleven existing growers licensed to sell recreational marijuana was African American, the city council's Black Caucus pushed back. Soon after the state legislature's legalized recreational marijuana, local African American legislators took issue with the obvious discrepancy.[266] Still, Chicago Mayor Lori Lightfoot, who received $123,000 from the marijuana industry in her contentious bid for mayor, suggested that those councilmembers take the issue up with the state legislators in Springfield. Legalization was implemented on schedule.

New Jersey State Senator Ronald Rice has been among the most vocal leaders against marijuana legalization. He wrote in an op-ed, "Seeing firsthand how drugs eviscerate urban communities—and understanding how marijuana legalization will impact the health, education, economics, business, liability, and litigation complexities of our densely-populated, metropolitan-bookended state—I fully oppose it."[267]

Legalization is not a blanket solution to social injustice. In fact, it may perpetuate it.

Impact on the Workforce

The legalization of marijuana has had serious ramifications for businesses and employers across the United States, particularly in states where marijuana is "legal." The prevalence of marijuana and its use has coincided with a dramatic increase in positive marijuana screens among employees in all industries across the country. Marijuana is the most commonly detected substance and has the highest drug positivity rate among all other tested substances across the majority of industry sectors in the United States.[268] In 2018, workforce marijuana positivity rates reached their highest levels since 2004.

In 2018, marijuana positivity increased in all workforce categories (general, federally mandated, safety-sensitive, and combined U.S. workforces). In 2018, positive marijuana urine tests increased 8 percent from the previous year (and have increased 17 percent since 2014). Positivity screens increased 53.3 percent among transportation and warehousing workers, 50 percent among mining workers, 47.1 percent among wholesale trade workers, 46.7 percent among construction workers, and 37.9 percent among accommodation and food services workers.[269] In particular, among the safety-sensitive workforce (aircraft pilots, bus drivers, and so forth) marijuana positivity in 2018 increased 5 percent from the previous year and nearly 24 percent since 2014.

The increase in national workforce marijuana positivity rates is led by states where marijuana is "legal." Rates in Oregon, Nevada, Massachusetts, Colorado, California, and Washington are several percentage points above the national average. In Oregon in particular, workforce marijuana positivity is nearly double the national rate.[270]

Further highlighting the impact of legalization on the workforce, marijuana positivity rates in "legal" states increased nearly 50 percent since legalization. These increases are particularly pronounced in Colorado, Nevada, Oregon, and Washington, where positivity rates have increased 76.5 percent, 48.1 percent, 115 percent, and 50 percent, respectively, since legalization.[271]

The prevalence of positive marijuana screens has important consequences for the average American workplace. A study conducted in Washington State from 2011–2014 found that the percentage of work-related injuries and illnesses was significantly higher among marijuana users (8.9 percent) compared to nonusers.[272] This poses a particular problem for employers, who may be confronted with liability claims following marijuana-related injuries or onsite illnesses.[273]

Though increased marijuana use among the workforce has exposed employers to liability, many states have moved to prevent marijuana screenings. A 2019 bill passed by the Nevada state legislature bans employers from refusing prospective employees who fail a marijuana test.[274] The New York City Council passed a similar measure in 2019, barring employers from testing applicants for marijuana.[275] Colorado is also considering such a measure.

Impact on Homelessness

Though the extent to which a correlation may exist between the increasing homeless population and the legalization of marijuana is unclear, some trends in this area are notable.

In Colorado, the homelessness rate appears to have increased with the expansion of recreational marijuana. The U.S. Department of Housing and Urban Development reported a 13 percent increase in Colorado's homeless population from 2015 to 2016, while the national average decreased 3 percent.[276] Business owners and officials in Durango, Colorado, have testified that the resort town "suddenly became a haven for recreational pot users, drawing in transients, panhandlers, and a large number of homeless drug addicts."[277]

A 2018 study, conducted by the Colorado Division of Criminal Justice, surveyed seven Colorado jail populations. It yielded results that further link homelessness and marijuana use.[278] The study, though small, found that 50.8 percent of respondents reported using marijuana 30 days prior to their time in jail. Additionally, 54.9 percent of respondents who were homeless prior to their jail time reported marijuana use 30 days prior to it (compared with 36.1 percent reporting alcohol use).

The study also found that of the respondents, 38.5 percent were Colorado natives and 61.5 percent were not. Of the non-Colorado natives surveyed, 35.1 percent reported marijuana as his or her reason for moving to Colorado after it was legalized in 2012.[279]

Considering the impact of homelessness on communities—and the resources required to help those impacted by it—it is worth investigating the correlation between homelessness and legalization.

Impact on Impaired Driving

Driving while under the influence of marijuana has proved an increasingly damaging phenomenon due to the legalization and normalization of marijuana in the United States. The Centers for Disease Control and Prevention found that, in 2018, 12 million U.S. residents reported driving under the influence of marijuana. This represents 4.7 percent of the driving population.[280]

In Michigan, a survey found that 51 percent of medical marijuana users admitted to driving while "a little high," and one in five of those surveyed admitted to driving while very high.[281] The reduced perception of risk and the prevalence of stoned drivers on the road bear consequences for road safety and raise questions for legislators and law enforcement going forward.

Driving under the influence of marijuana is dangerous. The National Institute on Drug Abuse holds that marijuana use impairs driving in a number of ways: by slowing reaction time, decreasing coordination, and impairing judgment of time and distance. Polysubstance use—using marijuana along with alcohol or another drug—compounds the risk of a vehicle crash more than the drugs being used alone.[282] Nevertheless, marijuana-impaired driving is rising while the perception of its negative consequences is decreasing.

A survey conducted by AAA found that only 70 percent of drivers perceived driving within an hour of using marijuana as extremely dangerous or very dangerous, compared to 95.1 percent who felt that driving under the influence of alcohol above the legal limit was extremely or very dangerous.[283] The number of respondents who completely or somewhat approved of driving shortly after using marijuana was 7.4 percent compared to 1.6 percent who completely or somewhat approved of driving under the influence of alcohol above the legal limit. The answers from younger drivers were even more alarming. Of respondents between the ages of 19 to 24, only 57.9 percent believed that driving under the influence of marijuana was extremely or very dangerous. Among drivers between the ages of 19 to 24, 20.4 percent completely or somewhat approved of driving shortly after using marijuana.[284] The downward trend in perception of risk has coincided with an increased percentage of marijuana-impaired drivers on the road.

According to the biological results of Washington's Roadside Survey, "... nearly one in five daytime drivers may be under the influence of marijuana, up from less than one in 10 drivers prior to the implementation of marijuana retail sales."[285]

The reduced perception of risk has reached young drivers in "legal" states as well. The Washington State Healthy Youth Survey found that in 2018, 16 percent of 12th graders drove after using marijuana and 24 percent rode with a driver who was using marijuana.[286] In Alaska, one in ten high school students had driven after using marijuana.[287]

In Colorado, DUIDs (driving under the influence of drugs) have risen in recent years. The percentage of drivers testing THC-only positive increased 16.1 percent from 2016 to 2017. Of these drivers in 2017, 39.4 percent were under the age of 18. What's more, the percentage of drivers testing positive for alcohol with THC increased 10.9 percent in a single year from 2016 to 2017.[288]

In a 2017 report of DUID data, marijuana was detected in 3,170 of all case filings where a cannabinoid screen was conducted after a driver was pulled over for demonstrating impaired driving. Of these positive screens, 84.4 percent tested positive for 1.0 to 5.0+ active THC.[289] What's more, 59 percent of those who tested positive for THC tested positive for extremely high levels of the drug (THC level of 5.0 or higher).

Additionally, some of these people found driving under the influence of marijuana (testing positive for 1.0 to 5.0+ THC) were also found to have a blood alcohol content (BAC) from 0.05 to 0.08 or higher in their system. Of the instances where THC was detected at

5.0 or higher and an alcohol screen was conducted, 47 percent of those drivers tested with a BAC of 0.08 or higher.[290]

Vehicle crashes and traffic fatalities have surged after the legalization of marijuana. Research by the Highway Loss Data Institute found that the legalization of recreational marijuana in Colorado, Oregon, and Washington coincided with an increase in collision claims.[291]

In Colorado, traffic fatalities increased over 31 percent since 2013. The rise in statewide traffic fatalities has coincided with a rise in instances of traffic fatalities where the driver tested positive for marijuana (active THC in the bloodstream). The number of traffic fatalities involving drivers who tested positive for marijuana in Colorado rose from 55 deaths in 2013 to 115 deaths in 2016. Twenty percent of all traffic fatalities in Colorado in 2018 involved a driver who tested positive for marijuana.[292]

A recent report released by AAA found that the number of drivers who tested positive for marijuana after a fatal crash doubled after legalization in Washington State. Researchers found that in the five years prior to legalization in the state, marijuana-impaired drivers comprised around 8.8 percent of all drivers implicated in traffic fatalities. In the years following, the rate jumped to around 18 percent.[293] The AAA writes, "AAA opposes the legalization of marijuana for recreational use because of its inherent traffic safety risks and because of the difficulties in writing legislation that protects the public and treats drivers fairly."[294]

Compounding the risk of an increasingly stoned driving population is the difficulty posed to law enforcement officers who attempt to stop and detain marijuana-impaired drivers. The smell of marijuana in a suspected driver's car is no longer enough to make an arrest in many states, even in states that have not yet legalized marijuana.[295] Technology to determine THC levels is underdeveloped and lacks the certainty of traditional breathalyzers. The quick metabolization of THC renders it difficult to detect and tests must be administered quickly in suspected cases.

Additionally, many states have struggled to create a standard level of impairment when THC is detected.[296] Studies are mixed regarding what level of THC constitutes impairment. Recently, scientists found that drivers may still be impaired from marijuana use well after intoxication, demonstrating an increased likelihood of poor driving performance, increased accidents, and decreased rule-following.[297]

Many of the marijuana "legal" states failed to establish laws or guidance prior to legalizing marijuana, leaving law enforcement officers in the dark as legislators played catch-up to dangerous trends. As a result, road safety is compromised.

Trends in Crime Since Legalization

Marijuana legalization advocates have argued that legalization will reduce overall crime. However, in states that have legalized marijuana crime rates have risen at a faster rate than other states across the country.

While it is difficult to say whether crime can be causally associated with marijuana legalization, some studies shed light on a correlation. A 2019 study conducted in Denver found that the existence of both recreational and medical marijuana dispensaries in Denver neighborhoods are significantly and positively associated with increased crime.[298]

Researchers found that Denver neighborhoods adjacent to marijuana businesses saw 84.8 more property crimes each year than those without a marijuana shop nearby.[299] The number of court filings charged with the Colorado Organized Crime Control Act that were linked to a marijuana charge increased 639 percent from 2013 to 2017.[300] Further, Crimes Against Society (such as drug violations) have increased 44 percent since 2014.[301]

Colorado's crime rate in 2016 increased 11 times faster than the 30 largest cities in the nation since legalization.[302] In 2018, data from the Colorado Bureau of Investigation demonstrates a 14.2 percent increase in property crime since 2013 (157,360 to 179,650) and a 36.5 percent increase in violent crime since 2013 (18,475 to 25,212).

Though arrests for marijuana offenses had declined in the years prior to legalization in Colorado, they are increasing again. In 2013, arrests for marijuana sales offenses were at a low of 337, having decreased 52.1 percent since 2008. From 2013 to 2018, arrests for marijuana sales offenses increased 29.4 percent. Additionally, prior to legalization, arrests for all drug sales offenses had declined 54.9 percent (from 2008 to 2013). In the years since, arrests for drug sales offenses have increased 11 percent.[303]

Overall, while increased crime has not been definitively linked to marijuana legalization, these upward trends in property crime and violent crime—as well as crimes against society—warrant further investigation.

A Thriving Underground Market

Commercialization advocates have long argued that legalization will reduce black market marijuana activity in "legal" states. However, the legalization and commercialization of marijuana has led to greater black-market activity than ever before. This is driven by a number of causes.

Illegal marijuana originating from "legal" states is uncovered at increasingly high rates. From July 2015 to January 2018, 14,550 pounds of illegally trafficked Oregon marijuana, worth approximately $48 million, was seized en route to 37 different states.[304] In 2018, Colorado law enforcement seized 12,150 pounds (6.1 tons) of bulk marijuana. Officials recorded 25 different states to which marijuana was destined.[305] In its 2019 National Drug Threat Assessment report, the Drug Enforcement Agency (DEA)[306] found that states with the highest marijuana removals came from states with major border crossings or states with medical or recreational marijuana markets. These states give cover to illegal activity; black market problems abound.

Many marijuana proponents argued that a slew of benefits would result from the legalization of marijuana. Two of these were that legal weed would drive out the black market and that taxed marijuana would provide money-dry states with much-needed revenue. Both have yet to pan out. Regulated marijuana is not the revenue cash cow for states that industry advocates promised. California's projected marijuana tax revenue by July 2019 was nearly half of what was originally expected when the state permitted retail sales in 2018.[307] In Colorado, marijuana tax revenue represented nine tenths of one percent of Colorado's 2018 statewide budget.[308] Even still, marijuana license holders complain that "marijuana-legal" states are too regulated and that taxes on the drug are too high.[309] They go as far as to say that regulation and taxes are the reason the black market continues to dominate.

That contention is ill-founded for several reasons. The regulatory and compliance systems instituted in the "legal" states were instituted with little foresight. State compliance officials are left on their heels while various regulatory and compliance issues become exposed. The Oregon Liquor Control Commission wrote in a 2018 report that, ". . . due to the legally required rapid implementation of the recreational program, OLCC has not been able to implement robust compliance monitoring and enforcement controls and processes for the recreational marijuana program."[310]

The lack of oversight also bears consequences for consumer safety. An independent investigation in San Diego found that nearly 30 percent of marijuana samples purchased from licensed retailers in Southern California tested positive in labs for pesticides.[311] States are ill-equipped to handle marijuana testing and even states with the most stringent regulatory requirements have demonstrated significant lapses, which has allowed contaminated marijuana products to reach the market.[312] As a result, the states themselves are blurring the lines between "legal" and illegal marijuana, by allowing "legal" operators to skirt regulation. Licensed marijuana retailers are not incentivized to comply with the law, and they benefit from that leeway while continuing to point fingers at the black market when problems arise.

Illicit activity has proliferated with marijuana legalization, much of it tied to "state-legal" marijuana. Many pro-marijuana figures have suggested the black market causes problems because other states have not legalized marijuana. This is not true. The unfettered black market will always be able to undercut the "legal" market.

The unchecked proliferation of the marijuana industry has abetted some of these significant problems. The market saturation and overproduction permitted and written into law by "marijuana-legal" states have caused tremendous problems for regulators and law enforcement. It is estimated that Oregon has a production capacity of approximately

2 million pounds, well over the estimated consumption capacity of the state, which is approximately 275,000 pounds.[313] A 2019 audit by Oregon's Secretary of State found that the volume of marijuana produced in Oregon is nearly 7 times its local consumption.[314] Adding to this issue, the same Oregon audit found that black market marijuana fetches prices several times higher than "legal" marijuana. As the U.S. Attorney in Oregon reported in 2018, the state has "an identifiable and formidable marijuana overproduction and diversion problem."[315] Still, marijuana proponents in numerous states seek faster license approvals and more marijuana licenses.[316]

In California, according to recent reports, the black market outsells the "legal" marijuana market at a rate of three to one. These illicit sellers have brazenly set up shop in cities across the state, hiding in plain sight and giving way to a perpetual game of "Whac-a-mole," as one law enforcement officer described it. These companies also advertise on the popular marijuana website, Weedmaps, blending in with "legal" sellers. When the state warned Weedmaps to stop permitting illegal operators to advertise, CEO Chris Beals complained that the problem was not his company's fault but rather a result of the state prohibiting more retail marijuana licenses.[317]

In "legal" states, illegal grow operations have easily blended their production facilities with "legal" ones and have taken advantage of rural cover to hide from law enforcement. Okanogan (WA) County Chief Criminal Deputy Steve Brown told NPR reporters that prior to legalization, operations of the kind he continues to uncover were "hidden up in the hills." Now he finds some just off of roads, within sight of neighbors. Other investigations have uncovered illegal operations run by people who were licensed in other "marijuana-legal" states.[318]

In a 60 Minutes story on marijuana in California, Sheriff Tom Allman took reporter Sharyn Alfonsi in a helicopter to survey a very obvious illegal grow site in "the emerald triangle"—an area of California known for marijuana. He was not surprised that the operation wasn't hidden. "Allman explained since Prop 64 and the legalization of marijuana, the black market suppliers try to blend in with legal pot farmers sometimes on the same property."[319]

Another major promise of marijuana proponents was that a "legal" market would eliminate black market weed and allow law enforcement officials to focus on other things. Allman laughed at the idea and told Alfonsi that he was "looking forward to that day."[320] The very creation of the "legal" marijuana market in California has ushered a more powerful illicit market that had never existed before. What's more, Allman believes that his department lacks resources to combat the illegal operations. He estimates that it only has the capacity to handle 10 percent of the illegal grows.

Local illicit actors are not the only beneficiaries of "legal" marijuana. The proliferation of black market marijuana bolsters the businesses of well-financed international cartels, which extend as far north as Alaska.[321] The DEA found that Asian DTOs [drug trafficking organizations] were operating grow facilities across the state of Washington.[322] Cartel presence in California has only expanded since legalization. In California, authorities suspect—based on phone records and wire transfer activity, as well as figurines commonly associated with cartels, such as those depicting Jesús Malverde—that illegal marijuana activity is tied to the Sinaloa and La Familia Michoacana cartels.[323] In 2018, the Oregon-Idaho High Intensity Drug Trafficking task force identified 58 DTOs with foreign as well as domestic connections. Between January and April of 2019, the Oregon-Idaho High Intensity Drug Trafficking Area task force identified 13 new DTOs.[324]

The Drug Enforcement Administration concluded in their National Drug Threat Assessment, published in early 2020: "Domestic production and trafficking of marijuana will likely increase as more states adopt or change current marijuana laws to establish medical or recreational marijuana markets, allowing criminals to exploit state legality."[325] "Legal" marijuana continues to boost the black market.

Final highlights:

- The DEA's marijuana-dedicated task force, the Domestic Cannabis Eradication/Suppression Program (DCE/SP), eradicated over 4 million marijuana plants from illegal indoor and outdoor grow operations in 2019. The DCE/SP exclusively targets DTOs in its operations.[326]
- In 2018, 174 marijuana extraction labs (used to manufacture BHO) were uncovered, with 57 percent found in California, 26 percent in Oregon, and 35 percent of those labs listed at residential locations—posing an enormous threat to public safety.[327]
- In 2018 in Colorado, there were 257 completed investigations into illicit marijuana activity, up from 144 in the previous year, with 192 felony arrests made.[328]
- The U.S. Postal Service intercepted 1,009 parcels containing marijuana mailed from Colorado to another state in 2017 alone.[329]
- Around three quarters of parcels interdicted by the Oregon-Idaho task force between 2016 to 2018 were marijuana-related.[330]
- In Alaska in 2017, the DEA seized 20.2 kilograms worth of illegal marijuana. Marijuana seizures ranked second among types of drug seized by amount in kilograms.[331]
- Law enforcement officers in California seized over $1.5 billion worth of illegally grown marijuana. Raids yielded over 950,000 plants from around 350 different sites; 150 people were arrested in connection with these raids.[332]
- In 2019, Massachusetts authorities arrested two brothers in connection with a multistate marijuana trafficking and money laundering scheme. Officers seized five cars, 100 pounds of illegal marijuana, over $300,000 in cash, and over $27,000 in casino chips, prepaid gift cards, jewelry, and drug ledgers.[333]
- In California, 7,200 marijuana vape cartridges were seized in a single bust of a warehouse tied to state-licensed Kushy Brands.[334]
- In early 2019, federal and local authorities teamed up in Colorado to bust what U.S. Attorney Jason Dunn deemed the largest marijuana drug enforcement action in the state, with 42 search warrants served and 80,000 plants and $2.1 million in cash seized in connection with the operation.[335]

Environmental Impact

Conversations regarding the legalization of marijuana have largely ignored the threat that the industry poses to the environment. Given the lack of data, it is difficult to predict the full extent of marijuana's impact. However, early indications point to damaging consequences.

The environment is at risk of pollution from both "legal" and illegal marijuana operations. Regulatory standards are lacking and enforcement is low. The lack of clarity in regulation has blurred the line between "legal" and illegal marijuana cultivation practices. Furthermore, limited resources have prevented law enforcement officials from investigating illegal grow sites—which are well disguised on state and federally protected land. In 2017 alone, for example, 80,826 plants were seized from Colorado public lands, compared to 4,980 plants seized in 2013.[336]

Surrounding communities and ecosystems are at stake. Marijuana facilities on federal land in California are estimated to contain up to 731,000 pounds of solid fertilizer, 491,000 ounces of liquid fertilizer, and 200,000 pounds of toxic pesticides.[337] These chemicals threaten the surrounding environment and have devastated local animal species. An illegal rodent poison has been associated with a rise in instances of death of the northern spotted owl, a threatened species native to the Northwest.[338]

In California, officials estimate that 70 percent of the illegal market is cultivated on public lands. According to one investigative report, 9 out of every 10 illegal marijuana farms raided in 2018 contained traces of carbofuran, an extremely toxic and banned chemical. From 2012 to 2017, six times as many chemicals have been found at these operations. "These places are toxic garbage dumps. Food containers attract wildlife, and the chemicals kill the animals long after the sites are abandoned," said Rich McIntyre, director of the Cannabis Removal on Public Lands (CROP) Project, which is dedicated to restoring lands devastated by criminal grow sites on state and federal property in California.[339] "We think there's a public health time bomb ticking," 60 percent of California's water comes from national forest land. The reclamation of such illegal grow sites costs an average of $40,000 per site.[340]

As marijuana legalization expands, so does the illicit market and the threat it poses to the environment. But illegal marijuana is not the only culprit. Marijuana cultivation uses a significant amount of power. The indoor cultivation of one kilogram of marijuana requires 5.2 megawatt hours of electricity and releases 4.5 metric tons of carbon dioxide emissions, comparable to that of a passenger car in one year.[341] Marijuana production is nearly four times more energy intensive than coal or oil production.[342]

A 2015 study on the impact of marijuana cultivation on watersheds in California found that individual marijuana plants require 22.7 liters of water—daily. Production facilities range in daily water demand from 523,144 liters to 724,016 liters.[343]

Additional studies have further highlighted the need for a better understanding of the consequences of marijuana farming. A 2016 study focused on marijuana production in Humboldt County, California, found that 68 percent of the grow sites were less than 500 meters from developed roads, introducing a risk of landscape fragmentation; that 22 percent of grows were on steep slopes, posing a risk for erosion, sedimentation, and landslide; and that 5 percent were less than 100 meters from threatened fish habitats.[344] A subsequent study found that marijuana farming has drastic impacts on its surrounding environment, an important observation as the industry seeks to expand.[345]

From 2012–2016, the number of marijuana farms in Northern California increased 58 percent and the total area under cultivation expanded 91 percent. Expansion of these farms occurred in locations of extreme environmental sensitivity. However, budgetary accommodations for regulating marijuana farm expansion were relatively low compared with other regulatory programs.[346]

Legalization has thus far resulted in extreme environmental damage, and the consequences may not be fully understood in time to prevent worse outcomes, as the industry expands.

Localities Opt-Out on Retail Marijuana

Though marijuana legalization has passed through ballots in several states, the picture at the local level is very different. The perception that legalization is welcomed by the citizens of marijuana-friendly states is not accurate.

Proposition 64, the marijuana ballot measure in California, received just over 57 percent of the vote when it appeared on the ballot in 2016. Yet 80 percent of California localities have denied marijuana businesses from setting up shop.[347] This means that the approximately 630 stores licensed by the state are concentrated within 20 percent of the towns and cities.

What's more, licensed operators have expressed frustration with the restrictive policies of the localities, prompting one legislator to craft a law that would require towns that opted out to permit at least one marijuana business for every four bars or restaurants. According to a Los Angeles Times report, that would result in nearly 2,200 new marijuana shops across the state.[348] The legislation runs counter to what the citizenry was promised in the ballot initiative.

The shocking discrepancy has been replicated across the country. When it comes to ballot measures regarding legalized marijuana, voters may think pot is not a big deal. The picture changes when legalization hits home. Voters choose to opt-out on marijuana in their communities in large numbers. This raises questions about the political process of legalization.

In Michigan, where recreational marijuana sales began in December 2019, more than 1,400 of Michigan's 1,773 municipalities opted out of recreational marijuana—with 40 of 83 counties reporting none of their municipalities allowing the sale of medical marijuana.[349] That amounts to around 79 percent of the state's municipalities opting out of marijuana. Detroit voted to extend its ban on marijuana sales through at least March 31, 2020.[350]

In Colorado, another state known to be marijuana-friendly, 64 percent of jurisdictions banned both recreational and medical marijuana sales.[351] As a result, nearly 59 percent of licensed medical and recreational marijuana locations are concentrated in four counties: Denver (345), El Paso (125), Boulder (68), and Pueblo (58).[352]

Over 60 percent of municipalities and counties in Oregon have opted out of marijuana sales. Though some of those jurisdictions voted after shops set up in their cities, no new marijuana retail stores are permitted. As such, 50 percent of Oregon dispensaries are concentrated in three counties, with a whopping 196 of the total 666 dispensaries located in the county of Multnomah.[353]

In Illinois, similar debates are raging, with more community mobilization than many legislators and community organizers have ever seen, according to a report by the Chicago Tribune.[354] The wave of anti-marijuana sentiment surprised some, since the measure passed fairly easily in the state legislature. That being said, an investigative report by Illinois-based newspapers found that—from January 2017 to spring 2019—marijuana companies, executives, and lobbyists donated over $630,000 to various politicians in the state.[355]

While it may pay to gain the favor of legislators, localities are far less certain about "legal" marijuana taking over their hometowns.

Recommendations

Policy makers and the public need real-time data both on the consequences of legalization and related monetary costs. Meanwhile, we should pause future legalization efforts and implement public health measures such as potency caps in places that have legalized the drug. In addition, the industry's influence on policy should be significantly curtailed. SAM recommends that research efforts and data collection focus on the following categories:

- Emergency room and hospital admissions related to marijuana.
- Marijuana potency and price trends in the "legal" and illegal markets.
- School incidents related to marijuana, including studies involving representative datasets.
- Extent of marijuana advertising toward youth and its impact.
- Marijuana-related car crashes, including THC levels even when testing positive for alcohol.

- Mental health effects of marijuana.
- Admissions to treatment and counseling intervention programs.
- Cost of implementing legalization from law enforcement to regulation.
- Cost of mental health and addiction treatment related to increased marijuana use.
- Cost of needing, but not receiving, treatment.
- Effect on the market for alcohol and other drugs.
- Cost to workplace and employers, including impact on employee productivity.
- Effect on minority communities, including arrests, placement of marijuana establishments, and quality of life indicators.
- Effect on the environment, including water and power usage.

Notes

Prologue: Exposed

1 National Academies of Sciences, Engineering, and Medicine, *The Health Effects of Cannabis and Cannabinoids: The Current State of Evidence and Recommendations for Research* (Washington, DC: The National Academies Press), 2017, https://doi.org/10.17226/24625.

2 National Academies of Sciences, Engineering, and Medicine.

3 "Suicide Prevention," Colorado Department of Public Health and Environment, accessed December 28, 2020, http://cdphe.colorado.gov/health/prevention-and-wellness/office-of-suicide-prevention.

4 Mike Kelly, "Ronald Rice's Lonely Quest to Block Legal Pot," The Record, NorthJersey, March 15, 2019, https://www.northjersey.com/story/news/columnists/mike-kelly/2019/03/15/nj-legal-weed-ronald-rices-lonely-quest-block-pot-kelly/3163204002/.

5 Star-Ledger Guest Columnist, "Sen. Rice: Legalizing Pot Won't Stop Social Injustice in the Black and Brown Community," Nj.com, October 22, 2019, https://www.nj.com/opinion/2019/10/sen-rice-legalizing-pot-wont-stop-social-injustice-in-the-black-and-brown-community.html.

6 Ronald L. Rice, "Legal Weed: A Money Grab, a Hustle and Pure Trickery," The Record, NorthJersey, September 23, 2019, https://www.northjersey.com/story/opinion/2019/09/23/opinion-legal-weed-money-grab-hustle-and-trickery/2385533001/.

7 Teresa Haley, "Legalizing Weed Won't Eliminate Risk of Discrimination: People of Color Still Will Be Disproportionately Targeted and Lose Their Jobs or Places

to Live," Chicagobusiness.com, November 25, 2019, https://www.chicagobusiness.com/forum-ideas-cannabis/legalizing-weed-wont-eliminate-risk-discrimination; Steven Spearie, "State NAACP Opposed to Recreational Marijuana," State Journal-Register, March 22, 2019, https://www.sj-r.com/news/20190322/state-naacp-opposed-to-recreational-marijuana.

Chapter One: Taking on Goliath

8 Elizabeth Williamson, "John Boehner: From Speaker of the House to Cannabis Pitchman," *New York Times*, June 3, 2019, https://www.nytimes.com/2019/06/03/us/politics/john-boehner-marijuana-cannabis.html.

9 Mark Kleiman, "The Marijuana Movement and the Marijuana Lobby," Samefacts.com, September 30, 2015, https://www.samefacts.com/52714/.

10 Substance Abuse and Mental Health Data Archive, Samhsa.gov, accessed December 28, 2020, https://datafiles.samhsa.gov/.

11 Howard S. Kim and Andrew A. Monte, "Colorado Cannabis Legalization and Its Effect on Emergency Care," *Annals of Emergency Medicine* 68, no. 1 (2016): 71–75; "Recreational Marijuana and Collision Claim Frequencies," Highway Loss Data Institute Bulletin (35), no. 8 (April 2018), https://www.iihs.org/media/e0028841-76ee-4315-a628-32a704258980/gmJeDw/HLDI%20Research/Bulletins/hldi_bulletin_35-08.pdf.

12 Michael T. Lynskey et al., "Major Depressive Disorder, Suicidal Ideation, and Suicide Attempt in Twins Discordant for Cannabis Dependence and Early-Onset Cannabis Use," National Library of Medicine, *Archives of General Psychiatry* 61, no. 10 (October 2004): 1026–1032, https://pubmed.ncbi.nlm.nih.gov/15466676/.

13 Marta Di Forti et al., "The Contribution of Cannabis Use to Variation in the Incidence of Psychotic Disorder across Europe (EU-GEI): A Multicentre Case-Control Study," *The Lancet Psychiatry* 6 (May 2019): 427–436, https://www.thelancet.com/journals/lanpsy/article/PIIS2215-0366(19)30048-3/fulltext.

14 "Cannabis' Pharma Futuremaker," Emblem Cannabis, January 4, 2018, https://emblemcannabis.com/cannabis-pharma-futuremaker/.

15 Dana Gentry, "Weed Whistleblower Turns to FBI," *Nevada Current*, January 14, 2020, https://www.nevadacurrent.com/2020/01/14/weed-whistleblower-turns-to-fbi/.

Chapter Three: Forces behind the Revolution

16 Rachel Ann Barry et al., "Waiting for the Opportune Moment: The Tobacco Industry and Marijuana Legalization: The Tobacco Industry and Marijuana Legalization," *The Milbank Quarterly* 92, no. 2 (June 2014), 207–242, https://www.milbank.org/quarterly/articles/waiting-for-the-opportune-moment-the-tobacco-industry-and-marijuana-legalization/.

17 Leonid Bershidsky, "Big Tobacco's Future: Big Pot: As Marijuana Gradually Becomes a Legal Drug, Big Tobacco Is Preparing to Dominate the Market,"

Bloomberg, February 20, 2015, http://www.bloombergview.com/articles/2015-02-20/big-tobacco-s-future-big-pot.

18 "MPP Chief Ready to Barter for Marijuana Campaign Donations," *Marijuana Business Daily*, April 28, 2017, https://mjbizdaily.com/mpp-chief-ready-barter-marijuana-campaign-donations/.

19 "Value for Money Audit: Alcohol and Gaming Commission of Ontario," Office of the Auditor General of Ontario, auditor.on.ca, December 2020, https://www.auditor.on.ca/en/content/annualreports/arreports/en20/20VFM_01AGCO.pdf.

20 Ben Schreckinger and Mona Zhang, "Lavish Parties, Greedy Pols and Panic Rooms: How the 'Apple of Pot' Collapsed," Politico.com, May 24, 2020, https://www.politico.com/news/magazine/2020/05/24/up-in-smoke-marijuana-med-men-249301.

21 Michelle L. Price, "Former Exec Says MedMen Made Illegal Campaign Donations to Sisolak; State Investigating," *Reno Gazette Journal*, May 28, 2020, https://www.rgj.com/story/news/2020/05/28/former-exec-says-medmen-made-illegal-campaign-donations-sisolak/5279317002/>.

22 Chad Sokol, "State Marijuana Regulators Fire Employee Who Leased Deer Park Land for Growing Operation," *The Spokesman-Review*, updated June 2, 2017, https://www.spokesman.com/stories/2017/jun/02/state-marijuana-regulators-fire-employee-who-lease/. Accessed 28 Dec. 2020.

23 Jeff Coen et al., "Illinois Marijuana Growers Spent about $600,000 on Political Giving Leading to the Pot Legalization Vote. Here's Where the Money Went," *Chicago Tribune*, August 2, 2019, https://www.chicagotribune.com/news/ct-marijuana-legalize-illinois-politics-campaign-funds-20190802-lfzjgrn5vnahdlbabfenuukpmi-story.html; Tina Sfondeles, "Pot Bill Sponsor Sees No Conflict in Spouse's New Job." *Chicago Sun-Times*, July 31, 2019, https://chicago.suntimes.com/cannabis/2019/7/31/20747754/marijuana-spouse-llinois-pot-bill-sponsor-kelly-cassidy-candace-gingrich-job-cannabis-revolution.

Chapter Four: Facts Matter, Money Talks

24 Elizabeth Stuyt, "The Problem with the Current High Potency THC Marijuana from the Perspective of an Addiction Psychiatrist," *Missouri Medicine* 115, no. 6 (November–December 2018): 482–486, https://www.ncbi.nlm.nih.gov/pmc/articles/PMC6312155/.

25 "National Survey on Drug Use and Health (NSDUH)," Substance Abuse and Mental Health Services Administration, accessed December 28, 2020, https://www.samhsa.gov/data/population-data-nsduh.

26 Deborah S. Hasin et al., "Prevalence of Marijuana Use Disorders in the United States between 2001–2002 and 2012–2013," *JAMA Psychiatry* 72, no. 12 (December 2015): 1235–1242, https://jamanetwork.com/journals/jamapsychiatry/fullarticle/2464591.

27 "Reports and Summaries," Colorado Department of Public Health and Environment (Monitoring Health Concerns Related to Marijuana), accessed December 28, 2020,

https://marijuanahealthinfo.colorado.gov/summary.

28 Andrew Gross, "Fatal Crashes Involving Drivers Who Test Positive for Marijuana Increase after State Legalizes Drug," AAA Newsroom, January 30, 2020, https://newsroom.aaa.com/2020/01/fatal-crashes-involving-drivers-who-test-positive-for-marijuana-increase-after-state-legalizes-drug/.

29 Archie Bleyer and Brian Barnes, "Opioid Death Rate Acceleration in Jurisdictions Legalizing Marijuana Use," *JAMA Internal Medicine* 178, no. 9 (September 2018): 1280–1281.

30 Tess L. Crume et al., "Cannabis Use During the Perinatal Period in a State with Legalized Recreational and Medical Marijuana: The Association between Maternal Characteristics, Breastfeeding Patterns, and Neonatal Outcomes," *Journal of Pediatrics* 197, (June 2018): 90–96, https://pubmed.ncbi.nlm.nih.gov/29605394/.

31 National Academies of Sciences, Engineering, and Medicine. *The Health Effects of Cannabis and Cannabinoids: The Current State of Evidence and Recommendations for Research* (Washington, DC: The National Academies Press), 2017, https://doi.org/10.17226/24625.

32 "Drug Testing IndexTM: Overall Positivity Rate in 2019," Quest Diagnostics, dtidrugmap.com, accessed December 28, 2020, http://www.dtidrugmap.com.

33 Gene Balk, "1 in 4 Marijuana Users Get High at Work in States with Legal Weed, Survey Says," *Seattle Times*, March 13, 2019, https://www.seattletimes.com/seattle-news/data/1-in-4-marijuana-users-with-a-job-get-stoned-at-work-survey-says/. Accessed 28 Dec. 2020.

34 Chloe Sorvino, "An inside Look at the Biggest Drug Reformer in the Country: George Soros," *Forbes* magazine, October 2, 2014, https://www.forbes.com/sites/chloesorvino/2014/10/02/an-inside-look-at-the-biggest-drug-reformer-in-the-country-george-soros/?sh=48a34ea81e29.

35 Jonathan Gornall, "Big Tobacco, the New Politics, and the Threat to Public Health," *BMJ* (Clinical Research Ed.) 365, (May 2019): l2164, https://www.bmj.com/content/365/bmj.l2164.

Chapter Five: A Mother's Job

36 Samuel T. Wilkinson et al., "Marijuana Use Is Associated with Worse Outcomes in Symptom Severity and Violent Behavior in Patients with Posttraumatic Stress Disorder," *Journal of Clinical Psychiatry* 76, no. 9 (September 2015): 1174–1180.

Chapter Seven: What's Been Unleashed

37 Liz Braun, "UN Ambassador Bob Rae Reveals He Has Invested in Pot Industry," *Strathroy Age Dispatch*, November 30, 2020, https://www.strathroyagedispatch.com/news/local-news/un-ambassador-bob-rae-buys-into-canadas-unique-position/wcm/c03e7fd9-6266-4e3b-81c2-ccb1d9414044. Accessed 28 Dec. 2020.

38 "58% of Mexicans Oppose Legalization of Marijuana: Poll," Mexico

News Daily, November 24, 2020, https://mexiconewsdaily.com/news/58-of-mexicans-oppose-legalization-of-marijuana-poll/.

Chapter Nine: Perpetuating Social Injustice

39 Ronald L. Rice, "Legal Weed: A Money Grab, a Hustle and Pure Trickery," The Record, NorthJersey, September 23, 2019, https://www.northjersey.com/story/opinion/2019/09/23/opinion-legal-weed-money-grab-hustle-and-trickery/2385533001/.

40 "Off-Premises Liquor Stores Targeted to Poor Urban Blacks," Johns Hopkins Bloomberg School of Public Health, January 6, 2000, https://www.jhsph.edu/news/news-releases/2000/alcohol-off-premises.html.

41 "Persons Arrested," FBI.gov: 2017 Crime in the United States, accessed December 28, 2020, https://ucr.fbi.gov/crime-in-the-u.s/2017/crime-in-the-u.s.-2017/topic-pages/persons-arrested; Nina Mulia et al., "Social Disadvantage, Stress, and Alcohol Use among Black, Hispanic, and White Americans: Findings from the 2005 U.S. National Alcohol Survey," *Journal of Studies on Alcohol and Drugs* 69, no. 6 (November 2008): 824–833, https://pubmed.ncbi.nlm.nih.gov/18925340/.

42 "Industry Documents Library," ucsf.edu, accessed December 29, 2020, https://www.industrydocuments.ucsf.edu/docs/qhhb0039.

43 Thomas R. Kirchner et al., "Tobacco Retail Outlet Advertising Practices and Proximity to Schools, Parks and Public Housing Affect Synar Underage Sales Violations in Washington, DC," *Tobacco Control* 24, no. e1 (2015): e52-8, https://tobaccocontrol.bmj.com/content/24/e1/e52.

44 Hannah Knowles and Laurie McGinley, "As Trump Tackles Vapes, African Americans Feel Stung by Inaction on Menthol Cigarettes," *Washington Post*, November 1, 2019, https://www.washingtonpost.com/national/health-science/as-trump-tackles-vapes-african-americans-feel-stung-by-inaction-on-menthol-cigarettes/2019/10/31/d06e93d2-e6ec-11e9-a331-2df12d56a80b_story.html.

45 "Cigarette Smoking and Tobacco Use among People of Low Socioeconomic Status," Centers for Disease Control and Prevention, March 2, 2020, https://www.cdc.gov/tobacco/disparities/low-ses/index.htm.

46 Mark Kleiman, "The arithmetic of drinking," Samefacts.com, July 13, 2003, http://www.samefacts.com/2003/07/health-and-medicine/medicare-health-and-medicine/the-arithmetic-of-drinking.

47 Kurt Kleiner, "Pleasure or Addiction?: The Reason Why Cigarette Companies Change the Levels of Nicotine in Tobacco Is at the Heart of an Investigation That Could See Smoking Banned in the US Once and for All," New Scientist, April 9, 1994, https://www.newscientist.com/article/mg14219202-200/.

48 Ronald L. Rice, "Legal Weed: A Money Grab, a Hustle and Pure Trickery," The Record, NorthJersey, September 23, 2019, https://www.northjersey.com/story/opinion/2019/09/23/

opinion-legal-weed-money-grab-hustle-and-trickery/2385533001/.

49 "Marijuana Activist Ed 'NJWeedman' Forchion Wages His Own War on Drugs, Holds Press Conference Announcing Federal Lawsuit against New Jersey Governor Phil Murphy," Morningstar.com, November 19, 2020, https://www.morningstar.com/news/pr-newswire/20201119ph97845/marijuana-activist-ed-njweedman-forchion-wages-his-own-war-on-drugs-holds-press-conference-announcing-federal-lawsuit-against-new-jersey-governor-phil-murphy.

50 David Migoya and Ricardo Baca, "Denver's Pot Businesses Mostly in Low-Income, Minority Neighborhoods," *Denver Post*, January 2, 2016, https://www.denverpost.com/2016/01/02/denvers-pot-businesses-mostly-in-low-income-minority-neighborhoods/.

51 Eli McVey, "Chart: Percentage of Cannabis Business Owners and Founders by Race," *Marijuana Business Daily*, September 11, 2017, https://mjbizdaily.com/chart-19-cannabis-businesses-owned-founded-racial-minorities.

52 Jennifer Peltz, "A Look at Efforts to Make Legal Pot Foster Social Justice," Associated Press, May 19, 2019, https://apnews.com/article/4940124fc72e40b28609e4634068317a.

53 "A Tale of Two Countries: Racially Targeted Arrests in the Era of Marijuana Reform," ACLU Research Report, aclu.org, accessed December 28, 2020, https://www.aclu.org/report/tale-two-countries-racially-targeted-arrests-era-marijuana-reform.

54 "Prison Population in AK, CO, DC, OR, and WA Since Legalization," learnaboutsam.org, accessed December 28, 2020, https://learnaboutsam.org/state-prison-populations.

55 Caislin Firth and Beatriz H. Carlini, "Cannabis Legalization and Racial Disparities in Washington State," Alcohol & Drug Abuse Institute, University of Washington, March 2019, http://adai.uw.edu/pubs/pdf/2019racialdisparities.pdf.

Chapter Ten: A Red Herring

56 Rachel Ann Barry et al., "Waiting for the Opportune Moment: The Tobacco Industry and Marijuana Legalization," *Millbank Quarterly* 92, no. 2 (June 2014): 207-242, https://www.milbank.org/quarterly/articles/waiting-for-the-opportune-moment-the-tobacco-industry-and-marijuana-legalization/.

57 Rachel Ann Barry et al., "Waiting for the Opportune Moment: The Tobacco Industry and Marijuana Legalization," *Millbank Quarterly* 92, no. 2 (June 2014): 207-242, https://www.milbank.org/quarterly/articles/waiting-for-the-opportune-moment-the-tobacco-industry-and-marijuana-legalization/.

58 The Emory Wheel, "NORML Chairman Keith Stroup Talks on Pot Issues," February 6, 1979, 19.

Chapter Eleven: Inconvenient Truths

59 Tom Huddleston Jr., "Pot Nation Gains New Territory, but Cashing in Requires Patience," Fortune, March 2, 2015, https://fortune.com/2015/03/02/

marijuana-alaska-dc-entrepreneurs.
60 Kenneth W. Boyd, "Deep Dive: Recreational Marijuana Tax Revenue in the United States, Alaska Marijuana Tax Revenue," ais-cpa.com, accessed December 28, 2020, https://www.ais-cpa.com/deep-dive-recreational-marijuana-tax-revenue-in-the-united-states/#Alaska_Marijuana_Tax_Revenue.
61 Dominic Holden, "WA Pot Initiative Could Generate $1.9 Billion in Revenue over Five Years," *The Stranger* (blog), August 10, 2012, https://www.thestranger.com/slog/archives/2012/08/10/i-502-could-generate-19-billion-in-state-revenue-over-five-years.
62 Jan Conway, "Excise Tax Revenue of Cannabis in Washington State, United States from 2015 to 2018," Statista.com, October 21, 2020, https://www.statista.com/statistics/731917/us-washington-state-marijuana-sales-taxes.
63 Kenn Finn and Rochelle Salmore, "The Hidden Costs of Marijuana Use in Colorado: One Emergency Department's Experience," *Journal of Global Drug Policy and Practice* 10, no. 2 (Summer 2016), https://www.researchgate.net/publication/314140400_The_Hidden_Costs_of_Marijuana_Use_in_Colorado_One_Emergency_Department's_Experience.
64 Andrew Gross, "Fatal Crashes Involving Drivers Who Test Positive for Marijuana Increase after State Legalizes Drug," AAA Newsroom, January 30, 2020, https://newsroom.aaa.com/2020/01/fatal-crashes-involving-drivers-who-test-positive-for-marijuana-increase-after-state-legalizes-drug/.
65 NYU Langone Health / NYU School of Medicine, "In States Where Recreational Marijuana is Legal, Problematic Use Increased Among Adults and Teens," ScienceDaily, November 13, 2019, www.sciencedaily.com/releases/2019/11/191113153049.htm.
66 "Patient Discharge and Emergency Department Data, 2017–2019," Office of Statewide Health Planning and Development, California, https://oshpd.ca.gov/data-and-reports/.
67 Kirk Mitchell, "Crime Rate in Colorado Increases Much Faster than Rest of the Country," *Denver Post*, July 11, 2017, https://www.denverpost.com/2017/07/11/colorado-sees-big-increase-crime-10-percent-higher-murder-rate/.
68 U.S. Department of Justice, Federal Bureau of Investigation, "Uniform Crime Reporting Handbook," 2004, https://ucr.fbi.gov/additional-ucr-publications/ucr_handbook.pdf/.
69 "Workforce Drug Testing Positivity Climbed to Highest Rate in 16 Years, New Quest Diagnostics Drug Testing IndexTM Analysis Finds," Quest Diagnostics, August 25, 2020, https://www.questdiagnostics.com/home/physicians/health-trends/drug-testing.
70 "2019 AHAR: Part 1—PIT Estimates of Homelessness in the U.S," Hud Exchange, January 2020, https://www.hudexchange.info/resource/5948/2019-ahar-part-1-pit-estimates-of-homelessness-in-the-us/.
71 "The Health and Social Effects of Nonmedical Cannabis Use," World Health

Organization, 2016, https://www.who.int/substance_abuse/publications/cannabis_report/en.

72 National Academies of Sciences, Engineering, and Medicine, *The Health Effects of Cannabis and Cannabinoids: The Current State of Evidence and Recommendations for Research* (Washington, DC: The National Academies Press), 2017, https://doi.org/10.17226/24625.

73 Archie Bleyer and Brian Barnes, "Opioid Death Rate Acceleration in Jurisdictions Legalizing Marijuana Use," *JAMA Internal Medicine* 178, no. 9 (September 2018): 1280–1281.

74 Gabrielle Campbell et al., "Effect of Cannabis Used in People with Chronic Non-Cancer Pain Prescribed Opioids: Findings from a 4-year Prospective Cohort Study," *Lancet Public Health* 3, no. e341 (July 2018), https://pubmed.ncbi.nlm.nih.gov/29976328/.

75 Betsy Dickson et al., "Recommendations from Cannabis Dispensaries about First-Trimester Cannabis Use," *Obstetrics and Gynecology* 131, no. 6 (June 2018): 1031–1038, https://pubmed.ncbi.nlm.nih.gov/29742676/.

76 "User Clip: Surgeon General on Marijuana," c-span.org, July 27, 2017, https://www.c-span.org/video/?c4678317/user-clip-surgeon-general-marijuana.

Chapter Twelve: Training for the Olympics

77 "July 2020 Public Meeting Packet," Cannabis Control Commission, Commonwealth of Massachusetts, accessed December 28, 2020, http://mass-cannabis-control.com/wp-content/uploads/july-2020-public-meeting-packet.pdf.

78 Bart Schaneman, "Proposed Pesticide, Heavy-Metal Testing Rules in Washington State Roil Marijuana Cultivators," *Marijuana Business Daily*, November 30, 2020, https://mjbizdaily.com/proposed-pesticide-heavy-metal-testing-rules-in-washington-state-roil-marijuana-cultivators.

Chapter Fourteen: Public Health Crisis

79 "Outbreak of Lung Injury Associated with E-cigarette Use, or Vaping," Centers for Disease Control and Prevention, February 25, 2020, https://www.cdc.gov/tobacco/basic_information/e-cigarettes/severe-lung-disease.html.

80 Gillian Flaccus, "Another Death Is Linked to Vaping, the 1st Tied to a Pot Shop," *USA Today*, September 5, 2019, https://www.usatoday.com/story/news/health/2019/09/05/vaping-death-oregon-man-dies-thc-vape-dispensary/2218501001/; Andrew Selsky, "2nd Death in Oregon from Vaping-related Illness, *Seattle Times*, September 26, 2019, https://www.seattletimes.com/seattle-news/health/2nd-oregonian-dies-from-vaping-related-illness/; WKRN, "Minnesota Native Identified as Tennessee's First Vaping-related Death," WKRN.com, October 17, 2019, https://www.wkrn.com/news/local-news/minnesota-man-identified-as-tennessees-first-vaping-related-death/.

81 Sascha Ellington et al., "Update: Product, Substance-Use, and Demographic Characteristics of Hospitalized Patients in a Nationwide Outbreak of E-cigarette, or Vaping, Product Use–Associated Lung Injury—United States, August 2019–January 2020," *Morbidity and Mortality Weekly Report* 69, no. 2 (January 2020): 44–49, DOI: http://dx.doi.org/10.15585/mmwr.mm6902e2.

82 Colton Grace, "Massachusetts Health Officials Confirm Vaping Illnesses Tied to 'Legal' Market Following SAM FOIA," Smart Approaches to Marijuana, December 17, 2019, https://learnaboutsam.org/massachusetts-health-officials-confirm-vaping-illnesses-tied-to-legal-market-following-sam-foia/.

83 Gus Burns, "Vitamin E–tainted Marijuana Vaping Cartridges Recalled in Michigan," Michigan Live, February 8, 2020, https://www.mlive.com/public-interest/2020/02/unclear-how-tainted-marijuana-vaping-cartridges-slipped-by-michigan-testing.html.

84 Gus Burns, "Michigan Marijuana Regulators Say They're Forbidden from Looking at Their Own Data," Michigan Live, January 28, 2020, https://www.mlive.com/public-interest/2020/01/michigan-marijuana-regulators-say-theyre-forbidden-from-looking-at-their-own-data.html.

Chapter Fifteen: An Intolerable Habit

85 UCSF Library Truth Initiative, Truth Tobacco Industry Documents, accessed January 6, 2021, https://www.industrydocuments.ucsf.edu/tobacco/.

86 Mikaela Conley, "Teen Drug Use Number One Health Problem: Study," ABC News, June 28, 2011, https://abcnews.go.com/Health/teen-drug-number-health-problem-america-study/story?id=13950339.

Chapter Seventeen: No Stopping for COVID

87 Thomas Mitchell, "Denver Pot Sales Jump 392 Percent During March 23 Shutdown Scare," Westword, March 29, 2020, https://www.westword.com/marijuana/denver-marijuana-sales-jump-392-percent-during-two-hour-shutdown-scare-11676288#:~:text=According%20to%20marijuana%20sales%20tracker,for%20a%20Monday%20in%202020.

88 Alexander Nieves, "California Cannabis Tax Revenues Explode During Pandemic," Politico.com, December 3, 2020.

Chapter Eighteen: Waging a Federal Fight

89 Vivian Wang and Nick Corasaniti, "Marijuana Legalization Hits a Wall: First in New Jersey, Then in New York," *New York Times*, May 13, 2019, https://www.nytimes.com/2019/05/13/nyregion/marijuana-legalization-ny-nj.html.

90 David Remnick, "Going the Distance: On and Off the Road with Barack Obama," *New Yorker*, January 20, 2014, https://www.newyorker.com/magazine/2014/01/27/going-the-distance-david-remnick.

91 Matt Spetalnick and Aileen Torres-Bennett, "Obama Tells Jamaicans to Go

Easy on the 'Ganja,'" Reuters, April 9, 2015, https://www.reuters.com/article/us-usa-caribbean-obama-idUSKBN0N02K520150409.

92 Liz Fields, "Obama Talks to VICE News about Climate Change, Marijuana Legalization, and the Islamic State." Vice.Com, March 16, 2015, https://www.vice.com/en/article/mbwmvq/obama-talks-to-vice-news-about-climate-change-marijuana-legalization-and-the-islamic-state.

93 Alexander Mooney, "Obama: Marijuana Is Not a Good Strategy to Spur Economy," CNN.com, March 26, 2009, https://politicalticker.blogs.cnn.com/2009/03/26/obama-marijuana-is-not-a-good-strategy-to-spur-economy/comment-page-12/?fbid=8WIXXRASUtq.

94 Barack Obama, *A Promised Land*, 1st edition (New York: Crown Publishing Group, 2020).

Chapter Nineteen: What More Is in Pandora's Box?

95 "A Guide to the Drug Legalization Movement," National Families in Action, accessed December 28, 2020, http://www.nationalfamilies.org/legalization/legalization_from_here.html.

96 Cynthia Cotts, "Smart Money," *Rolling Stone*, (May 5, 1994), 42-43.

97 Ethan Nadelmann, "Should We Legalize Drugs? History Answers Yes," *American Heritage*, (February-March 1993), 41-56.

98 Robb London, "Is the war on drugs succeeding?" (July 1, 2005), https://today.law.harvard.edu/feature/war-drugs-succeeding/).

99 Sasha Issenberg, "Ballot Measures Don't Tell Us Anything About What Voters Really Want," *Washington Post*, November 25, 2020, https://www.washingtonpost.com/outlook/referenda-ballot-measures-democrats/2020/11/25/d5984964-2e69-11eb-bae0-50bb17126614_story.html. "Vote No on Measure 110," *John Kitzhaber* (blog), October 18, 2020, https://blog.johnkitzhaber.com/vote-no-on-measure-110/.

100 "Vote No on Measure 110," *John Kitzhaber* (blog), October 18, 2020, https://blog.johnkitzhaber.com/vote-no-on-measure-110/.

101 "Behind Bars II: Substance Abuse and America's Prison Population," Partnership to End Addiction, February 2010, https://www.centeronaddiction.org/addiction-research/reports/behind-bars-ii-substance-abuse-and-america's-prison-population.

102 N. Fertig, P. Demko, and M. Zhang, "The Movement to Change Drug Laws for Psychedelics is Following the Pot Playbook," *Politico Pro's Morning Cannabis*, Politico.com, December 8, 2020.

103 Adam Owens et al., "Market Size and Demand for Marijuana in Colorado 2017 Market Update," Colorado Department of Revenue, released August 2018, https://www.colorado.gov/pacific/sites/default/files/MED%20Demand%20and%20Market%20%20Study%20%20082018.pdf.

Appendix: SAM Lessons Learned from State Legalization Impact Report

104 Controlled Substances Act, 21 U.S.C. § 801 et. seq., Pub.L. 91–513, 84 Stat. 1236, enacted October 27, 1970.

105 Alaska State Troopers, "Alaska State Troopers Annual Drug Report, 2016," https://dps.alaska.gov/getmedia/f259530b-5277-408e-9d45-4999958fe530/2016-Annual-Drug-Report-6-28-17final;.aspx; Darrin T. Grondel, Staci Hoff, and Dick Doane, "Marijuana Use, Alcohol Use, and Driving in Washington State," Washington Traffic Safety Commission, April 2018, http://wtsc.wa.gov/wp-content/uploads/dlm_uploads/2018/05/Marijuana-and-Alcohol-Involvement-in-Fatal-Crashes-in-WA_FINAL.pdf; Oregon-Idaho High Intensity Drug Trafficking Area, "Threat Assessment and Strategies," 2020, http://oridhidta.org/reports; Oregon Liquor Control Commission, "Marijuana Market Data," Oregon.gov, 2020, https://www.oregon.gov/olcc/marijuana/Documents/CTS/OregonCannabisTrackingSystemData.pdf; Oregon Public Health Division, "Marijuana report: Marijuana Use, Attitudes and Health Effects in Oregon," 2016, https://www.oregon.gov/oha/ph/PreventionWellness/marijuana/Documents/oha-8509-marijuana-report.pdf; Oregon State Police Drug Enforcement Section, "A Baseline Evaluation of Cannabis Enforcement Priorities in Oregon," 2017, https://mass-cannabis-control.com/wp-content/uploads/2017/12/A-Baseline-Evaluation-of-Cannabis-Enforcement-Priorities-in-Oregon_.pdf; Rocky Mountain High Intensity Drug Trafficking Area (RMHIDTA), "The Legalization of Marijuana in Colorado: The impact," 2019, https://rmhidta.org/files/D2DF/FINAL-Volume6.pdf; Washington Office of Financial Management, "Monitoring Impacts of Recreational Marijuana Legalization: 2019 Update Report," 2019, https://www.ofm.wa.gov/pubs-reports/monitoring-impacts-recreational-marijuana-legalization-2019-update-report.

106 Mary Catherine Cash et al., "Mapping Cannabis Potency in Medical and Recreational Programs in the United States," PLOS One, March 26, 2020, https://doi.org/10.1371/journal.pone.0230167

107 Office of the Surgeon General, "U.S. Surgeon General's Advisory: Marijuana Use and the Developing Brain," U.S. Department of Health & Human Services, August 29, 2019, https://www.hhs.gov/surgeongeneral/reports-and-publications/addiction-and-substance-misuse/advisory-on-marijuana-use-and-developing-brain/index.html.

108 John Cornyn and Dianne Feinstein, "Marijuana and America's Health: Questions and Issues for Policy Makers," U.S. Senate Caucus on International Narcotics Control (public hearing), 2019, https://www.youtube.com/watch?v=bYEgAyK-2W90&=&feature=youtu.be.

109 Cornyn and Feinstein, "Marijuana and America's Health."

110 "Surgeon General's Advisory on E-cigarette Use Among Youth," Centers for Disease Control and Prevention, April 9, 2019, https://www.cdc.gov/tobacco/basic_information/e-cigarettes/surgeon-general-advisory/index.html.

111 Oregon Liquor Control Commission, Colorado Dept. of Revenue, Washington Liquor

and Cannabis Board, Alaska Alcohol and Marijuana Control Office.

112 Colorado Department of Revenue, "MED licensed facilities," 2019, https://www.colorado.gov/pacific/enforcement/med-licensed-facilitiesmed-licensed-facilities

113 Suman Chandra et al., "New Trends in Cannabis Potency in USA and Europe During the Last Decade (2008–2017)," *European Archives of Psychiatry and Clinical Neuroscience* 269 (2019): 5–15, https://doi.org/10.1007/s00406-019-00983-5.

114 Mark A. Prince and Bradley T. Conner, "Examining Links Between Cannabis Potency and Mental and Physical Health Outcomes," *Behaviour Research and Therapy* 115 (2019): 111–120, https://doi.org/10.1016/j.brat.2018.11.008.

115 Francois R. Lamy et al., "'Those Edibles Hit Hard': Exploration of Twitter Data on Cannabis Edibles in the U.S," *Drug and Alcohol Dependence* 164 (2016): 64–70, https://doi.org/10.1016/j.drugalcdep.2016.04.029; Michael Peace et al., "Evaluation of Two Commercially Available Cannabidiol Formulations for Use in Electronic Cigarettes," *Frontiers in Pharmacology* 7 (2016), https://doi.org/10.3389/fphar.2016.00279; Dave Yates and Jessica Speer, "Over and Under-regulation in the Colorado Cannabis Industry: A Data-analytic Perspective," *International Journal of Drug Policy* 59 (2018): 63–66, https://doi.org/10.1016/j.drugpo.2018.06.001

116 Oregon Liquor Control Commission, "Marijuana Market Data," Oregon.gov, 2020, https://www.oregon.gov/olcc/marijuana/Documents/CTS/OregonCannabisTrackingSystemData.pdf.

117 Michael Peace et al., "Evaluation of Two Commercially Available Cannabidiol Formulations for Use in Electronic Cigarettes," *Frontiers in Pharmacology* 7 (2016), https://doi.org/10.3389/fphar.2016.00279.

118 Sean O'Connor and Sam Méndez, "Concerning Cannabis-infused Edibles: Factors that Attract Children to Foods," University of Washington School of Law, June 28, 2016, https://lcb.wa.gov/publications/Marijuana/Concerning-MJ-Infused-Edibles-Factors-That-Attract-Children.pdf.

119 John Ayers et al., "The Need for Federal Regulation of Marijuana Marketing," *JAMA* 321, no. 22 (2019): 2163–2164, https://doi.org/10.1001/jama.2019.4432; Kimber P. Richter and Sharon Levy, "Big Marijuana: Lessons from Big Tobacco," *New England Journal of Medicine* 371, no. 5 (2014): 399–401, https://doi.org/10.1056/NEJMp1406074.

120 Angelica LaVito and Lauren Hirsch, "Altria Looks to a Future Beyond Cigarettes but Investors Aren't Cheering its $15 Billion Bet," CNBC, December 21, 2018. https://www.cnbc.com/2018/12/20/juul-cronos-investments-could-diversify-altria-beyond-cigarettes.html.

121 Jessica Murphy, "Ex-Big Pharma Executive Behind OxyContin Sells Medical Marijuana," BBC News, Toronto, November 25, 2016, https://www.bbc.com/news/world-us-canada-38083737.

122 Carly Helfand, "Teva Inks Trailblazing Cannabis Pact with Israel's Syqe Medical," Fierce Pharma, November 28, 2016, https://www.fiercepharma.com/marketing/teva-inks-trailblazing-cannabis-pact-israel-s-syqe-medical.

123 RTT News, “TLRY Teams Up with Novartis, TLSA to Report Data in Q2, RARX Marches Ahead,” Nasdaq, December 18, 2018, https://www.nasdaq.com/articles/tlry-teams-novartis-tlsa-report-data-q2-rarx-marches-ahead-2018-12-18.

124 Michael Sheetz, “Corona Beer Maker Constellation Ups Bet on Cannabis with $4 Billion Investment in Canopy Growth,” CNBC, August 15, 2018, https://www.cnbc.com/2018/08/15/corona-maker-constellation-ups-bet-on-cannabis-with-4-billion-investm.html.

125 Trevor Hughes, “Blue Moon’s Brewer Launching Marijuana-infused ‘Beer,’” *USA Today*, March 28, 2018, https://www.usatoday.com/story/news/2018/03/28/blue-moon-brewer-marijuana-infused-beer/467110002/; Ben Miller, “Molson Coors Makes Cannabis-infused Beverage Deal in Canada,” CNBC, August 1, 2018. https://www.cnbc.com/2018/08/01/molson-coors-makes-cannabis-infused-beverage-deal-in-canada.html.

126 “Concern Over Industry Support for Wider Access to Medical Cannabis,” BMJ, March 18, 2020, https://www.bmj.com/company/newsroom/concern-over-industry-support-for-wider-access-to-medical-cannabis/.

127 Nora D. Volkow et al., “Adverse Health Effects of Marijuana Use,” *New England Journal of Medicine* 370, no. 23 (2014): 2219–2227, https://doi.org/10.1056/NEJMra1402309.

128 Jodi M. Gilman et al., “Cannabis Use is Quantitatively Associated with Nucleus Accumbens and Amygdala Abnormalities in Young Adult Recreational Users,” *Journal of Neuroscience* 34, no. 16 (2014): 5529–5538, https://doi.org/10.1523/JNEUROSCI.4745-13.2014.

129 Deborah S. Hasin et al., “Cannabis Withdrawal in the United States: Results from NESARC,” *Journal of Clinical Psychiatry* 69, no. 9 (2008): 1354–1363, https://doi.org/10.4088/jcp.v69n0902; Anees Bahji et al., “Prevalence of Cannabis Withdrawal Symptoms Among People with Regular or Dependent Use of Cannabinoids: A Systematic Review and Meta-analysis,” *JAMA Network Open* 3, no. 4 (2020): e202370, https://jamanetwork.com/journals/jamanetworkopen/fullarticle/2764234.

130 National Institute on Drug Abuse, “Is Marijuana Addictive?,” July 2020, https://www.drugabuse.gov/publications/research-reports/marijuana/marijuana-addictive.

131 Timothy G. Freels et al., “Vaporized Cannabis Extracts Have Reinforcing Properties and Support Conditioned Drug-seeking Behavior in Rats,” *Journal of Neuroscience* 40, no. 9 (2020): 1897–1908, https://doi.org/10.1523/JNEUROSCI.2416-19.2020.

132 Cécile Henquet et al., “Prospective Cohort Study of Cannabis Use, Predisposition for Psychosis, and Psychotic Symptoms in Young People,” *BMJ* (Clinical Research Ed.) 330, no. 7481 (2005): 11, https://pubmed.ncbi.nlm.nih.gov/15574485/; Arianna Marconi et al., “Meta-analysis of the Association Between the Level of Cannabis Use and Risk of Psychosis,” *Schizophrenia Bulletin* 42, no. 5 (2016): 1262–1269, https://doi.org/10.1093/schbul/sbw003; Antti Mustonen et al., “Adolescent Cannabis Use, Baseline Prodromal Symptoms and the Risk of Psychosis,” *British Journal of Psychiatry* 212, no. 4 (2018): 227–233, https://doi.org/10.1192/bjp.2017.52; Jussi A. Niemi-Pynttäri

et al., "Substance-induced Psychoses Converting into Schizophrenia: A Register-based Study of 18,478 Finnish Inpatient Cases," *Journal of Clinical Psychiatry* 74, no. 1 (2013): e94–99, https://doi.org/10.4088/JCP.12m07822.

133 Arpana Agrawal et al., "Major Depressive Disorder, Suicidal Thoughts and Behaviours, and Cannabis Involvement in Discordant Twins: A Retrospective Cohort Study," *The Lancet Psychiatry* 4, no. 9 (2017): 706–714, https://doi.org/10.1016/S2215-0366(17)30280-8; Jacqueline Duperrouzel et al., "The Association Between Adolescent Cannabis Use and Anxiety: A Parallel Process Analysis," *Addictive Behaviors* 78 (March 2018): 107–113, https://doi.org/10.1016/j.addbeh.2017.11.005; Gabriella Gobbi et al., "Association of Cannabis Use in Adolescence and Risk of Depression, Anxiety, and Suicidality in Young Adulthood: A Systematic Review and Meta-analysis," *JAMA Psychiatry* 76, no. 4 (2019): 426, https://doi.org/10.1001/jamapsychiatry.2018.4500.

134 Marta Di Forti et al., "The Contribution of Cannabis Use to Variation in the Incidence of Psychotic Disorder Across Europe (EU-GEI): A Multicentre Case-control Study," *The Lancet Psychiatry* 6, no. 5 (2019): 427–436, https://doi.org/10.1016/S2215-0366(19)30048-3.

135 Bonnie Leadbeater et al., "Age-varying Effects of Cannabis Use Frequency and Disorder on Symptoms of Psychosis, Depression and Anxiety in Adolescents and Adults," *Addiction* 114, no. 2 (2019): 278–293, https://doi.org/10.1111/add.14459.

136 L. Cinnamon Bidwell et al., "Exploring Cannabis Concentrates on the Legal Market: User Profiles, Product Strength, and Health-related Outcomes," *Addictive Behaviors Reports* 8 (2018): 102–106, https://doi.org/10.1016/j.abrep.2018.08.004; Marta Di Forti et al., "The Contribution of Cannabis Use to Variation in the Incidence of Psychotic Disorder Across Europe (EU-GEI): A Multicentre Case-control Study," *The Lancet Psychiatry* 6, no. 5 (2019): 427–436, https://doi.org/10.1016/S2215-0366(19)30048-3; Benedikt Fischer et al., "Lower-risk Cannabis Use Guidelines: A Comprehensive Update of Evidence and Recommendations," *American Journal of Public Health* 107, no. 8 (2017): e1–e12, https://doi.org/10.2105/AJPH.2017.303818; Joseph Pierre et al., "Cannabis-induced psychosis associated with high potency 'wax dabs,'" *Schizophrenia Research* 172, no 1–3 (April 2016): 211–212, https://doi.org/10.1016/j.schres.2016.01.056.

137 Substance Abuse and Mental Health Services Administration, "National Survey on Drug Use and Health 2018 (NSDUH-2018-DS0001)," Substance Abuse and Mental Health Data Archive, 2019, https://www.datafiles.samhsa.gov/study-dataset/national-survey-drug-use-and-health-2018-nsduh-2018-ds0001-nid18758.

138 Magdelena Cerdá et al., "Association Between Recreational Marijuana Legalization in the United States and Changes in Marijuana Use and Cannabis Use Disorder from 2008 to 2016," *JAMA Psychiatry* 77, no. 2 (2020): 165, https://doi.org/10.1001/jamapsychiatry.2019.3254.

139 Substance Abuse and Mental Health Services Administration, "National Survey on Drug Use and Health 2018 (NSDUH-2018-DS0001)," Substance Abuse and Mental Health Data Archive, 2019, https://www.datafiles.samhsa.gov/study-dataset/

national-survey-drug-use-and-health-2018-nsduh-2018-ds0001-nid18758.

140 L. Bigay-Gamé et al., "Characteristics of Lung Cancer in Patients Younger than 40 Years: A Prospective Multicenter Analysis in France," *Oncology* 95, no. 6 (2018): 337–343, https://doi.org/10.1159/000489784; Wayne Hall et al., "Evaluating the Public Health Impacts of Legalizing Recreational Cannabis Use in the United States," *Addiction* 111, no. 10 (2016): 1764–1773, https://doi.org/10.1111/add.13428; Pal Pacher et al., "Cardiovascular Effects of Marijuana and Synthetic Cannabinoids: The Good, the Bad, and the Ugly," *Nature Reviews Cardiology* 15, no. 3 (2018): 151–166, https://doi.org/10.1038/nrcardio.2017.130.

141 Chao Liu et al., "Cannabinoids Promote Progression of HPV-positive Head and Neck Squamous Cell Carcinoma Via p38 MAPK Activation," *Clinical Cancer Research* 26, no. 11 (June 2020), https://doi.org/10.1158/1078-0432.CCR-18-3301.

142 Mehrnaz Ghasemiesfe et al., "Association Between Marijuana Use and Risk of Cancer: A Systematic Review and Meta-analysis," *JAMA Network Open* 2, no. 11 (2019): e1916318, https://doi.org/10.1001/jamanetworkopen.2019.16318; J. Gurney et al., "Cannabis Exposure and Risk of Testicular Cancer: A Systematic Review and Meta-analysis," *BMC Cancer* 15, no. 1 (2015): 897, https://doi.org/10.1186/s12885-015-1905-6.

143 Kat McAlpine, "Male Marijuana Use Might Double the Risk of Partner's Miscarriage," *The Brink*, Boston University, October 16, 2019, http://www.bu.edu/articles/2019/marijuana-use-and-miscarriage-risk/.

144 Anja C. Huizink and Eduard J. H. Mulder, "Maternal Smoking, Drinking or Cannabis Use During Pregnancy and Neurobehavioral and Cognitive Functioning in Human Offspring," *Neuroscience & Biobehavioral Reviews* 30, no. 1 (2006): 24–41, https://pubmed.ncbi.nlm.nih.gov/16095697/; George Sam Wang et al., "Marijuana and Acute Health Care Contacts in Colorado," *Preventive Medicine* 104 (2017): 24–30, https://doi.org/10.1016/j.ypmed.2017.03.022.

145 Robert Frau et al., "Prenatal THC Exposure Produces a Hyperdopaminergic Phenotype Rescued by Pregnenolone," *Nature Neuroscience* 22, no. 12 (October 2019): 1975–1985, https://doi.org/10.1038/s41593-019-0512-2.

146 J. K. L. Gunn et al., "Prenatal Exposure to Cannabis and Maternal and Child Health Outcomes: A Systematic Review and Meta-analysis," *BMJ Open* 6, no. 4 e009986 (2016), https://doi.org/10.1136/bmjopen-2015-009986; Elyse Olshen Kharbanda et al., "Birth and early developmental screening outcomes associated with cannabis exposure during pregnancy," *Journal of Perinatology* 40, no. 3 (2020): 473–480, https://doi.org/10.1038/s41372-019-0576-6.

147 "Premature birth: Symptoms and causes," Mayo Clinic, December 21, 2017, https://www.mayoclinic.org/diseases-conditions/premature-birth/symptoms-causes/syc-20376730.

148 Alaska Department of Health and Social Services, "Marijuana Use and Public Health in Alaska," 2020, http://dhss.alaska.gov/dph/Director/Documents/marijuana/MarijuanaUse_PublicHealth_Alaska_2020.pdf.

149 Michael Nedelman, "Marijuana Shops Recommend Products to Pregnant Women, Against Doctors' Warnings," CNN, May 10, 2018, https://www.cnn.com/2018/05/10/health/cannabis-marijuana-dispensaries-pregnancy-study/index.html.

150 Nora D. Volkow et al., "Marijuana Use During Stages of Pregnancy in the United States," *Annals of Internal Medicine* 166, no. 10 (2017): 763–764, https://doi.org/10.7326/L17-0067.

151 Office of the Surgeon General, "U.S. Surgeon General's Advisory: Marijuana Use and the Developing Brain," U.S. Department of Health & Human Services, August 29, 2019, https://www.hhs.gov/surgeongeneral/reports-and-publications/addiction-and-substance-misuse/advisory-on-marijuana-use-and-developing-brain/index.html.

152 Connie Bao and Shiping Bao, "Neonate Death Due to Marijuana Toxicity to the Liver and Adrenals," *American Journal of Case Reports* 20 (2019): 1874–1878, https://doi.org/10.12659/AJCR.919545.

153 Office of the Surgeon General, "U.S. Surgeon General's Advisory: Marijuana Use and the Developing Brain," U.S. Department of Health & Human Services, August 29, 2019, https://www.hhs.gov/surgeongeneral/reports-and-publications/addiction-and-substance-misuse/advisory-on-marijuana-use-and-developing-brain/index.html.

154 Nicholas P. Allan et al., "Interactive Effects of PTSD and Substance Use on Suicidal Ideation and Behavior in Military Personnel: Increased Risk from Marijuana Use," *Depression and Anxiety* 36, no. 11 (2019): 1072–1079, https://doi.org/10.1002/da.22954; E. L. Gentes et al., "Prevalence and Correlates of Cannabis Use in an Outpatient VA Posttraumatic Stress Disorder Clinic," *Psychology of Addictive Behaviors* 30, no. 3 (2016): 415–421, https://doi.org/10.1037/adb0000154.

155 Mad Money, "MedMen CEO: Forget 'Stoner?'" YouTube, June 21, 2018, https://www.youtube.com/watch?v=aOm2yCy6V20.

156 "Opioid Overdose: Understanding the Epidemic," Centers for Disease Control and Prevention, March 19, 2020, https://www.cdc.gov/drugoverdose/epidemic/index.html.

157 "Alcohol facts and statistics," National Institute on Alcohol Abuse and Alcoholism, updated October 2020, https://www.niaaa.nih.gov/publications/brochures-and-fact-sheets/alcohol-facts-and-statistics.

158 Marcus A. Bachhuber et al., "Medical Cannabis Laws and Opioid Analgesic Overdose Mortality in the United States, 1999–2010," *JAMA Internal Medicine* 174, no. 10 (2014): 1668–1673, https://doi.org/10.1001/jamainternmed.2014.4005.

159 Chelsea L. Shover et al., "Association Between Medical Cannabis Laws and Opioid Overdose Mortality Has Reversed Over Time," *Proceedings of the National Academy of Sciences* 116, no. 26 (2019): 12624–12626, https://doi.org/10.1073/pnas.1903434116.

160 Theodore L. Caputi, "Medical Marijuana, Not Miracle Marijuana: Some Well-publicized Studies about Medical Marijuana Do Not Pass a Reality Check," *Addiction* 114, no. 6 (2019): 1128–1129, https://doi.org/10.1111/add.14580.

161 Maria Ellgren et al., "Adolescent Cannabis Exposure Alters Opiate Intake and Opioid

Limbic Neuronal Populations in Adult Rats," *Neuropsychopharmacology* 32, no. 3 (2007): 607–615, https://doi.org/10.1038/sj.npp.1301127.

162 Roberto Secades-Villa et al., "Probability and Predictors of the Cannabis Gateway Effect: A National Study," *International Journal of Drug Policy* 26, no. 2 (2015): 135–142, https://doi.org/10.1016/j.drugpo.2014.07.011.

163 Sunday Azagba et al., "Trends in Opioid Misuse among Marijuana Users and Non-users in the U.S. from 2007–2017," *International Journal of Environmental Research and Public Health* 16, no. 22 (2019): 4585, https://doi.org/10.3390/ijerph16224585.

164 Mark Olfson et al., "Cannabis Use and Risk of Prescription Opioid Use Disorder in the United States," *American Journal of Psychiatry* 175, no. 1 (2018): 47–53, https://doi.org/10.1176/appi.ajp.2017.17040413.

165 Olfson, "Cannabis Use and Risk of Prescription Opioid Use"; Robert Secades-Villa et al., "Probability and predictors of the cannabis gateway effect: A national study," *International Journal of Drug Policy* 26, no. 2 (2015): 135–142, https://doi.org/10.1016/j.drugpo.2014.07.011.

166 U.S. Department of Health and Human Services, Substance Abuse and Mental Health Services Administration, "Center for Behavioral Health Statistics and Quality, 2018, National Survey on Drug Use and Health 2016 (NSDUH-2016-DS0001)," Substance Abuse and Mental Health Data Archive, accessed December 28, 2020, https://datafiles.samhsa.gov/.

167 Kristin Salottolo et al., "The Grass is Not Always Greener: A Multi-institutional Pilot Study of Marijuana Use and Acute Pain Management Following Traumatic Injury," *Patient Safety in Surgery* 12, no. 1 (2018): 16, https://doi.org/10.1186/s13037-018-0163-3.

168 Deborah S. Hasin, et al., "U.S. Adults with Pain, a Group Increasingly Vulnerable to Nonmedical Cannabis Use and Cannabis Use Disorder: 2001–2002 and 2012–2013," *American Journal of Psychiatry* 177, no. 7 (July 2020): 611–618, https://doi.org/10.1176/appi.ajp.2019.19030284.

169 Rocky Mountain High Intensity Drug Trafficking Area (RMHIDTA), "The Legalization of Marijuana in Colorado: *The Impact*," September 2019, https://rmhidta.org/files/D2DF/FINAL-Volume6.pdf.

170 Gabrielle Campbell et al., "Effect of Cannabis Use in People with Chronic Non-cancer Pain Prescribed Opioids: Findings from a 4-year Prospective Cohort Study," *The Lancet Public Health* 3, no. 7 (2018): e341–e350, https://doi.org/10.1016/S2468-2667(18)30110-5.

171 Michael B. Sauter and Samuel Stebbins, "States Drinking the Most Beer," 24/7 Wall St., updated January 12, 2020, https://247wallst.com/special-report/2018/04/30/states-drinking-the-most-beer-2.

172 Colorado Department of Revenue, "MED licensed facilities," 2019, https://www.colorado.gov/pacific/enforcement/med-licensed-facilities; Colorado Department of Revenue, "Liquor Excise Tax Reports," 2019, https://cdor.colorado.gov/data-and-reports/liquor-data/liquor-excise-tax-reports.

173 Sarah Haughwout et al., "Apparent per capita alcohol consumption: National, state, and region trends, 1977–2014," National Institute on Alcohol Abuse and Alcoholism (NIAAA), March 2016, https://pubs.niaaa.nih.gov/publications/surveillance104/CONS14.htm.

174 Thomas Pellechia, "Does Legalizing Marijuana Threaten Wine (and Beer) Consumption?" *Forbes*, February 12, 2018, https://www.forbes.com/sites/thomaspellechia/2018/02/12/does-legalizing-marijuana-threaten-wine-and-beer-consumption/#3e9a73b77dfb

175 Katherine M. Keyes et al., "Historical Trends in the Grade of Onset and Sequence of Cigarette, Alcohol, and Marijuana Use among Adolescents from 1976–2016: Implications for 'Gateway' Patterns in Adolescence," *Drug and Alcohol Dependence* 194 (2019): 51–58, https://doi.org/10.1016/j.drugalcdep.2018.09.015.

176 Vanessa Morris et al., "Elevated Behavioral Economic Demand for Alcohol in Co-users of Alcohol and Cannabis," *Journal of Studies on Alcohol and Drugs* 79, no. 6 (November 2018): 929–934, https://pubmed.ncbi.nlm.nih.gov/30573024/.

177 Andrea Weinberger et al., "Is Cannabis Use Associated with an Increased Risk of Onset and Persistence of Alcohol Use Disorders? A Three-year Prospective Study among Adults in the United States," *Drug and Alcohol Dependence* 161 (2016): 363–367, https://doi.org/10.1016/j.drugalcdep.2016.01.014.

178 "Outbreak of Lung Injury Associated with E-cigarette Use, or Vaping," Centers for Disease Control and Prevention, February 25, 2020, https://www.cdc.gov/tobacco/basic_information/e-cigarettes/severe-lung-disease.html.

179 CNN, "Teen Receives Double Lung Transplant after Vaping-related Illness," CNN Wire, November 13, 2019, https://fox8.com/news/teen-receives-double-lung-transplant-after-vaping-related-illness/.

180 "Outbreak of Lung Injury Associated with E-cigarette Use, or Vaping," Centers for Disease Control and Prevention, February 25, 2020, https://www.cdc.gov/tobacco/basic_information/e-cigarettes/severe-lung-disease.html.

181 R. A. Miech et al., "National Adolescent Drug Trends Press Release: Text & Tables," Monitoring the Future, 2019, http://www.monitoringthefuture.org/data/19data.html#2019data-drugs.

182 Yasmeen M. Butt et al., "Pathology of Vaping-associated Lung Injury," *New England Journal of Medicine* 381, no. 18 (2019): 1780–1781, https://doi.org/10.1056/NEJMc1913069.

183 Andrew Selsky, "2nd Death in Oregon from Vaping-related Illness," *Seattle Times*, September 26, 2019, https://www.seattletimes.com/seattle-news/health/2nd-oregonian-dies-from-vaping-related-illness/.

184 WKRN, "Minnesota Native Identified as Tennessee's First Vaping-related Death," WKRN.com, October 17, 2019, https://www.wkrn.com/news/local-news/minnesota-man-identified-as-tennessees-first-vaping-related-death/.

185 Erika Edwards, "Not Just Counterfeit: Legal THC Vaping Products Linked to Lung

Illnesses," NBC News, December 6, 2019, https://www.nbcnews.com/health/vaping/not-just-counterfeit-legal-thc-vaping-products-linked-lung-illnesses-n1097011; Elizabeth Janney, "23 Vaping-related Lung Illnesses Reported in Maryland," Patch: Baltimore, MD, October 3, 2019, https://patch.com/maryland/baltimore/23-vaping-related-lung-illnesses-reported-maryland; Meredith Newman, "State: Delawarean Believed to Have Died from Vaping-related Lung Injury," Delaware Online, October 3, 2019, https://www.delawareonline.com/story/news/health/2019/10/03/state-delawarean-believed-have-died-vaping-related-lung-injury/3850705002/; Jayne O'Donnell, "Sketchy THC Vape Products. Sneaky Teens. How Patchwork Regulations on E-cigarettes Led to Health Crisis," *USA Today*, September 23, 2019, https://www.usatoday.com/story/news/health/2019/09/23/vaping-illnesses-crisis-teens-black-market-thc-no-regulation/2209009001/; Kate Snyder, "Maumee Man's Hospitalization Possibly Linked to Vaping THC," The Blade, October 18, 2019, https://www.toledoblade.com/news/medical/2019/10/18/vaping-respiratory-illness-ban-e-cigarette-lung-raphael-rodriguez/stories/20191018120; Will Stone, "Some States with Legal Weed Embrace Vaping Bans, Warn of Black Market Risks," NPR, October 26, 2019, https://www.npr.org/sections/health-shots/2019/10/26/770377080/some-states-with-legal-weed-embrace-vaping-bans-warn-of-black-market-risks.

186 M. A. ElSohly et al., "Potency Trends of Delta9-THC and Other Cannabinoids in Confiscated Marijuana from 1980–1997," *Journal of Forensic Sciences* 45, no. 1 (January 2000): 24–30, https://pubmed.ncbi.nlm.nih.gov/10641915/.

187 Suman Chandra et al., "New Trends in Cannabis Potency in USA and Europe During the Last Decade (2008–2017)," *European Archives of Psychiatry and Clinical Neuroscience* 269, no. 1 (2019): 5–15, https://doi.org/10.1007/s00406-019-00983-5.

188 Rosanna Smart et al., "Variation in Cannabis Potency and Prices in a Newly Legal Market: Evidence from 30 Million Cannabis Sales in Washington State," *Addiction* 112, no. 12 (2017): 2167–2177, https://doi.org/10.1111/add.13886.

189 Oregon Liquor Control Commission, "Marijuana Market Data," Oregon.gov, 2020, https://www.oregon.gov/olcc/marijuana/Documents/CTS/OregonCannabisTrackingSystemData.pdf.

190 Marta Di Forti et al., "The Contribution of Cannabis Use to Variation in the Incidence of Psychotic Disorder Across Europe (EU-GEI): A Multicentre Case-control Study," *The Lancet Psychiatry* 6, no. 5 (2019): 427–436, https://doi.org/10.1016/S2215-0366(19)30048-3.

191 Gary C. K. Chan et al., "User characteristics and effect profile of Butane Hash Oil: An extremely high-potency cannabis concentrate," *Drug and Alcohol Dependence* 178 (September 2017): 32–38, https://doi.org/10.1016/j.drugalcdep.2017.04.014.

192 Oregon-Idaho High Intensity Drug Trafficking Area, "Threat Assessments and Strategies," oridhidta.org, accessed January 4, 2021, http://oridhidta.org/reports.

193 Oregon-Idaho High Intensity Drug Trafficking Area, "Threat Assessments and Strategies."

194 Oregon-Idaho High Intensity Drug Trafficking Area, "An Initial Assessment of Cannabis Production, Distribution, and Consumption in Oregon 2018—An Insight Report," August 6, 2018, https://static1.squarespace.com/static/579bd717c534a564c72ea7bf/t/5b69d694f950b7f0399c4bfe/1533662876506/An+Initial+Assessment+of+Cannabis+Production+Distribution+and+Consumption+in+Oregon+2018_OR-ID+HIDTA_8-6-18.pdf.

195 Yuyan Shi and Di Liang, "The Association Between Recreational Cannabis Commercialization and Cannabis Exposures Reported to the US National Poison Data System," *Addiction* 115, no. 10 (February 2020), https://doi.org/10.1111/add.15019.

196 Wayne Hall and Daniel Stjepanović, "Commentary on Shi & Liang (2020): Has Cannabis Legalization Increased Acute Cannabis–related Harms?," *Addiction* 115, no. 10 (April 2020): 1900–1901, https://doi.org/10.1111/add.15064.

197 Colorado Department of Public Health and Environment, "Colorado Hospital and Emergency Department Discharges with Marijuana-Related Billing Codes," Colorado.gov, 2019, https://marijuanahealthinfo.colorado.gov/health-data/colorado-hospital-association-cha-data.

198 Colorado Department of Public Health and Environment, "Suicides in Colorado: Counts," 2019, https://www.cohealthdata.dphe.state.co.us/Data/Details/11.

199 Rocky Mountain Poison and Drug Center, personal phone call with RMHIDTA, 2019; see also Rocky Mountain High Intensity Drug Trafficking Area (RMHIDTA), "The Legalization of Marijuana in Colorado: *The Impact*," 2019, https://rmhidta.org/files/D2DF/FINAL-Volume6.pdf.

200 Colorado Department of Public Health and Environment, "Monitoring Health Concerns Related to Marijuana in Colorado 2018: Summary," 2018, https://marijuanahealthinfo.colorado.gov/summary.

201 Rocky Mountain High Intensity Drug Trafficking Area (RMHIDTA), "The Legalization of Marijuana in Colorado: The Impact," 2019, https://rmhidta.org/files/D2DF/FINAL-Volume6.pdf.

202 Jennifer M. Whitehill et al., "Incidence of Pediatric Cannabis Exposure among Children and Teenagers Aged 0 to 19 Years Before and After Medical Marijuana Legalization in Massachusetts," *JAMA Network Open* 2, no. 8 (2019): e199456, https://doi.org/10.1001/jamanetworkopen.2019.9456.

203 Anita A. Thomas et al., "Unintentional Pediatric Marijuana Exposures Prior to and After Legalization and Commercial Availability of Recreational Marijuana in Washington State," *Journal of Emergency Medicine* 56, no. 4 (March 2019): 398–404. https://doi.org/10.1016/j.jemermed.2019.01.004.

204 "2018 Annual Data Report: Cannabis," Washington Poison Center, 2018, https://www.wapc.org/data/data-reports/cannabis-data-report/.

205 Alaska Department of Health and Social Services, "Marijuana Use and Public Health in Alaska," 2020, http://dhss.alaska.gov/dph/Director/Documents/marijuana/MarijuanaUse_PublicHealth_Alaska_2020.pdf.

206 Rosie McCall, "Just a Week After Recreational Marijuana was Legalized in Illinois, Chicago Doctors Report a Spike in ER Visits," *Newsweek*, January 9, 2020, https://www.newsweek.com/recreational-weed-legalized-illinois-chicago-doctors-reporting-spike-er-visits-1481226.

207 Sanjay Bhandari et al., "Recent Trends in Cyclic Vomiting Syndrome–Associated Hospitalisations with Liberalisation of Cannabis Use in the State of Colorado," *Internal Medicine Journal* 49, no. 5 (2019): 649–655, https://doi.org/10.1111/imj.14164.

208 Mahra Nourbakhsh et al., "Cannabinoid Hyperemesis Syndrome: Reports of Fatal Cases," *Journal of Forensic Sciences* 64, no. 1 (2019): 270–274, https://doi.org/10.1111/1556-4029.13819.

209 Bertha K. Madras et al., "Associations of Parental Marijuana Use with Offspring Marijuana, Tobacco, and Alcohol Use and Opioid Misuse," *JAMA Network Open* 2, no. 11 (2019): e1916015, https://doi.org/10.1001/jamanetworkopen.2019.16015.

210 Substance Abuse and Mental Health Services Administration, "National Survey on Drug Use and Health 2018 (NSDUH-2018-DS0001)," Substance Abuse and Mental Health Data Archive, 2019, https://www.datafiles.samhsa.gov/study-dataset/national-survey-drug-use-and-health-2018-nsduh-2018-ds0001-nid18758.

211 Washington State Healthy Youth Survey, "Healthy Youth Survey," Fact Sheets, 2018, https://www.askhys.net/FactSheets.

212 "Violations Dataset," Washington State Liquor and Cannabis Board, 2020, https://data.lcb.wa.gov/dataset/Violations-Dataset/dx3i-tzh2/data.

213 Julia Dilley et al., "Marijuana Use, Attitudes and Health Effects in Oregon," Oregon Health Authority, January 2016, https://www.oregon.gov/oha/ph/PreventionWellness/marijuana/Documents/oha-8509-marijuana-report.pdf.

214 Oregon Health Authority, "Oregon Healthy Teens Survey," 2017, https://www.oregon.gov/oha/PH/BIRTHDEATHCERTIFICATES/SURVEYS/OREGONHEALTHYTEENS/Pages/2017.aspx.

215 Pamela J. Trangenstein et al., "Active Cannabis Marketing and Adolescent Past-year Cannabis Use," *Drug and Alcohol Dependence* 204 (2019): 107548, https://doi.org/10.1016/j.drugalcdep.2019.107548.

216 Washington State Healthy Youth Survey, "Healthy Youth Survey," Fact Sheets, 2018, https://www.askhys.net/FactSheets.

217 Substance Abuse and Mental Health Services Administration, "National Survey on Drug Use and Health 2018 (NSDUH-2018-DS0001)," Substance Abuse and Mental Health Data Archive, 2019, https://www.datafiles.samhsa.gov/study-dataset/national-survey-drug-use-and-health-2018-nsduh-2018-ds0001-nid18758.

218 R. A. Miech et al., "National Adolescent Drug Trends Press Release: Text & Tables," Monitoring the Future, 2019, http://www.monitoringthefuture.org/data/19data.html#2019data-drugs.

219 "Surgeon General's Advisory on E-cigarette Use Among Youth," Centers for Disease Control and Prevention, April 9, 2019, https://www.cdc.gov/tobacco/

basic_information/e-cigarettes/surgeon-general-advisory/index.html.

220 Nicholas Chadi et al., "Association Between Electronic Cigarette Use and Marijuana Use among Adolescents and Young Adults: A Systematic Review and Meta-analysis," *JAMA Pediatrics* 173, no. 10 (2019): e192574, https://doi.org/10.1001/jamapediatrics.2019.2574; Sarah D. Kowitt et al., "Vaping Cannabis among Adolescents: Prevalence and Associations with Tobacco Use from a Cross-sectional Study in the USA," *BMJ Open* 9, no. 6 (2019): e028535, https://doi.org/10.1136/bmjopen-2018-028535.

221 R. A. Miech et al., "National Adolescent Drug Trends Press Release: Text & Tables," Monitoring the Future, 2019, http://www.monitoringthefuture.org/data/19data.html#2019data-drugs.

222 Substance Abuse and Mental Health Services Administration, "State Data Tables and Reports from the 2017–2018 NSDUH," 2019, https://www.samhsa.gov/data/nsduh/state-reports-NSDUH-2018.

223 Substance Abuse and Mental Health Services Administration, "State Data Tables and Reports."

224 Alaska Department of Health and Social Services, "Marijuana Use and Public Health in Alaska," 2020, http://dhss.alaska.gov/dph/Director/Documents/marijuana/MarijuanaUse_PublicHealth_Alaska_2020.pdf.

225 Substance Abuse and Mental Health Services Administration, "State Data Tables and Reports from the 2017–2018 NSDUH," 2019, https://www.samhsa.gov/data/nsduh/state-reports-NSDUH-2018.

226 Substance Abuse and Mental Health Services Administration, "State Data Tables and Reports."

227 Jacob T. Borodovsky et al., "U.S. Cannabis Legalization and Use of Vaping and Edible Products among Youth," *Drug and Alcohol Dependence* 177 (2017): 299–306, https://doi.org/10.1016/j.drugalcdep.2017.02.017.

228 Andy Hatch, "Researchers Tracking Public Health Impacts of Marijuana Legalization," Washington State University, April 14, 2017, https://nursing.wsu.edu/2017/04/14/13255

229 Charles Wohlforth, "Marijuana School Suspensions More than Doubled After Legalization," opinion, *Anchorage Daily News*, January 11, 2018, https://www.adn.com/opinions/2018/01/11/marijuana-school-suspensions-more-than-doubled-after-legalization/.

230 Washington State Healthy Youth Survey, "Healthy Youth Survey," Fact Sheets, 2018, https://www.askhys.net/FactSheets.

231 Ernesto Munoz et al., "Summary of Law Enforcement and District Attorney Reports of Student Contacts," Colorado Department of Public Safety, 2017, https://cdpsdocs.state.co.us/ors/docs/reports/2017-HB15-1273-StudentContacts.pdf.

232 Alaska Department of Health and Social Services, "Marijuana Use and Public Health in Alaska," 2020, http://dhss.alaska.gov/dph/Director/Documents/marijuana/

MarijuanaUse_PublicHealth_Alaska_2020.pdf.

233 Magdalena Cerdá et al., "Association Between Recreational Marijuana Legalization in the United States and Changes in Marijuana Use and Cannabis Use Disorder from 2008 to 2016," *JAMA Psychiatry* 77, no. 2 (2020): 165, https://doi.org/10.1001/jamapsychiatry.2019.3254.

234 Washington State Healthy Youth Survey, "Healthy Youth Survey," Fact Sheets, 2018, https://www.askhys.net/FactSheets.

235 Jiries Meehan-Atrash et al., "Toxicant Formation in Dabbing: The Terpene Story," *ACS Omega* 2, no. 9 (2017): 6112–6117, https://doi.org/10.1021/acsomega.7b01130.

236 Catherine Orr et al., "Grey Matter Volume Differences Associated with Extremely Low Levels of Cannabis Use in Adolescence," *Journal of Neuroscience* 39, no. 10 (2019): 1817–1827, https://doi.org/10.1523/JNEUROSCI.3375-17.2018.

237 Carolyn Coffey and George C. Patton, "Cannabis Use in Adolescence and Young Adulthood: A Review of Findings from the Victorian Adolescent Health Cohort Study," *Canadian Journal of Psychiatry* 61, no. 6 (2016): 318–327, https://doi.org/10.1177/0706743716645289.

238 A. M. Arria et al., "The Academic Consequences of Marijuana Use During College," *Psychology of Addictive Behaviors* 29, no. 3 (2015): 564–575, https://doi.org/10.1037/adb0000108; Madeline H. Meier et al., "Persistent Cannabis Users Show Neuropsychological Decline from Childhood to Midlife," *Proceedings of the National Academy of Sciences* 109, no. 40 (October 2012): E2657–E2664, https://doi.org/10.1073/pnas.1206820109; Madeline H. Meier et al., "Associations of Adolescent Cannabis Use with Academic Performance and Mental Health: A Longitudinal Study of Upper Middle Class Youth," *Drug and Alcohol Dependence* 156 (2015): 207–212, https://doi.org/10.1016/j.drugalcdep.2015.09.010; Rochelle Salmore and Ken Finn, "The Hidden Costs of Marijuana Use in Colorado: One Emergency Department's Experience," *Journal of Global Drug Policy and Practice* 10 (Summer 2016): 1–26, https://www.researchgate.net/publication/314140400_The_Hidden_Costs_of_Marijuana_Use_in_Colorado_One_Emergency_Department's_Experience; Randi Melissa Schuster et al., "One Month of Cannabis Abstinence in Adolescents and Young Adults is Associated with Improved Memory," *Journal of Clinical Psychiatry* 79, no. 6 (2018), https://doi.org/10.4088/JCP.17m11977; Edmund Silins et al., "Young Adult Sequelae of Adolescent Cannabis Use: An Integrative Analysis," *The Lancet Psychiatry* 1, no. 4 (2014): 286–293, https://doi.org/10.1016/S2215-0366(14)70307-4.

239 Gabriella Gobbi et al., "Association of Cannabis Use in Adolescence and Risk of Depression, Anxiety, and Suicidality in Young Adulthood: A Systematic Review and Meta-analysis," *JAMA Psychiatry* 76, no. 4 (2019): 426, https://doi.org/10.1001/jamapsychiatry.2018.4500; Edmund Silins et al., "Young Adult Sequelae of Adolescent Cannabis Use: An Integrative Analysis," *The Lancet Psychiatry* 1, no. 4 (2014): 286–293, https://doi.org/10.1016/S2215-0366(14)70307-4.

240 John Daley, "The Rate of Teen Suicide in Colorado Increased by 58% in 3 Years,

Making it the Cause of 1 in 5 Adolescent Deaths," Colorado Public Radio, September 17, 2019, https://www.cpr.org/2019/09/17/the-rate-of-teen-suicide-in-colorado-increased-by-58-percent-in-3-years-making-it-the-cause-of-1-in-5-adolescent-deaths/.

241 Colorado Department of Public Health and Environment, "Suicides in Colorado: Counts," 2019, https://www.cohealthdata.dphe.state.co.us/Data/Details/11.

242 Substance Abuse and Mental Health Services Administration, "National Survey on Drug Use and Health 2018 (NSDUH-2018-DS0001)," Substance Abuse and Mental Health Data Archive, 2019, https://www.datafiles.samhsa.gov/study-dataset/national-survey-drug-use-and-health-2018-nsduh-2018-ds0001-nid18758.

243 Substance Abuse and Mental Health Services Administration, "National Survey."

244 Substance Abuse and Mental Health Services Administration, "National Survey."

245 Substance Abuse and Mental Health Services Administration, "State Data Tables and Reports from the 2017–2018 NSDUH," 2019, https://www.samhsa.gov/data/nsduh/state-reports-NSDUH-2018.

246 Substance Abuse and Mental Health Services Administration, "State Data Tables and Reports."

247 Jacob T. Borodovsky et al., "U.S. Cannabis Legalization and Use of Vaping and Edible Products Among Youth," *Drug and Alcohol Dependence* 177 (2017): 299–306, https://doi.org/10.1016/j.drugalcdep.2017.02.017; Bonnie J. Leadbeater et al., "Age-varying Effects of Cannabis Use Frequency and Disorder on Symptoms of Psychosis, Depression and Anxiety in Adolescents and Adults," *Addiction* 114, no. 2 (2019): 278–293, https://doi.org/10.1111/add.14459.

248 David C. R. Kerr et al., "Changes in Undergraduates' Marijuana, Heavy Alcohol and Cigarette Use Following Legalization of Recreational Marijuana Use in Oregon," *Addiction* 112, no. 11 (2017): 1992–2001, https://doi.org/10.1111/add.13906.

249 Colorado Division of Criminal Justice, "Offense/Arrest/Court Filing," Colorado.gov, September 3, 2019, https://www.colorado.gov/pacific/dcj-ors/Offense/Arrest/CourtFiling.

250 Colorado Division of Criminal Justice, "A Study of Homelessness in Seven Colorado Jails," June 2018, https://cdpsdocs.state.co.us/ors/docs/reports/2018_Jail_Homelessness_Study.pdf.

251 Colorado Division of Criminal Justice, "Offense/Arrest/Court Filing," Colorado.gov, September 3, 2019, https://www.colorado.gov/pacific/dcj-ors/Offense/Arrest/CourtFiling.

252 Metropolitan Police Department of the District of Columbia, "MPD Adult Arrests (2013–2017)," mpdc.dc.gov, January 1, 2019, https://mpdc.dc.gov/node/1379551.

253 Metropolitan Police Department of the District of Columbia, "MPD Adult Arrests."

254 Chris Morrison et al., "The Economic Geography of Medical Cannabis Dispensaries in California," *International Journal of Drug Policy* 25, no. 3 (2014): 508–515, https://doi.org/10.1016/j.drugpo.2013.12.009.

255 Crystal Thomas and Bridget Freisthler, "Evaluating the Change in Medical Marijuana

Dispensary Locations in Los Angeles Following the Passage of Local Legislation," *Journal of Primary Prevention* 38, no. 3 (2017): 265–277, https://doi.org/10.1007/s10935-017-0473-8.

256 Kevin Hamm, "Marijuana in Denver: Map of Pot-related Businesses by Neighborhood with Income Data, School Locations," *Denver Post*, January 2, 2016, https://www.denverpost.com/2016/01/02/marijuana-in-denver-map-of-pot-related-businesses-by-neighborhood-with-income-data-school-locations/.

257 Eli McVey, "Chart: Recreational Marijuana Stores are Clustered in Low-income Areas of Denver, Seattle," *Marijuana Business Daily*, July 31, 2017, https://mjbizdaily.com/chart-recreational-marijuana-stores-clustered-low-income-areas-denver-seattle/.

258 Elizabeth Kneebone and Scott W. Allard, "A Nation in Overdose Peril: Pinpointing the Most Impacted Communities and the Local Gaps in Care," Brookings Institution, September 25, 2017, https://www.brookings.edu/research/pinpointing-opioid-in-most-impacted-communities/.

259 Truth Initiative, "'Worth More' Campaign Exposes Big Tobacco for Its Manipulation of Lower-income Communities," January 25, 2018, https://truthinitiative.org/research-resources/targeted-communities/worth-more-campaign-exposes-big-tobacco-its-manipulation.

260 Substance Abuse and Mental Health Services Administration, "National Survey on Drug Use and Health 2018 (NSDUH-2018-DS0001)," Substance Abuse and Mental Health Data Archive, 2019, https://www.datafiles.samhsa.gov/study-dataset/national-survey-drug-use-and-health-2018-nsduh-2018-ds0001-nid18758.

261 Substance Abuse and Mental Health Services Administration, "National Survey."

262 American College of Obstetricians and Gynecologists, "Marijuana Use During Pregnancy and Lactation," Committee opinion number 722, October 2017, https://www.acog.org/Clinical-Guidance-and-Publications/Committee-Opinions/Committee-on-Obstetric-Practice/Marijuana-Use-During-Pregnancy-and-Lactation?IsMobileSet=false.

263 Shira Schoenberg, "Boston Grapples with Diversity in Marijuana Industry," MassLive, updated January 29, 2019, https://www.masslive.com/politics/2018/12/boston_grapples_with_lack_of_d.html.

264 U.S. Census Bureau, "QuickFacts: Boston, Massachusetts," census.gov, 2019, https://www.census.gov/quickfacts/fact/table/bostoncitymassachusetts/RHI225218.

265 Todd Wallack and Dan Adams, "Massachusetts Marijuana Regulators Investigating Whether Companies Violated License Limits," *Boston Globe*, March 27, 2019, https://www.bostonglobe.com/metro/2019/03/27/massachusetts-marijuana-regulators-investigating-whether-companies-violating-ownership-limits/jshf4znu16AaNxD3P1NdBK/story.html.

266 Jay Koziarz, "Amid Calls for More Minority Participation, Marijuana Ordinance Passes City Council," Curbed Chicago, October 16, 2019, https://chicago.curbed.com/2019/10/16/20917215/

chicago-recreational-marijuana-city-council-zoning-black-caucus.

267 Ronald L. Rice, "Sen. Rice: Legalizing Pot Won't Stop Social Injustice in the Black and Brown Community," opinion, NJ.com, October 22, 2019, https://www.nj.com/opinion/2019/10/sen-rice-legalizing-pot-wont-stop-social-injustice-in-the-black-and-brown-community.html.

268 "Drug Testing Index™: Overall Positivity Rate in 2018," Quest Diagnostics, http://www.dtidrugmap.com/#/all/2018.

269 Quest Diagnostics, "Workforce Drug Positivity Increases in More than One-third of U.S. Industry Sectors Examined, According to Quest Diagnostics Multi-year Analysis," Quest Diagnostics Newsroom, September 11, 2019, https://newsroom.questdiagnostics.com/2019-09-11-Workforce-Drug-Positivity-Increases-in-More-Than-One-Third-of-U-S-Industry-Sectors-Examined-According-to-Quest-Diagnostics-Multi-Year-Analysis.

270 Quest Diagnostics, "Workforce Drug Positivity."

271 Quest Diagnostics, "Workforce Drug Positivity."

272 Jennifer L. Marcum et al., "Self-reported Work-related Injury or Illness—Washington, 2011–2014," *Morbidity and Mortality Weekly Report* 66, no. 11 (2017): 302–306, https://doi.org/10.15585/mmwr.mm6611a6.

273 George C. Hlavac and Edward J. Easterly, "Legal Issues: Marijuana in the Workplace," National Association of Colleges and Employers, February 1, 2016, https://www.naceweb.org/public-policy-and-legal/legal-issues/legal-issues-marijuana-in-the-workplace/.

274 Ken Ritter, "Nevada law prevents most employers from rejecting pot-users," AP News, June 12, 2019, https://apnews.com/0fe555109df746afb2e76924cbb26175.

275 Michael Gold, "Marijuana Testing of Job Applicants is Barred by City in Groundbreaking Measure," *New York Times*, April 11, 2019, https://www.nytimes.com/2019/04/11/nyregion/marijuana-drug-testing-nyc.html.

276 Kelly David Burke and Alicia Acuna, "Colorado Tries to Fight Homeless Problem that May Have Been Triggered by Pot Law," Fox News, July 10, 2017, https://www.foxnews.com/us/colorado-tries-to-fight-homeless-problem-that-may-have-been-triggered-by-pot-law.

277 Joseph J. Kolb, "Legalized Marijuana Turns Colorado Resort Town into Homeless Magnet," Fox News, May 16, 2017, https://www.foxnews.com/us/legalized-marijuana-turns-colorado-resort-town-into-homeless-magnet.

278 Colorado Division of Criminal Justice, "A Study of Homelessness in Seven Colorado Jails," June 2018, https://cdpsdocs.state.co.us/ors/docs/reports/2018_Jail_Homelessness_Study.pdf.

279 Colorado Division of Criminal Justice, "A Study of Homelessness."

280 Alejandro Azofeifa et al., "Driving Under the Influence of Marijuana and Illicit Drugs among Persons Aged ≥16 Years—United States, 2018," *Morbidity and Mortality Weekly Report* 68, no. 50 (2019): 1153–1157, https://doi.org/10.15585/mmwr.mm6850a1.

281 CBS, "Police Struggle to Address Driving While High on Marijuana," CBS Morning Rounds, January 19, 2019, https://www.cbsnews.com/video/police-struggle-to-address-driving-while-high-on-marijuana/.

282 National Institute on Drug Abuse, "Drugged Driving DrugFacts," December 2019, https://www.drugabuse.gov/publications/drugfacts/drugged-driving.

283 AAA Foundation for Traffic Safety, "2018 Traffic Safety Culture Index," June 2019, https://us.vocuspr.com/Newsroom/ViewAttachment.aspx?SiteName=AAACS&Entity=PRAsset&AttachmentType=F&EntityID=110440&AttachmentID=dac31258-48b7-4707-8ec6-186932cffb96.

284 AAA Foundation for Traffic Safety, "2018 Traffic Safety Culture Index."

285 Darrin Grondel et al., "Marijuana Use, Alcohol Use, and Driving in Washington State," Washington Traffic Safety Commission, April 2018, http://wtsc.wa.gov/wp-content/uploads/dlm_uploads/2018/05/Marijuana-and-Alcohol-Involvement-in-Fatal-Crashes-in-WA_FINAL.pdf.

286 Washington State Healthy Youth Survey, "Healthy Youth Survey," Fact Sheets, 2018, https://www.askhys.net/FactSheets.

287 Alaska Department of Health and Social Services, "Marijuana Use and Public Health in Alaska," 2020, http://dhss.alaska.gov/dph/Director/Documents/marijuana/MarijuanaUse_PublicHealth_Alaska_2020.pdf.

288 Becky Bui and Jack K. Reed, "Driving Under the Influence of Drugs and Alcohol," Colorado Division of Criminal Justice, June 2019, http://cdpsdocs.state.co.us/ors/docs/reports/2019-DUI_HB17-1315.pdf.

289 Bui and Reed, "Driving Under the Influence."

290 Bui and Reed, "Driving Under the Influence."

291 Highway Loss Data Institute, "Recreational Marijuana and Collision Claim Frequencies," Bulletin 35, no. 8 (April 2018), https://www.iihs.org/media/e0028841-76ee-4315-a628-32a704258980/gmJeDw/HLDI%20Research/Bulletins/hldi_bulletin_35-08.pdf.

292 David Migoya, "Exclusive: Traffic Fatalities Linked to Marijuana are Up Sharply in Colorado. Is Legalization to Blame?," *Denver Post*, updated December 28, 2018, denverpost.com/2017/08/25/colorado-marijuana-traffic-fatalities/.

293 Andrew Gross, "Fatal Crashes Involving Drivers Who Test Positive for Marijuana Increase after State Legalizes Drug," AAA NewsRoom, January 30, 2020, https://newsroom.aaa.com/2020/01/fatal-crashes-involving-drivers-who-test-positive-for-marijuana-increase-after-state-legalizes-drug/.

294 Gross, "Fatal Crashes."

295 Vanessa Romo, "Maryland Court Rules Marijuana Odor Not Enough to Search a Person," NPR, August 16, 2019, https://www.npr.org/2019/08/16/751783763/maryland-court-rules-marijuana-odor-not-enough-to-search-a-person.

296 James Queally and Sarah Parvini, "For Police, Catching Stones Drivers Isn't So Easy," *Los Angeles Times*, March 22, 2018, https://www.latimes.com/local/lanow/

la-me-ln-marijuana-dui-20180322-story.html.

297 M. Kathryn Dahlgren et al., "Recreational Cannabis Use Impairs Driving Performance in the Absence of Acute Intoxication," *Drug and Alcohol Dependence* 208 (March 2020): 107771, https://doi.org/10.1016/j.drugalcdep.2019.107771

298 Lorine A. Hughes et al., "Marijuana Dispensaries and Neighborhood Crime and Disorder in Denver, Colorado," *Justice Quarterly* 37, no. 3 (2019): 1–25, https://doi.org/10.1080/07418825.2019.1567807.

299 Bridget Freisthler et al., "From Medical to Recreational Marijuana Sales: Marijuana Outlets and Crime in an Era of Changing Marijuana Legislation," *Journal of Primary Prevention* 38, no. 3 (2017): 249–263, https://doi.org/10.1007/s10935-017-0472-9.

300 Rocky Mountain High Intensity Drug Trafficking Area (RMHIDTA), "The Legalization of Marijuana in Colorado: *The Impact*," September 2019, https://rmhidta.org/files/D2DF/FINAL-Volume6.pdf.

301 Rocky Mountain High Intensity Drug Trafficking Area (RMHIDTA), "The Legalization of Marijuana."

302 Kirk Mitchell, "Crime Rate in Colorado Increases Much Faster than the Rest of the Country," *Denver Post*, updated July 12, 2017, https://www.denverpost.com/2017/07/11/colorado-sees-big-increase-crime-10-percent-higher-murder-rate/.

303 Federal Bureau of Investigation, "Crime data explorer: Colorado," 2018, https://crime-data-explorer.fr.cloud.gov/explorer/state/colorado/arrest.

304 Drug Enforcement Administration, "Intelligence," El Paso Intelligence Center, 2018, https://www.dea.gov/ops/intel.shtml#EPIC.

305 Rocky Mountain High Intensity Drug Trafficking Area (RMHIDTA), "The Legalization of Marijuana in Colorado: *The Impact*," September 2019, https://rmhidta.org/files/D2DF/FINAL-Volume6.pdf.

306 Drug Enforcement Administration, "2019 National Drug Threat Assessment," December 2019, https://www.dea.gov/sites/default/files/2020-01/2019-NDTA-final-01-14-2020_Low_Web-DIR-007-20_2019.pdf.

307 Michael R. Blood, "Weaker-Than-Expected Marijuana Sales Ding California Budget," U.S. News & World Report, May 9, 2019, https://www.usnews.com/news/best-states/california/articles/2019-05-09/weaker-than-expected-marijuana-sales-ding-california-budget; Thomas Fuller, "Now for the Hard Part: Getting Californians to Buy Legal Weed," *New York Times*, January 2, 2019, https://www.nytimes.com/2019/01/02/us/buying-legal-weed-in-california.html.

308 Colorado Joint Budget Committee, "Budget in Brief Fiscal Year 2018–19," https://leg.colorado.gov/sites/default/files/fy18-19bib.pdf.

309 Sharyn Alfonsi, "How Red Tape and Black Market Weed are Buzzkills for California's Legal Marijuana Industry," 60 Minutes, October 27, 2019, https://www.cbsnews.com/news/marijuana-in-california-black-market-weed-buzzkills-for-california-legal-weed-industry-60-minutes-2019-10-27/.

310 Oregon Liquor Control Commission, "Cannabis Information Systems Properly

Functioning but Monitoring and Security Enhancements are Needed," Oregon.gov, February 2018, https://sos.oregon.gov/audits/documents/2018-07.pdf.

311 Joel Grover and Amy Corral, "Poisonous Pot Found in Some Los Angeles-area Stores," NBC Los Angeles, February 26, 2019, https://www.nbclosangeles.com/news/local/marijuana-poison-pot-investigation/5913/.

312 Noelle Crombie, "Contaminated Marijuana Still Reaching Consumers in Oregon," Oregonlive, *Oregonian*, June 17, 2017, https://www.oregonlive.com/marijuana/2017/06/contaminated_marijuana_still_r.html.

313 Oregon Liquor Control Commission, "2019 Recreational Marijuana Supply and Demand Legislative Report," January 2019, http://opb-imgserve-production.s3-website-us-west-2.amazonaws.com/original/2019_supply_and_demand_legislative_report_final_for_legislators_1548964723484.pdf.

314 Oregon Secretary of State, "Oregon's framework for Regulating Marijuana Should be Strengthened to Better Mitigate Diversion Risk and Improve Laboratory Testing," Oregon Audits Division, 2019, https://sos.oregon.gov/audits/Documents/2019-04.pdf.

315 Gillian Flaccus, "US Prosecutor: Oregon Has Big Pot Overproduction Problem," AP News, February 2, 2018, https://apnews.com/833bc51a456d4819b1e9882cb17b46ef/US-prosecutor:-Oregon-has-big-pot-overproduction-problem.

316 Sharyn Alfonsi, "How Red Tape and Black Market Weed are Buzzkills for California's Legal Marijuana Industry," 60 Minutes, October 27, 2019, https://www.cbsnews.com/news/marijuana-in-california-black-market-weed-buzzkills-for-california-legal-weed-industry-60-minutes-2019-10-27/.

317 Dennis Romero, "California's Cannabis Black Market Has Eclipsed its Legal One," NBC News, September 20, 2019, https://www.nbcnews.com/news/us-news/california-s-cannabis-black-market-has-eclipsed-its-legal-one-n1053856.

318 Martin Kaste, "Despite Legalization, Marijuana Black Market Hides in Plain Sight," NPR, May 16, 2018, https://www.npr.org/2018/05/16/610579599/despite-legalization-marijuana-black-market-hides-in-plain-sight.

319 Sharyn Alfonsi, "How Red Tape and Black Market Weed are Buzzkills for California's Legal Marijuana Industry," 60 Minutes, October 27, 2019, https://www.cbsnews.com/news/marijuana-in-california-black-market-weed-buzzkills-for-california-legal-weed-industry-60-minutes-2019-10-27/.

320 Alfonsi, "How Red Tape and Black Market Weed are Buzzkills."

321 Alaska State Troopers, "Alaska State Troopers Annual Drug Report, 2016," https://dps.alaska.gov/getmedia/f259530b-5277-408e-9d45-4999958fe530/2016-Annual-Drug-Report-6-28-17final;.aspx.

322 Drug Enforcement Administration, "2019 National Drug Threat Assessment," December 2019, https://www.dea.gov/sites/default/files/2020-01/2019-NDTA-final-01-14-2020_Low_Web-DIR-007-20_2019.pdf.

323 Johnny Magdaleno, "Mexican Drug Cartels May Use Legal Marijuana to Increase Their

Presence in Northern California," *Newsweek*, January 10, 2018, https://www.newsweek.com/2018/01/19/mexican-drug-cartels-taking-over-california-legal-marijuana-775665.html.

324 Oregon-Idaho HIDTA Program, "Drug Threat Assessment: Program Year 2020," Oregon-Idaho High Intensity Drug Trafficking Area, June 2019, https://static1.squarespace.com/static/579bd717c534a564c72ea7bf/t/5d08088507db5c0001ed3f21/1560807567416/PY+2020+OREGON-IDAHO+HIDTA+Threat+Assessment_FINAL_061719.pdf.

325 Drug Enforcement Administration, "2019 National Drug Threat Assessment," December 2019, https://www.dea.gov/sites/default/files/2020-01/2019-NDTA-final-01-14-2020_Low_Web-DIR-007-20_2019.pdf.

326 Drug Enforcement Administration, "Domestic Cannabis Suppression/Eradication Program," 2020, https://www.dea.gov/domestic-cannabis-suppression-eradication-program.

327 Drug Enforcement Administration, "2019 National Drug Threat Assessment," December 2019, https://www.dea.gov/sites/default/files/2020-01/2019-NDTA-final-01-14-2020_Low_Web-DIR-007-20_2019.pdf.

328 Rocky Mountain High Intensity Drug Trafficking Area (RMHIDTA), "The Legalization of Marijuana in Colorado: *The Impact*," September 2019, https://rmhidta.org/files/D2DF/FINAL-Volume6.pdf.

329 U.S. Postal Inspection Service, retrieved from Rocky Mountain High Intensity Drug Trafficking Area (RMHIDTA), "The Legalization of Marijuana in Colorado: *The Impact*," 2019, https://rmhidta.org/files/D2DF/FINAL-Volume6.pdf.

330 Oregon-Idaho High Intensity Drug Trafficking Area, "Threat Assessments and Strategies," oridhidta.org, accessed January 4, 2021, http://oridhidta.org/reports.

331 Alaska State Troopers, "2017 Annual Drug Report," Statewide Drug Enforcement Unit, 2017, https://dps.alaska.gov/getmedia/1c42905b-dc16-453e-aad5- cfc99d9b-c425/2017-Annual-Drug-Report-Final-UPDATED-090718.pdf.

332 Associated Press, "California seizes $1.5 billion in illegally grown marijuana plants, CBS News, November 4, 2019, https://www.cbsnews.com/news/marijuana-drug-raid-california-seizes-1-5-billion-illegally-grown-marijuana-2019-11-04/.

333 Office of Attorney General Maura Healey, "Two Braintree Brothers Arrested, Arraigned in Connection with Major Money Laundering and Marijuana Trafficking Operation," press release, Mass.gov, June 27, 2019, https://www.mass.gov/news/two-braintree-brothers-arrested-arraigned-in-connection-with-major-money-laundering-and#:~:text=Quincy%20%E2%80%94%20Two%20Braintree%20brothers%20have,General%20Maura%20Healey%20announced%20today.&text=Wai%20Eng%20and%20Aibun%20Eng,12.

334 Jennifer Peltz, "Marijuana Vaping Busts on Rise; Over 500K Seized in 2 Years. U.S. News & World Report, December 3, 2019, https://www.usnews.com/news/us/articles/2019-12-03/over-500k-pot-vapes-seized-in-2-years-as-busts-rise-in-us.

335 Megan Trimble, "Feds, Police Bust Marijuana Grow Houses in Colorado," U.S. News & World Report," January 31, 2019, https://www.usnews.com/news/national-news/articles/2019-01-31/federal-agents-police-bust-suspected-marijuana-grow-houses-in-colorado.

336 Colorado Division of Criminal Justice, "A Study of Homelessness in Seven Colorado Jails," June 2018, https://cdpsdocs.state.co.us/ors/docs/reports/2018_Jail_Homelessness_Study.pdf.

337 Sharon Bernstein, "Toxic Waste from U.S. Pot Farms Alarms Experts," Reuters, August 6, 2017, https://www.reuters.com/article/us-usa-marijuana-environment-idUSKBN1AM0C3

338 Alan B. Franklin et al., "Grass is Not Always Greener: Rodenticide Exposure of a Threatened Species Near Marijuana Growing Operations," *BMC Research Notes* 11, no. 1 (2018): 94, https://doi.org/10.1186/s13104-018-3206-z.

339 Christopher Weber, "Illegal Pot Farm Leaves 'Toxic Garbage Dump' in Northern California National Forest," OregonLive, *Oregonian*, November 17, 2019, https://www.oregonlive.com/nation/2019/11/illegal-pot-farm-leaves-toxic-garbage-dump-in-northern-california-national-forest.html.

340 Weber, "Illegal Pot Farm."

341 Katherine Curl Reitz, "An Environmental Argument for a Consistent Federal Policy on Marijuana," *Arizona Law Review* 57, 2015, http://arizonalawreview.org/pdf/57-4/57arizlrev1085.pdf.

342 Evan Mills, "The Carbon Footprint of Indoor *Cannabis* Production," *Energy Policy* 46 (July 2012): 58–67, https://www.sciencedirect.com/science/article/abs/pii/S0301421512002228.

343 Scott Bauer et al., "Impacts of Surface Water Diversions for Marijuana Cultivation on Aquatic Habitat in Four Northwestern California Watersheds," *PLOS ONE* 10, no. 3 (March 2015): e0120016, https://doi.org/10.1371/journal.pone.0120016.

344 Van Butsic and Jacob C. Brenner, "Cannabis (*Cannabis sativa* or *C. indica*) Agriculture and the Environment: A Systematic, Spatially-explicit Survey and Potential Impacts," *Environmental Research Letters* 11, no. 4 (April 2016): 044023, https://doi.org/10.1088/1748-9326/11/4/044023.

345 Ian J. Wang et al., "Cannabis, an Emerging Agricultural Crop, Leads to Deforestation and Fragmentation," *Frontiers in Ecology and the Environment* 15, no. 9 (2017): 495–501, https://doi.org/10.1002/fee.1634.

346 Van Butsic et al., "The Emergence of Cannabis Agriculture Frontiers as Environmental Threats," *Environmental Research Letters* 13, no. 12 (2018): 124017, https://doi.org/10.1088/1748-9326/aaeade

347 Sharyn Alfonsi, "How Red Tape and Black Market Weed are Buzzkills for California's Legal Marijuana Industry," 60 Minutes, October 27, 2019, https://www.cbsnews.com/news/marijuana-in-california-black-market-weed-buzzkills-for-california-legal-weed-industry-60-minutes-2019-10-27/.

348 Patrick McGreevy, "California Might Triple the Number of Marijuana Shops Across State," *Los Angeles Times*, May 13, 2019, https://www.latimes.com/politics/la-pol-ca-california-pot-shops-liquor-stores-legislature-mandate-20190513-story.html.

349 WXYZ Detroit, "Here's a List of the 1,400+ Communities That Have Opted Out of Recreational Marijuana," November 26, 2019, https://www.wxyz.com/news/heres-a-list-of-the-1-300-communities-that-have-opted-out-of-recreational-marijuana.

350 Corey Williams, "Detroit City Council Extends Temporary Ban on Pot Sales," AP News, January 28, 2020, https://apnews.com/0683c9e3a1aede7be8340f120b6f5fbd.

351 Colorado Marijuana Enforcement Division, "Local Authority Status List, 2019," https://drive.google.com/file/d/1GcdE3drg3xf74ix48ZsSME2s0rEw2-g0/view.

352 Colorado Department of Revenue, "MED Licensed Facilities," colorado.gov, 2019, https://www.colorado.gov/pacific/enforcement/med-licensed-facilities.

353 Oregon Liquor Control Commission, "Marijuana Market Data," Oregon.gov, 2020, https://www.oregon.gov/olcc/marijuana/Documents/CTS/OregonCannabisTrackingSystemData.pdf.

354 Robert McCoppin et al., "When Illinois Legalized Marijuana, it Sparked a Backlash from Suburban Residents Who Don't Want Pot Shops in Their Towns," *Chicago Tribune*, November 19, 2019, https://www.chicagotribune.com/marijuana/illinois/ct-illinois-marijuana-opt-out-feud-20191119-hbkeqeug6nc67fturytz5x7lay-story.html.

355 Colton Grace, "Big Marijuana, Big Money, Big Politics: Part One–Illinois," SAM: Smart Approaches to Marijuana, September 6, 2019, https://learnaboutsam.org/big-marijuana-big-money-big-politics-part-one-illinois/.